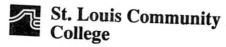

Parody as Film Genre

An informal moment on the set of the classic reaffirmation parody *Butch Cassidy and the Sundance Kid* (1969), with Robert Redford, Katharine Ross, and Paul Newman.

Parody as Film Genre

"Never Give a Saga an Even Break"

Wes D. Gehring

Foreword by Scott R. Olson

Contributions to the Study of Popular Culture, Number 69

Greenwood Press
Westport, Connecticut • London

Library of Congress Cataloging-in-Publication Data

Gehring, Wes D.
  Parody as film genre : "never give a saga an even break" / Wes D.
Gehring ; foreword by Scott R. Olson.
    p. cm.—(Contributions to the study of popular culture,
ISSN 0198–9871 ; no. 69)
  Filmography: p.
  Includes bibliographical references and index.
  ISBN 0–313–26186–5 (alk. paper)
  1. Comedy films—History and criticism. 2. Parody in motion
pictures. I. Title. II. Series.
PN1995.9.C55G426 1999
791.43'617—dc21   99–18592

British Library Cataloguing in Publication Data is available.

Library of Congress Catalog Card Number: 99–18592
ISBN: 0–313–26186–5
ISSN: 0198–9871

First published in 1999

Greenwood Press, 88 Post Road West, Westport, CT 06881
An imprint of Greenwood Publishing Group, Inc.
www.greenwood.com

Printed in the United States of America

The paper used in this book complies with the
Permanent Paper Standard issued by the National
Information Standards Organization (Z39.48–1984).

10 9 8 7 6 5 4 3 2 1

Every reasonable effort has been made to trace the owners of copyright materials in this book,
but in some instances this has proven impossible. The author and publisher will be glad to
receive information leading to more complete acknowledgments in subsequent printings of
the book and in the meantime extend their apologies for any omissions.

To
Joe & Maria Pacino

BLAZING FRANKENSTEIN

In the world according to
Babbling Brooks, parody is
Merely "anarchy by accident,"
Or "Jewish novocaine."

If Mel had been around
To collaborate with D. W. Griffith,
America's first epic film would
Have been *Mirth of a Nation*.

Still, thanks to one scene
In *Blazing Saddles* Brooks
Had several critics calling
Him "the Farter of his country."

Dig deeper and *Blazing Saddles'*
Sideswiping of violence and
Racism show us how
Far we haven't come.

Or, chill out to Dr. Frankenstein
And his creation donning top hat
And tails to perform "Puttin'
On the Ritz," or is it "The Monster Mash"?

Think sci-fi spoofing and Mel's
Space Balls beams up . . . but his
Whole oeuvre might be called
The Invasion of the GENRE Snatchers.

Wherever Brooks' time-tripping takes
Us bank on a Mel milieu in which
Things are never what they seem
And too far is just far enough.

          —Wes D. Gehring

Contents

Illustrations

Foreword:
Puncturing and Reaffirmation

You're about to read a very important book, because dominant genres reveal a lot about culture. Ours is a time of parody. Wes Gehring's timing couldn't be better, since parody is often associated with the end of a genre's natural life cycle, the step right before it arises like a phoenix from its own ashes. After all, *Pale Rider* (1985) and *Unforgiven* (1992) somehow followed the devastation of *Blazing Saddles* (1974). We're now at the *fin de siecle* of not only a century, but of a millennium, and the parodies are coming fast and furious. The phoenix may mutate, but it doesn't die.

Part of that mutation is a blurring of the definition of what parody is. Dr. Gehring makes an important distinction between the parody of overt puncturing and the parody of reaffirmation that gets to the heart of the current vitality of the parody form. This is a critical difference, because it separates films and television shows that are clearly spoofs, such as those of Mel Brooks that broadly skewer the idiosyncrasies of their target, from that fuzzier breed of media that adores its object even as it mimics it, such as one sees in *Scream* (1996) or *The Brady Bunch Movie* (1995). As Dr. Gehring demonstrates, overt puncturing has been with us for a long time. But that other creature, the reaffirmation, seems to be coming into its own just now.

Pastiche, the affectless, nonsatiric, and seemingly random appropriation of intertextual material, is the main device of reaffirmative parody. It's important because the parody of pastiche is considered by many cultural critics to be a major symptomatic condition of the postmodern age (Jameson 1992). When Disney parodies its own film *The Lion King* (1994)

at the end of its film *George of the Jungle* (1997) by having George ascend
Pride Rock to present his newborn child to the animals, its goal is not to
provoke a response of "Boy, is that film convention stupid," so much as
"Hey, I recognize that!" *The Lion King* is reaffirmed, not punctured. It
helps sell more videos.

So although puncturing is still around, there's a lot of reaffirmation on
television and in the movies. Television has always been a haven for parody
since before Milton Berle and *Texaco Star Theater*, but the sort of parody
one sees now on television is more focused, less broad, and more subtly
referential, more respectful and even reverent toward its targets. One good
television example of postmodern reaffirmative pastiche is the animated
sitcom *The Simpsons* (Fox), which is difficult to appreciate or even follow
without specific knowledge of the source material it targets. In one episode,
Homer and Marge hire Sherry Bobbins, a British nanny whose name
prompts one character to say, "Don't you mean Mary Pop——?" before
being cut off. That truncated line of dialogue makes the reference clear
without miring Fox in a lawsuit with notoriously litigious Disney. In contrast to the restorative family therapy enacted by the eponymous character
in the film *Mary Poppins* (1964), Sherry Bobbins fails to improve the Simpson clan, causing a self-satisfied Homer Simpson to sing in a parody of a
Sherman and Sherman tune that

> I'd rather drink a beer
> Than win "Father of the Year."
> I'm happy with things the way they are!

Another episode parodies the Superman character through the attempts of
a Hollywood studio to shoot a film called *Radioactive Man* in the Simpsons' hometown. The actor who plays Radioactive Man, a caricature of
Arnold Schwarzenegger called McBain, has an Austrian accent so thick that
he can't get the character's signature line right; despite extensive directorial
coaching, he keeps saying, "Up and at them!" instead of the important
catchphrase "Up and Atom!" In another episode, the science fiction film
The Planet of the Apes (1968) is affectionately sent up as "Planet of the
Apes—The Musical!," which concludes with actor Troy McClure singing
a Lloyd Webber style, pull-out-the-stops finale called "You Really Made a
Monkey Out of Me!" in front of the ruins of the Statue of Liberty. There
is no derision or social criticism here, though—it's only wistful affection,
as if the folks at Gracie Films wished that once in a while a Disney pro-
tagonist couldn't overcome adversity, or that there really was a superhero
sidekick called Fallout Boy or a simian spectacular up for a Tony. One
never gets the sense that the producers of *The Simpsons* have any feeling
but love for the pop culture icons they parody.

The very meticulousness with which some parody is crafted bespeaks the affirmative motives behind it. Perhaps the best of all the television parody shows was *SCTV* (syndicated, NBC, HBO), which parodied not only other television programs, but also television networks themselves. Interwoven with its lampoons of cooking shows, news shows, game shows, and soap operas was the behind-the-scenes chaos of the SCTV network and its colorful executives and talent. In one memorable episode, a Soviet television satellite maliciously co-opts SCTV's broadcasting band and begins showing "Three-C-P One Russian Television" to startled Americans as a kind of reverse cultural imperialism. Each of these CCCP-1 programs is a parody distortion of some American genre; the Russian game show is a Cyrillic alphabet soup patterned after Scrabble called "Uposcrabblnyk," and a bland, amiable, laugh-tracked Russian sitcom is called "Hey, Giorgy!" The precision of this parody is so fine, it can be hard to tell if one is supposed to laugh or not. The French philosopher Jean Baudrillard (1990) has argued that at the end of the twentieth century, the line between an original and its simulacrum is getting pretty fuzzy. For him, the social condition created by that blurred division between what is real and what is mimetic is the most distinctive component of American culture. One could argue that affirmative parody is the very thing that makes American culture American.

What sets postmodern parody apart from its modernist precursor, then, is its razor-close aesthetic proximity to the thing it parodies. One of Milton Berle's overt parody commercials could not be easily mistaken for a real commercial, but the "Itchy and Scratchy" cartoons on *The Simpsons* or the horror spoof *Scream* (1996) look an awful lot like the real thing, and in some ways they *are* the real thing. A lot of young people I know who have never seen *Psycho* (1960), *Halloween* (1978), or *A Nightmare on Elm Street* (1984) were completely oblivious to any spoofing elements in *Scream* whatsoever, but no matter; it worked for them just fine as a horror movie. It is hard to imagine anyone mistaking the overt lampooning of *Blazing Saddles* (1974) for a real Western, even if they had never seen a Western before, but then, Brooks has the aesthetic distance of a Modernist. The essence of postmodern parody lies in its inability to distance itself.

That affectionate proximity can be evident even in more overt parodies such as *Police Squad!* (ABC) and its cinematic sibling *The Naked Gun* (1988). Consider, for example, the casting of Leslie Nielsen as Detective Frank Drebin. Unlike Uncle Miltie or Mel Brooks, Nielsen is the real thing, having starred in straight dramas such as *The Man Behind the Badge* (CBS) in the 1950s and *The New Breed* (ABC) and *The Protectors* (ABC) in the 1960s. He plays the character of Frank Drebin straight, like any other cop role. This lends a weird authenticity and verisimilitude that one doesn't find when watching the Marx Brothers in *Go West* (1940) or Mel Brooks in *High Anxiety* (1977). It's as if Clint Eastwood had starred in *Blazing Saddles*. The use of actors such as Lloyd Bridges, Peter Graves, and William Shatner in the *Airplane* movies or Charlie Sheen in the *Hot Shots!* films lends a similar authenticity. Milton Berle (or Jerry Lewis or Mel Brooks or Rick Moranis) in the same roles would have had a rather different effect.

As Dr. Gehring points out, satire is often wrongly equated with parody. They aren't the same thing, but puncturing parody often makes use of satire. Reaffirmative parody almost never does. Reaffirmation is incompatible with the derision and contempt that satiric parody shoots at its target. Postmodern parody relies instead on metafiction and intertextuality. Paradoxically, *Scream* as much epitomizes a slasher film as parodies one. It takes to a new level the interest director Wes Craven exhibited in metafiction in the film *Wes Craven's New Nightmare* (1994), a nonparodic reworking and culmination of the *Nightmare on Elm Street* series that blended real life with the fiction. *Scream* is not satire. It's adoration. Rather than make fun of the slasher subgenre, *Scream* (and Craven) enshrine and worship it in a pure, elemental form.

The same can be said of the film version of *The Brady Bunch Movie* (1995) or *A Very Brady Sequel* (1996). Can something so reverent to its source material be considered a parody, even a reaffirmative parody, or is it just a further and purer iteration of the original? These two films are so faithful to the original text, that apart from cast changes and anachronism gags, there is little difference between the simulation and the original. Plot lines and dialogue from the series are transferred whole and verbatim to the "parody." It would, after all, be hard to parody any show with spin-offs such as *The Brady Brides* (ABC) and *A Very Brady Christmas* (ABC). Merely quoting them is sufficient.

Blurring the line between the real and its spoof even further is the rock group Spinal Tap, spawned from the film *This is Spinal Tap* (1984), Rob Reiner's parody of heavy metal bands and the "rockumentaries" about them. Spinal Tap defies almost any attempt to define them as something other than an actual band. Although the film refers to numerous phony Spinal Tap albums, the band has since then actually released five albums: "This is Spinal Tap" (1984), "Christmas With the Devil EP" (1984), "Bitch School EP" (1992), "The Majesty of Rock EP" (1992), and "Break Like the Wind" (1993). It has done two national concert tours. It has produced several music videos. It did a corporate endorsement for IBM. By most definitions, Spinal Tap is at least as "real" as the nonparody synthetic bands The Monkees or The New Kids On The Block or Milli Vanilli or Spice Girls. At least Spinal Tap writes and performs its own music.

In short, parody is the literary form that most embodies postmodernism, and therefore best exemplifies the fuzzy, mutating, recombinant times in which we live. Like many other aspects of our environment, parody is at heart a language game. *Ilinx* is a term Roger Caillois (1962) uses to characterize dizzying and disorienting games, and elsewhere (1987) I've talked about the *ilinx*-like games found in the postmodern media. It is a descriptive label to slap on most of the parody found in the media today. Hitchcock liked to play this game, of course, as Thomas M. Leitch (1991) has pointed out. But as the game speeds up, as the references and intertextuality get more complex, the game is making us all dizzier. After all, *George of the Jungle* was supposed to be a parody of Tarzan. What's *The Lion King* doing in there? Trying to keep track of the pastiche in *Scream* or *The Simpsons* is a stupefying and vertiginous challenge. The essential postmodern question of "what's real?" is getting very hard to answer.

Because parody is such a representative literary form for our time, Wes Gehring (a pseudonym for Wes Craven? Note the lengthy discussion of *Scream* in this book . . . has anyone ever seen Wes Gehring and Wes Craven together at the same time?) does the world of film studies a service by taking a careful look at it. Knowing and understanding parody's devices is essential for informed and critical media viewership. Dr. Gehring is in a great position to do that needed analysis, given his extensive writings about film comedy and film genres. I suspect that when you finish the book, you'll be better able to make sense of these postmodern times. Since Dr. Gehring is passionate about helping us understand movies, the parody genre is likely to survive his scrutiny and dissection reaffirmed, not punctured.

Scott R. Olson

REFERENCES

Baudrillard, J. *America*. Trans. C. Turner. New York: Verso, 1988.

Caillois, R. *Man, Play, and Games*. London: Thames and Hudson, 1962.

Jameson, F. *Postmodernism, or the Cultural Logic of Late Capitalism*. Durham, NC: Duke University Press, 1992.

Leitch, T. *Find the Director and Other Hitchcock Games*. Athens: University of Georgia Press, 1991.

Olson, S. "Meta-television: Popular postmodernism." *Critical Studies in Mass Communication* 4, no. 3 (1987): 284–300.

Preface

In *Hot Shots!* (1991) pilot Topper Harley (Charlie Sheen) cannot believe his psychiatrist and eventual lover Ramada (Valeria Golino) is grounding him. When he tells her she must be joking, she replies, "Look, if I were joking I would have said, 'What do you do with an elephant with three balls? [Topper has no response.] You walk him and pitch to the rhino.' "

In 1988 my *Handbook of American Film Genres* was published. The catalyst for this volume, for which I was editor and chief contributor, was the chance to write chapters on what I saw as the five comedy genres—personality, screwball, parody, dark, and populist. I had been influenced by a statement from comedy theorist Jim Leach. With amusing insight he observed, "A genre which encompasses the visions of Jerry Lewis *and* Ernest Lubitsch is already in trouble."[1] Leach was encouraging a more ambitious look at *multiple* comedy genres, noting what most disciples of laughter have long believed: "If a genre is defined too loosely [as in the case of comedy], it ceases to be of any value as a critical tool."[2]

Accomplishments frequently beget new accomplishments, or at least greater aspirations. When the *Handbook* was published, my goal became to write a genre book about each of the five comedy types previously noted. With the completion of the text in hand, I have reached that objective.

The examination of American film parody that follows is divided into five chapters and an epilogue. Chapter 1 both scrutinizes the genre's numerous components and provides a historical overview of the spoofing tradition in American movies.

Chapter 2 studies the manner in which several pivotal comedians addressed Western parody at the height of America's golden film age, the years just prior to the country's entry into World War II (1941). The Western slant is important both for its significance at that time and its ongoing premier status (among genre targets) throughout the history of American movie parody.

The movies perused in Chapter 2 include Laurel & Hardy's *Way Out West* (1937), W. C. Fields and Mae West's *My Little Chickadee* (1940), and the Marx Brothers' *Go West* (1940). Besides these traditionally broad spoofs of the Western, the chapter also examines a film from the period, *Destry Rides Again* (1939), which assumes a more complex take on burlesque. The latter approach, called parody of reaffirmation, balances comic deflation with an eventual celebration of the genre under affectionate attack. The chapter closes with *Destry*'s comparison to the ultimate Western reaffirmation burlesque, *Butch Cassidy and the Sundance Kid* (1969).

Chapter 3 focuses on the central American parody artist prior to Mel Brooks—Bob Hope. His spoof career is briefly surveyed before the chapter quickly moves to analysis of my Hope trilogy: *The Road to Utopia* (1945), *My Favorite Brunette* (1947), and *The Paleface* (1948). *Utopia* is the best of the seven *Road* pictures he made with Bing Crosby, which burlesque action adventure movies. *Brunette* is a takeoff on film noir, and *Paleface* parodies the Western. Consistent with the latter genre's importance in spoof history, as reviewed in Chapter 2, *Paleface* was *the* critical and commercial hit of Hope's career. That portion of the chapter also compares *Paleface* with its very popular sequel, *Son of Paleface* (1952). This Hope portion of the text closes with a look at the comedian's number one parody disciple, Woody Allen, and his film *Play It Again, Sam* (1972).

Chapter 4 chronicles the burlesque misadventures of the genre's unofficial king, Mel Brooks. After an overview of Brooks' parody roots, the chapter closely examines his two greatest works, *Blazing Saddles* (1974) and *Young Frankenstein* (1974). Of particular interest, with regard to the preceeding chapters, is the watershed Western parody nature of *Blazing Saddles*, especially Brooks' comic mining of what Italian director Sergio Leone had stumbled into with his 1960s spaghetti Western trilogy.

Chapter 5 views spoof films in the 1990s by way of two representative works—the traditionally broad burlesque, *Hot Shots! Part Deux* (1993), and the parody of reaffirmation, *Scream* (1996). A special chapter slant addresses the genre's self-referential tendencies. Though this direction did not start in the 1990s, deconstruction is now both more apt to occur, and more ambitious in scope.

These chapters are followed by an Epilogue, a brief summing up, in which I reiterate some key points and add a few closing reflections on parody. On the heels of this are a selective bibliography and filmography.

Besides being driven by a fascination for all things comic, alluded to in my opening comments, this text has also been an attempt to balance a theoretical take on parody with a look at several special parody auteurs. Although cognizant of theorist Scott R. Olson's insightful warning about subsuming genre within authorship, I feel it is also essential to scrutinize those artists whose films help define, and/or redefine, whatever genre is under the microscope.[3] Parody, like all genres, is forever a work in transition. And theory must always find symmetry with the important practioners.

Because parody plays upon—spoofs—a pre-established artistic structure, it often does not receive the recognition visited upon other comedy genres. My closing wish for the text in hand would be that it helps redress this misconception. Funny here is just as special as funny elsewhere.

NOTES

1. Jim Leach, "The Screwball Comedy," in *Film Genres and Criticism*. ed. Barry K. Grant (Metuchen, NJ: Scarecrow Press, 1977), p. 75.

2. Ibid.

3. Scott R. Olson, "College Course File: Studies in Genre—Horror," *Journal of Film and Video*, Spring-Summer 1996, p. 74.

Acknowledgments

In Woody Allen's science fiction parody *Sleeper* (1973), he awakens 200 years in the future and is asked to join a revolution. His character responds, "I'm not the heroic type. I was beaten up by Quakers."

Film comedy has always held an honored position in my family. My dad and both grandfathers loved all things comic, and happily both my daughters, Sarah and Emily, are also predisposed along these lines. Thus, family tradition helped me get here, as well as providing an ongoing pleasant working environment for finishing the book in hand.

Some would suggest that examining comedy, whether parody or populism, destroys the magic. To them I would respectfully say, "Poppycock," or words to that effect. A better understanding of what makes you laugh enhances your hold on life. No one ever gets out with all the answers, but a handle on humor makes the stay much more palatable.

Besides family tradition and encouragement, there are several professional colleagues to thank. My department chairperson, "Dr. Joe" Misiewicz, assisted with both securing release time for me and facilitating university financial help. I greatly appreciate the ongoing support of Ball State University Provost Warren C. Vander Hill, as well as the backing of Earl Conn, former dean of the College of Communication, Information, and Media. Janet Warrner, my local copyeditor, was forever available and insightful. The computer preparation of the manuscript was done by Jean Thurman. And teaching friends Joe and Maria Pacino and Conrad Lane were often helpful, as was my new Dean of Communication, Scott R. Olsen, who wrote the foreword.

Research for this book also involved several important archives and their invariably helpful staffs. These include the New York Public Library System, especially the Billy Rose Theatre Collection at Lincoln Center; the Film Stills Archive of the Museum of Modern Art (New York); the Archives of the Performing Arts (Doeheny Library) at the University of Southern California (Los Angeles, with a special thank you to head archivist Ned Comstock); the Margaret Herrick Library at the Academy of Motion Picture Arts and Sciences (Beverly Hills); and Ball State University's Bracken Library (Muncie, Indiana). In writing a dozen film comedy texts prior to this one, I was also able to draw from a large private collection of movie files and stills.

Coming back full circle to family, a special thank-you is in order for both my daughters and my parents. Their love and support make demanding book projects like this possible.

Wes D. Gehring, Ph.D.

1

Parody Overview

After the appearance of a giant chicken in *Sleeper* (1973), Miles (Woody Allen) asks Luna (Diane Keaton) if 2173 has any weird futuristic animals—"like something with the body of a crab and the head of a social worker."

When *Young Frankenstein's* (1974) monster (Peter Boyle) stops making love to the doctor's fiancée (Madeline Kahn), she says, "Oh, you men are all alike. Seven or eight quick ones and you're off with the boys to boast and brag. Well, YOU BETTER KEEP YOUR MOUTH SHUT!"

American film parody is a comic, yet generally affectionate and distorted, imitation of a given genre, auteur, or specific work. These parody variations are best demonstrated by the 1970s Pied Piper of the genre, Mel Brooks. His *Blazing Saddles* (1974) is an inspired takeoff on the Western genre. *High Anxiety* (1977) parodies the mystery/thriller work of auteur Alfred Hitchcock. *Young Frankenstein* (1974) is largely a comic undercutting (or should one say distortion?) of the classic horror film *Frankenstein* (1931) and some of its sequels, especially *Bride of Frankenstein* (1935).

There is nothing inherently new about the genre, whether one goes back to Aristophanes (448?–380? B.C.) spoofing the writing styles of Aeschylus and Euripides in the *Frogs*, or Cervantes' undercutting of the medieval romance genre in his early seventeenth-century novel *Don Quixote*, whose title character argumentatively is Western culture's greatest comic figure.

Cleavon Little and Gene Wilder make with the liquid happiness in Mel Brooks' *Blazing Saddles* (1974).

Unlike other American film comedy genres, such as the 1930s Depression birth of screwball comedy, or the front and center emergence of dark comedy in the 1960s, parody has been a mainstream part of American film comedy since the beginning. It was, in fact, a pivotal ingredient in the works of Mack Sennett, America's film comedy father. This comedy pioneer was at his best when spoofing the melodramatic adventure films of his mentor, D. W. Griffith. For instance, Sennett's *Teddy at the Throttle* (1917) is a delightful takeoff on Griffith's propensity for the last-minute rescue, such as the close of his celebrated but still controversial *Birth of a Nation* (1915).

In this chapter's examination of seven basic characteristics of parody, Sennett's significance to the genre is underscored by frequent references to his work along with those of other pivotal directors, such as Brooks, or the director/writer team of Jim Abrahams, David Zucker, and Jerry Zucker (commonly known as the ZAZ team) of *Airplane!* (1980) fame. First, parody should be funny even without viewer expertise on the subject under comic attack. An example would be the extended bean-induced farting scene in *Blazing Saddles*. For decades cinema cowboys have been gobbling up this gas-producing meal without one reference to its natural powers. (Brooks accepts the nickname "vulgar primitive."[1]) Yes, parody often has one foot in reality. It should be obvious, however, that the genre is progressively more entertaining the greater one's familiarity with the subject being spoofed. Consequently, because Sennett was a former Griffith writer, his parody of the master has an added comic edge for students of that director. Film comedy historian Gerald Mast reminds us that Sennett's *Help! Help!* (1912) is a "specific parody" of Griffith's *Lonely Villa* (1909), which Sennett had written.[2] As an added footnote to the bean segment, *Help! Help!* is a good example of parody treating a low subject (melodramatic rescue) with mock dignity. Conversely, the genre also handles serious situations in a trivial manner. In *Blazing Saddles* the latter approach could be exemplified by any of the scenes in which the oversexed governor (played by Brooks) "works" on "affairs" of state. His scantily attired assistant comically reduces all official government action into hurried interruptions in the governor's all but nonstop sex life.

The genre that easily seems to have inspired the greatest number of American film parodies is also, fittingly, considered the most inherently American (incomparably familiar)—the Western. Thus, the vast majority of major American screen comedians have found time for a Western spoof, such as Buster Keaton's *Go West* (1925), Laurel & Hardy's *Way Out West* (1937), W. C. Fields and Mae West's *My Little Chickadee* (1940), the Marx Brothers' *Go West* (1940), Abbott & Costello's *The Wistful Widow of Wagon Gap* (1947), and Martin & Lewis's *Pardners* (1956). Bob Hope even managed to do three Western spoofs: *The Paleface* (1948), *Son of Paleface* (1952), and *Alias Jesse James* (1959), with Hope's version of the often-adapted *Ruggles of Red Gap—Fancy Pants* (1950)—sometimes counted as a fourth. Naturally, the most celebrated of all parodies remains Brooks' *Blazing Saddles*, though Western spoofs continue, be they the Saturday matinee variety of the Steve Martin/Chevy Chase/Martin Short *¡Three Amigos!* (1986), or the bawdy camp of *Lust in the Dust* (1985, starring late gross-out leader of women impersonators, Divine, of John Waters shock comedy fame).

Second, though the fundamental goal of parody is to be *funny* (something that should never be lost on the scholar), this genre is also an educational tool. This might best be defined as "creative criticism."[3] That is, to create effective parody one must be thoroughly versed in the subject under attack. (For this reason, parody is often comically affectionate in nature, since the artist is frequently a student of the target genre or auteur.) Thus, parody is the most palatable of *critical approaches*, offering insights through laughter. I frequently apply this in the classroom by teaching a genre course in which parody films are sometimes used to better define specific genres under discussion. Along the same lines, one better understands Griffith after viewing Sennett parodies of his work. Moreover, such parodies also provide a historical tenor of the time. In the case of Griffith, Sennett's period parodies demonstrate the initial popularity of this serious artist and also anticipate how Griffith could become passé during the roaring 1920s Jazz Age, when he seemed incapable of moving beyond the nineteenth-century melodramatic structure that Sennett spoofed.

The "creative criticism" significance of parody is important to keep in mind, because the genre often has been considered as something less than important; it has been defined as a parasitic growth on true works of art or as a literary elitist form of Trivial Pursuit, in which one needs to know an unnecessarily detailed collection of facts before even understanding the parody. The act of spoofing is more than a comic replication of close-up scenes from a given genre. Parody theorist Joe Lee Davis probably best demonstrated the genre's less-than-lofty image when he drew the following analogy: "As the pun [an abbreviated parody] has been called the lowest form of wit, so parody may often seem the lowest form of literary art."[4] Yet it takes just as much creative talent to both perceive a given structure and then effectively parody it as it does to create a structure in the first place. Parody is simultaneously something old and something new: kid a traditional structure, have fun with the content. That is, the parodist replicates the familiar pattern of a given genre or auteur while subjecting it to a fresh comic twist, such as the mysterious "elevator killer" of the Carl Reiner/Steve Martin film *The Man with Two Brains* (1983) turning out to be talk show host Merv Griffin. Besides being incongruously hilarious (Griffin's normally nice but boring persona is seemingly based in avoiding all controversy), it also offers comic insight about the contemporary horror predator—since *Psycho* (1960), it could be anyone.

Interestingly enough, one need not take the critic's "creative position" on the educational significance of parody. It is the *law*. In 1994 the United States Supreme Court ruled that the rap group 2 Live Crew could not be stopped from spoofing the Ray Orbison hit "Pretty Woman." (Acuff-Rose Music owns the rights to the song.) The company was concerned, as were many recording artists, that it would lose revenue by spoofs destroying future markets for the originals. Overruling a lower court decision, the Supreme Court declared that parody "can provide social benefit, by shedding light on an earlier work, and, in the process, creating a new one."[5] Though directed at the music industry, it is a watershed ruling applicable to all the arts, including motion pictures. As one article title (see note 5) on the subject, comically punned, "Parody Hits Right Note with the Court," spoofing artists were more than a little happy, too.

Ironically, parody's focus on artistic structure would eliminate it from the traditional axiom that "art imitates life." As parody scholar David Kiremidjian observed, whereas "Hamlet argues that art should hold the mirror up to nature ... parody ... holds the mirror not up to nature but to another work of art."[6] Yet the modern era has never been limited by this axiom. Indeed, as early as Oscar Wilde's essay "The Decay of Lying" (1889), with its insightfully tongue-in-cheek observation "Life Imitates Art far more than Art Imitates Life," defining the arts has been anything but traditional.[7] In today's world of self-conscious art, years after the "birth" of Andy Warhol's soup cans, there is no debating parody's artistic credentials. Indeed, parody embraces the first and still most controversial axiom of modern art: get away from the limitations of a single perspective. Brooks observes, "What I did when the [*Blazing Saddles*] gunfight spilled over onto the Busby Berkeley set with fifty dancers was what Picasso did when he painted the two eyes on the same side of the head."[8] Though one might not normally think of Brooks and Picasso in the same sentence, the comedy filmmaker's point is well taken. That is, in the cubism of Picasso, traditional perspective and illusion are abandoned in favor of analysis of a subject from numerous angles simultaneously.

Third, in a continued underlining of the significance of parody, the genre should *not* be confused with satire, of which it has sometimes been considered a lesser subcategory. As genre theorist Joseph A. Dane observed, "The norms in parody and satire are different; parody deals with literary [or cinematic] norms (collective understanding of a text or genre), while satire deals with social norms."[9] Spoofing has affectionate fun at the expense of a given form or structure; satire more aggressively attacks the flaws and follies of mankind. (And dark comedy—beyond satire—only hopes to steal an occasional laugh before *the* end.)

So why the confusion between parody and satire? Parody scholar Linda Hutcheon addresses this question in her seminal book, *A Theory of Parody*: "The obvious reason for the confusion of parody and satire, despite this major difference between them, is the fact that the two genres are often used together."[10] For example, Woody Allen uses his science fiction parody *Sleeper* (1973), in which the comedian's screen persona awakens 200 years in the future, as a perfect "historical setting" to also satirically refute the values of early 1970s America. And Brooks' *Blazing Saddles* makes pointed satirical comments on racism and violence in the one-time glorified American West. A much milder example of social satire in a Brooks parody is his *Spaceballs* (1987) attack on the mega merchandising aspects of the *Star Wars* trilogy. (And naturally this satire on marketing is applicable to most other action/adventure films of this type.) Although Brooks' work is primarily an affectionate spoof of George Lucas' films (indeed, Lucas' company did the special effects for Brooks), *Spaceballs* does have a deliciously self-conscious segment in which Brooks, as the Yoda-type character Yogurt, steps out of the story line to hawk a seemingly limitless supply of *Spaceballs* items. This is satirically compounded by reference to the punning sequel: *Spaceballs II: The Search for More Money*.

Still, the difference between parody and satire should be kept firmly in mind, with the understanding that the two need not go hand in hand. Indeed, the vast majority of American film parodies are much more concerned with undercutting the structure of a given genre and/or auteur, from the pioneer work of Sennett and the majority of Brooks, to the Zucker

Brothers and Jim Abrahams's *Airplane!* and the "Naked Gun" series, such as *Naked Gun: From the Files of Police Squad* (1988) and *Naked Gun 2 1/2: The Smell of Fear* (1991). In Abrahams's solo pictures, such as *Hot Shots!* (1991) and *Hot Shots! Part Deux* (1993), there is more likely to be some satire, such as Saddam Hussein's appearance in the *Hot Shots!* sequel. (The 1991 vehicle spoofs *Top Gun* (1986) and *Part Deux* tackles the Rambo trilogy—*First Blood*, 1982, *Rambo: First Blood Part II*, 1985, and *Rambo III*, 1988.) Still, Abrahams's scattergun lampooning (the basic parody norm) stays primarily in the spoofing mode.

One receives the form-over-social-comment message in the parody films of the underrated Bob Hope, who starred in a number of classic 1940s and 1950s examples of the genre. These included numerous solo spoofs, such as takeoffs of film noir or the Western as well as his *Road* pictures with Bing Crosby, in which the parody was often of the adventure film. The best of these was the *Road to Utopia* (1945), with the inspired use of humorist/actor Robert Benchley as a sometimes comic antiheroic narrator. In fact, Hope even scooped Brooks' *High Anxiety* spoof of Hitchcock by decades, having starred in the excellent 1942 parody of Hitchcock's *The 39 Steps* (1935). The film, *My Favorite Blonde*, co-starred Madeline Carroll, who had a similar co-starring role in the original. This emphasis on dismantling structure over social statement is present in the frequently neglected work of such comedy talents as Steve Martin (often in collaboration with Carl Reiner) and former Brooks disciples Gene Wilder and Marty Feldman. See especially the Martin/Reiner *The Man with Two Brains* (1983), Wilder's *The Adventures of Sherlock Holmes' Smarter Brother* (1975, Wilder directed, wrote, and starred), and Feldman's *The Last Remake of Beau Geste* (1977, Feldman directed, co-wrote, and starred). As a side note, when Abrahams and the Zucker Brothers attempted to include too much satire in their *Top Secret!* (1984), a collision of Elvis musicals and cold war espionage in East Germany, it was neither a critical nor commercial success.

Fourth, there are essentially two kinds of film parodies—the broad and obvious puncturing of a genre or auteur, and a more subdued approach that manages comic deflation with an eventual reaffirmation of the subject under attack. Again, one might think of Sennett as a personification of the first and most mainstream of parody types. In fact, Sennett parodies, and those of rival silent comedy producer Hal Roach, were sometimes so broad one need not go beyond their titles. For instance, both men produced short parodies later the same year of the 1923 epic silent Western *The Covered Wagon*. Sennett's version was *The Uncovered Wagon*; Roach countered with *Two Wagons, Both Covered*. One should also be aware of the wonderfully overt Sennett parodies starring cross-eyed comic Ben Turpin. The pun-titled *The Shriek of Araby* (1923, which spoofs Valentino) and *A Harem Knight* (1926, a parody of Erich von Stroheim) are comic joys.

Indeed, there is a special parody payoff just in seeing the diminutive, cross-eyed Turpin in the patented Stroheim white uniform and monocled or in the desert robes of Valentino's sheik. More recently, many spoof titles also leave little doubt that comedy is the message, such as *Naked Gun 2 ½: The Smell of Fear*. One of Gene Wilder's parodies, outside his work with Brooks, also is a Valentino takeoff—*The World's Greatest Lover* (1977). Even the obvious parody tradition of Turpin's comedy deformity lives on in the comic bulging eyes of Brooks disciple Marty Feldman, whose *Young Frankenstein* character of Igor is pronounced "Eye-gore."

Parodies of reaffirmation are not so obvious. They are often confused with the genre being undercut. A perfect example of this is John Landis' *An American Werewolf in London* (1981), in which broad parody (such as the use of songs such as "Bad Moon Rising" and several versions of "Blue Moon") alternates with shocking horror (graphic violence and painfully realistic werewolf transformations). This produces a fascinating tension between genre expectations (in this case, horror—to be scared) and a parody that is comic without deflating the characters involved. This is opposed to the more traditional horror parody of a *Young Frankenstein*, in which, for example, Feldman's Igor, with those eyes and a roving hump on his back, can never be taken seriously. Thus, the reaffirmation approach adds a poignancy not normally associated with parody. One is truly saddened by the death of the American werewolf (David Naughton). The closing deaths of the central heroes in the reaffirmation parody classics *Bonnie and Clyde* (1967) and *Butch Cassidy and the Sundance Kid* (1969) elicit even more deep-felt emotions. Yet for many, *Bonnie and Clyde* is merely a violently offbeat gangster film, and *Butch Cassidy and the Sundance Kid* is no more than another 1960s revisionist look at the Western. But as with the later *American Werewolf in London*, both these films maintain a mesmerizing tension between genre expectations (the crime and violence of gangster and Western outlaws) and an endearing sense of parody that encourages viewer identification. Consequently, Butch and Sundance are bumbling outlaws who make their living by comically *avoiding* shoot-outs. Butch shows genuine concern for their victims, is not particularly good with a gun, and has everyone wanting to protect him from the law. Indeed, my correspondence with the film's screenwriter (William Goldman, who won an Oscar for best original screenplay) revealed that these things were what really fascinated him about the story:

Here was this incredibly charming man, uncatchable (he just rode into farmhouses and said, "Hello, my name is Butch Cassidy, the law's on my tail, mind if I hide in your basement?" and they'd say, "Sure." . . . People *adored* Cassidy; he was just that amiable. . . . Couple that fact with his job as head of the biggest most successful gang in western history and he wasn't good at any of the things gang members were good at; well, I think that's interesting.[11]

A "vaudeville" interlude in *Butch Cassidy and the Sundance Kid* (1969), with Katharine Ross and Paul Newman.

Along similar lines, *Bonnie and Clyde* are outlaws who manage to exist quite nicely outside the gangster norm of the predatory—asphalt jungle—city at night, frequently behaving like Sennett's Keystone Cops in their slapstick, broad daylight chases with accompanying upbeat banjo soundtrack music. Indeed, a revisionist might be moved to call it a dark comedy.

The reaffirmation parody of *Butch Cassidy* is reminiscent of the tongue-in-cheek humor found in the swashbuckling adventure film. In fact, the Goldman correspondence reveals that a key influence was the often-comic banter between Cary Grant, Victor McLaglen, and Douglas Fairbanks, Jr., in *Gunga Din* (1939).[12] For more on these two movies, see Chapter 2.

It is not necessary, however, to limit oneself to modern (after 1960) cinema for examples of the more complex reaffirmation parodies. Though neither as obvious nor as prevalent as the traditional spoof movie, they, too, have always been there. Buster Keaton, silent film comedy's only rival to Charlie Chaplin, often used this method. Appropriately, Keaton's greatest and now most acclaimed film, *The General* (1927), uses this approach, with the comedian having a Civil War backdrop of epically real proportions. Unfortunately for Keaton, period critics and audiences did not appreciate this more subtle approach to parody (a common risk in reaffir-

Buster Keaton's masterpiece, the reaffirmation parody *The General* (1927).

mation work), and *The General* was a critical and commercial failure. As if to underline the ambiguity between comedy and drama in the reaffirmation parody, Disney later did the same story straight as *The Great Train Robbery* (1956.)

Keaton, of course, was a master of both parody methods. His first film, *The Three Ages* (1923), was a direct takeoff on D. W. Griffith's *Intolerance* (1916), as well as an interesting parody guide to Keaton's transition from short subjects to features. The epic *Intolerance*, with its examination of man's bigotry through the ages (ancient Babylon, the Judea of Christ, Renaissance France, and modern America), was a perfect parody invitation for Keaton to loosely join three short examples into one feature. Parodying Griffith's historical structure, Keaton looks at love in three periods (the Stone Age, ancient Rome, and modern America).

Keaton's direct parody ease of transition here, from short to features, is actually a phenomenon more frequently associated with the ambiguous reaffirmation method. For instance, film comedy historian Mast, though not addressing this basic parody dichotomy, has observed that since modern film parodies generally need to maintain their often-slender premise for feature length (as opposed to an earlier period when short subjects were the norm), it is much easier to sustain viewer interest by actually blending in the real thrills and chills of the genre under comic attack.[13]

One final parody aside on Keaton: for him, as for Sennett and a number of other silent film parodists, Griffith represented a favored target. Though Griffith was seldom so baldly spoofed as in *The Three Ages*, Keaton (again like Sennett) was fond of skewering those Griffith crosscutting conclusions, such as Keaton's athletically drawn out coming-to-the-rescue of the heroine in *College* (1927). Indeed, the fact that the *College* girl is actually being cornered in her own room by the film heavy is reminiscent of the cornered woman in *The Lonely Villa* (1909). A parody well done is always a pleasure to view. But there is an added comic joy when Griffith is the target, because as great as his pioneer significance was for early cinema, the master's many gifts did *not* include humor. And for that matter, spoofed film artists of the period were not as likely to be flattered, as is today's norm. For example, Keaton's dark comedy spoof of celebrated silent movie cowboy William S. Hart (*The Frozen North*, 1922) had the six-gun star not talking to the comedian for two years.

Fifth, film parody, like other comedy approaches, is a genre of indeterminate time and space. It is not limited to one period and place, as is more apt to occur in a determinate time and place genre such as the Western, which generally occurs on the American frontier from sometime after the Civil War (1861–65) until the turn of the century. The determinate genre Western generally has its hero enter a specific physically contested space, achieve a definite resolution, then exit said space. Thus, in an archetypal Western such as John Ford's *My Darling Clementine* (1946), Wyatt Earp (Henry Fonda) and his brothers ride into a contested space in the American West called Tombstone, a town suffering under the archetypal evil Clantons (led by the father, Walter Brennan). After a battle at the legendary O. K. Corral, in which the Clantons are killed and Tombstone's conflict is fully resolved, Wyatt Earp and one surviving brother move on.

A parody, therefore, might spoof the science fiction genre by focusing on another galaxy in the twenty-second century. Or one could parody the Western and go back to Dodge City in 1875. *But*, unlike the other comedy genres, once a specific parody choice has been made, time and place and all the icons that go with it (six-guns and ten-gallon hats, or space helmets and laser guns) are of the utmost importance. Because parody is based on triggering a viewer's prior knowledge of a given genre or auteur, it is naturally important to showcase early on (through icons) which particular subject has been nominated for the user-friendly hot spot. Again, this accents the point that parody focuses on having fun with a given structure or text.

The parodies of Brooks have been especially detailed in their attention to icons of a specific genre. In fact, he was even able to find and use the original laboratory set of the 1931 *Frankenstein* for *Young Frankenstein*.

(This historic set had been stored for years in the garage of its original designer, Kenneth Strictfaden!) Marty Feldman goes one step further in *The Last Remake of Beau Geste*. Through the use of actual footage from the 1939 *Beau Geste*, creative editing, and close attention to original set design, Feldman's character (Beau's *twin* brother Digby!) is able to share a scene with Gary Cooper's title character. Carl Reiner and Steve Martin push the envelope further in their film noir parody *Dead Men Don't Wear Plaid* (1982). The movie is constructed around extensive real footage from numerous 1940s noir classics, with Martin "interacting" with a who's who of the genre, including Humphrey Bogart and Alan Ladd. Though this one-gag parody eventually wears thin, the technical magic of matching new footage to old clips remains a fascinating achievement. It also reminds one that the technically authentic look of the film parody goes hand in hand with the icons. Again, *Young Frankenstein* is an excellent primer. Brooks apes the look of the 1930s film world by shooting his horror parody in black and white, using the old screen size and resurrecting such archaic transitions as the iris-out and the wipe.

Sometimes an old technique, such as the wipe, contributes humor beyond adding an amusing period atmosphere. This effect at its most basic is when one scene appears to be wiped off the screen by the progressive revelation of another scene—a vertical dividing line (separating the two) advancing across the screen from left to right. Brooks' revival of this "now you see it now you don't" technique is all the funnier since it is being used to spoof a genre, the horror film, in which black capes, moving dark shadows, ever-descending nightfalls . . . are mere iconographic variations of the wipe.

Another variation on parody recycling of a genre's icons involves casting cameo appearances by performers strongly associated with the type of film under friendly attack. Thus, Bob Hope's film noir parody *My Favorite Brunette* opens with a pivotal cameo from celebrated noir performer Alan Ladd; his Western parody *Alias Jesse James* closes with a corral full of Western cameos, ranging from Jay Silverheels (Tonto, of *Lone Ranger* fame) to Gary Cooper.

A further twist of actor-as-icon occurs in those film parodies in which a performer imitates a classic screen persona, such as Madeline Kahns' inspired takeoff on Marlene Dietrich in *Blazing Saddles*. At its most ambitious, such films treat the actor as auteur, basing their parody on high points in the performer's career. For instance, Humphrey Bogart has been used so often along these lines, he has nearly become a parody subgenre by himself. The Neil Simon–authored *Cheap Detective* (1978) has a Peter Falk–Bogart parodying his way through most of the tough guy's classics and those of a few others. *Variety* affectionately called it "Son of Casablanca" (June 7, 1978). The film was no doubt inspired by the earlier Simon parody *Murder By Death* (1976), in which a Falk–Bogart joins a parody collection of celebrated detectives, though the names have all been

changed (or at least slightly jiggled) to protect the "innocent"—the pro-
ducers. Thus, Falk's Sam Spade is called Sam Diamond, David Niven and
Maggie Smith's *Thin Man* couple Nick and Nora Charles become Dick and
Dora Charleston, and so on.

The Black Bird (1975), as more than suggested by the title, is a parody
of *The Maltese Falcon*, with George Segal starring as Sam Spade, Jr. *The
Man with Bogart's Face* (1980) has Robert Sacchi playing Bogart in a
private-eye case also suspiciously like *The Maltese Falcon*. And Woody
Allen's *Play It Again, Sam* has Jerry Lacy's Bogart advising Allen on his
love life, heavily filtered through *Casablanca* (1942; a clip from the close
acts as the start of the Allen film). Allen also periodically assumes Bogart's
mannerisms, voice, and *Casablanca* dialogue in the film, always with incongruously funny results, from attempting to drink bourbon to trying to
be a great lover. Fittingly, *Sam*'s runway close is patterned after the ending
of *Casablanca*. (Sam's basic spoofing premise of getting romantic cues off
the screen is also reminiscent of Keaton's wonderful *Sherlock Jr.*, 1924,
when the great "Stone Face" plays a movie projectionist who learns about
love via film.)

Bogart himself was directly involved in a send-up of *The Maltese Falcon*–
type films. He starred in John Huston's now-celebrated film *Beat the Devil*
(1954, scripted by Truman Capote and Huston, supposedly an adaptation
of James Helvick's novel). Capote said, "John and I decided to kid the
story, to treat it as a parody. Instead of another *Maltese Falcon* [which
Huston had adapted and directed in 1941], we turned it into a . . . [spoof]
on this type of film."[14] The Capote quote is included because the film is
sometimes mistakenly described as a specific parody of *The Maltese Falcon*.
Today, it would best be labeled a subtle parody of reaffirmation, which,
although critically well received, was over the heads of most 1954 viewers,
though a cult following soon started. Bogart himself was unhappy with the
results, though it is hardly likely, as is sometimes suggested, that he also
was unaware of its parody nature. After all, the man had lines such as,
"Without money I become dull, listles, and have trouble with my com-
plexion." As the old critical axiom states, "Trust the tale not the teller." If
Beat the Devil now works for the viewer as a parody of reaffirmation, that
in itself is sufficient evidence of its genre. If quotes like Capote's add to
one's argument, so much the better. But one's view of the art object is the
overriding concern.

It should be added that like a handful of other influential stars, such as
John Wayne in the Western, Cary Grant in screwball comedy, Gene Kelly
in the musical . . . the Bogart persona actually goes beyond being just another film noir icon. As movie critic Colin McArthur suggests, when certain
performers have appeared numerous times in one particular genre, they
have sometimes helped shape the evolution of the genre itself.[15] Thus, Bogart is such a film noir factor that the parody of this genre can result not

only from imitating his persona but also from doing just the opposite. For instance, Robert Altman's spoofing adaptation of Raymond Chandler's *The Long Goodbye* (1973), with a delightfully laid-back Elliott Gould as Philip Marlowe, still has the viewer often laughingly thinking about how different Bogart's Marlowe was in *The Big Sleep* (1946). When spoofing film noir, Bogart is hard to deny.

Parody itself has a few of these icon players. Writer/director/actor Mel Brooks is one such figure. Though not always casting himself in his pictures, it is hard not to think of parody when he *is* on-screen. Still, parody's most high-profile actor icon probably would be Leslie Nielsen. Star of *Airplane*! and the *Naked Gun* spoofs, he is able to use his parody connection even in nonfilm markets. For example, in 1993 he wrote (with David Fisher) the ironically titled autobiography *The Naked Truth*, with the marketing pitch: "At Last! The Hero of *The Naked Gun* Tells His Incredible Life Story—Uncensored, Uninhibited, and Totally Made Up!" Fittingly, the "autobiography" also included doctored stills of Nielsen allegedly hobnobbing with the film elite, including director Alfred Hitchcock and actor Steve McQueen. It is a funny parody of a life, just not his. For example, he and his brothers grew up on the Arctic Circle and "played all the usual childhood games—cowboys and Eskimos, Eskimos in space—but our favorite game was hide-and-seek. It wasn't because we particularly liked hide-and-seek, but rather because we loved hearing someone say 'You're getting warmer.' "[16] Appropriately enough, however, the book is also peppered with "creative criticism." For instance, Nielsen is constantly sharing stories about films he was allegedly in. But invariably, his comic commentary has some basis in fact, such as when he reveals that Warren Beatty told him, "*Bonnie and Clyde* is actually a strong anti-war statement."[17] And although he has lots of fun at the expense of this and other films, valid insights are interwoven at no extra cost.

The sixth characteristic of film parody repeatedly involves a compounding phenomenon. Although parody usually has a focus genre or auteur under comic attack, it frequently is peppered with eclectic references to other structures or texts. For instance, although *Airplane*! makes parody mincemeat of the *Airport* movies, it still has irreverent time for other film targets, from a wonderful opening credit deflating of *Jaws* to later sendups of John Travolta's white-suited solo dance number in *Saturday Night Fever* (1977), as well as the Burt Lancaster/Deborah Kerr beach scene in *From Here to Eternity* (1953). The latter example is such a prized parody target, it has turned up in several spoof films.

The term *compounding* was selected because of the current interest in what is considered a *compound genre*, in which one film displays strong characteristics of two or more genres. A comparable *compound parody* also occasionally occurs when two or more genres share the parody focus. Though it is not as common as the general parody phenomenon of stock-

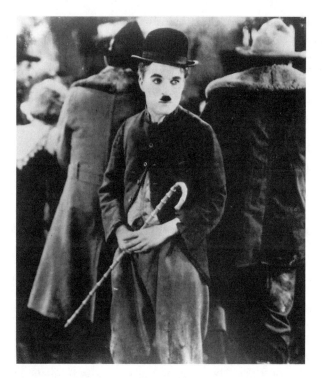

Charlie Chaplin's "little fellow" hits the frontier saloon
scene in *The Gold Rush* (1925).

piling short comic references to other genres, examples have always existed.
For instance, an excellent model from the early days would be the aforementioned short *The Frozen North* (1922). Though best celebrated as a
comic assault on silent Western star William S. Hart, the icy setting and
related humor demonstrate more than a passing awareness of an earlier
1922 cinema sensation—Robert Flaherty's *Nanook of the North*, which is
sometimes considered the beginning of the documentary movement. The
film includes a consistent peppering of other parody elements, such as the
comic broadside to the flamboyant 1920s actor/auteur Erich von Stroheim,
whose *Foolish Wives* (1921) was his current most recent period sensation.
(Stroheim remained a popular parody target throughout the 1920s, being
dissected in the Sennett two-reeler *The Pride of Pikeville*, 1927, in which
cross-eyed, anemic Ben Turpin emulates the virile star so successfully that
he accidentally manages—thanks to those eyes—to flirt with two women
simultaneously.) *The Frozen North* also anticipates the Klondike Western
parody elements of Chaplin's later classic, *The Gold Rush* (1925).

A modern era example of a compound parody is the superb *The Man
with Two Brains*, which does a comedy blitz of both the mad scientist

horror movie *and* film noir. The latter parody is largely through the in-spired casting of Kathleen Turner, who does a comedy send-up of her clas-sic predator noir woman from *Body Heat* (1981). Steve Martin, as the gifted surgeon with the unpronounceable comic name Michael Hfuhruhurr, inventor of the revolutionary screw-top brain operation, becomes roman-tically involved with a brain in a jar, losing interest in his bad news buffet wife (Turner). As "wild and crazy" as the premise seems (to use Martin's famous catchphrase from his earlier stand-up comedy period), the film then proceeds to showcase a laugh wave of "creative criticism" about the focus genres. For instance, when parodying a mad scientist (doctors such as Frankenstein, Jekyll, and Moreau, who risk the wrath of God and man for pure knowledge), what is more comically appropriate than having one fall in love with an actual brain in a jar? And what a refreshing twist this provides for the obligatory horror film search for available bodies, as Mar-tin seeks a beautiful "home" for his steady brain. Martin even does a brief comic imitation of the perennial assistant in such horror film searches—Igor.

The film also manages to close with a comic homage to the traditional message of mad scientist movies: man should not play God. After Martin has successfully placed the brain (voice by Sissy Spacek) in Turner's body, it is revealed through a flashback that his new ideal woman is a compulsive eater, and the sensual Turner body has turned to blubber.

It should be noted that Woody Allen often pursues the compound parody approach in a less obvious manner, with one of his target genres not being typical mainstream cinema audience fare. For instance, in his directing de-but, *Take the Money and Run* (1969), he mixes prison film parody with the conventions of the cinema vérité documentary. In what he once called his favorite film, *Love and Death* (1975, which certainly focuses on Allen's two central themes), his parody takes on the romantic costume drama war film and art house cinema (particularly the works of Allen idols Ingmar Bergman and Sergei Eisenstein, besides every nineteenth-century Russian novel this side of a college literature class). Even his more general audience parody grab bag, *Everything You Always Wanted to Know About Sex (But Were Afraid to Ask)* (1972), includes a takeoff on the Italian films of di-rector Michelangelo Antonioni.

Seventh, a frequent additional trait of film parody is self-consciously to draw attention to the fact that films about moviemaking, often called "genre genre" cinema, are parodies. To honestly be incorporated into a parody format, this self-consciousness must be used to complement an already-ongoing attack on a target genre or auteur. For instance, Brooks' brilliant (though then-controversial, see Chapter 4) conclusion to *Blazing Saddles* has the parody becoming so broad that it quite literally breaks out of the film. It first spills over into a musical being shot on another set, then comically invades the Warner Brothers lot and Hollywood proper. A smaller but just as exquisite Brooks example occurs in his Hitchcock parody, *High Anxiety*, when the famed director's fondness for the tracking shot is undercut. Whereas Hitchcock's camera obliquely travels through windows and walls, the Brooks camera attempts this only to break the window glass and draw the attention of all the actors before it embarrassedly backs out of the scene. (Film critic Pauline Kael said it most succinctly: "His [Brooks'] humor is a show-business comment on show business."[18])

In either case, such movie self-consciousness represents the ultimate parody prick, since nothing affectionately deflates a celebrated genre or auteur faster than a comic reminder that this is, indeed, only a movie. Moreover, since parody is based on self-consciousness about a given subject, such filmmaking interjections represent a logical culmination of the parody experience—the comic deathblow to any remaining vestiges of the viewer's suspension of disbelief. In addition, as implied by theory historian Margaret A. Rose, the self-consciousness is one other way of "signaling" the audience that this is indeed a parody.[19]

These, then, are the seven pivotal characteristics of parody: a humor based on the distorted imitation of a familiar genre or auteur; "creative criticism"—offering educational insights; distinctive from satire (an attack on structure, not society); two basic types—overt parody and reaffirmation; a genre of indeterminate time and place *but* with a difference; the compounding of more than one target subject; and self-consciousness about the filmmaking experience. As demonstrated by the preceding overview, those traits have remained consistent from silents through sound.

I am tempted to add a corollary to this list. It is not to be thought of as point eight but rather as a sometime occurrence. Mel Brooks has observed of parody: "Never try to be funny! The actors must be serious. Only the situation must be absurd. Funny is in the writing, not in the performing. And another thing, the more serious the situation, the funnier the comedy can be."[20] Although this is a sometimes-insightful statement by a pivotal parody auteur, it just does not always apply, even in Brooks' work. In fact, one of the most entertaining exceptions is played by Brooks himself in *Blazing Saddles*—the oversexed governor William J. LePetomane. His scenes are very broadly performed, to the point of Brooks comically crossing his eyes, reminiscent of the aforementioned work of silent comedy's cross-eyed parodist Ben Turpin. (Marty Feldman's bubble-eyed Igor, complete with roving hump, even steals the show in *Young Frankenstein*.) Conversely, some critics (such as Pauline Kael) have felt that a pivotal role in *Blazing Saddles* (Cleavon Little as the black marshal) was flawed by casting an underplaying actor instead of an over-the-top comic, such as Richard Pryor. Indeed, Pryor worked on the script and was originally meant to play that role. More typical of the film is the self-conscious direct address of Harvey Korman: "Why am I telling you [the viewer] this? You already know it."

The most entertaining exceptions to underplaying occur in Bob Hope's numerous spoofs. In *My Favorite Brunette* the comedian plays at being a film noir detective, sharing an early scene with Alan Ladd, a real-life film noir star at the time. Besides the immediate comedy contrast between Hope's essentially cowardly figure and his attempts to be a tough guy, the two men have blatantly different acting styles. Hope is a fully animated, over-the-top comedian. Ladd, like most noir figures, embraces a minimalist style of body and dialogue, with the latter element both brief and pithy. Noir is an existentialist world in which protecting one's self means personally exposing very little. Thus, the success of all the Hope parodies plays upon his figure being anything but serious. And Hope's parody work has greatly influenced the movies of major comedy auteur Woody Allen. An excellent companion piece to *Brunette* is Allen's own film noir spoof *Play It Again, Sam*, where Bogart is the model and Allen is anything but. Also, Allen's takeoff on science fiction, *Sleeper* (1973), showcases the actor at his most visually demonstrative best, including his inspired operation of the electric wheelchair with the thought police near *Sleeper*'s start, or the later speeded-up action of the robot repair scene, in which Allen the mechanical figure nearly loses his head.

Still, playing-it-straight parody performances frequently remain. In contrast to a Hope, the poker face dominates in the spoofing world of Jim Abrahams and Jerry and David Zucker. They felt so strongly that their "remake of *Zero Hour* [*Airplane!*] must be deadpan to be funny, they turned down one chance to do the film because the company putting up the money wanted to use established comedians like . . . [the over-the-top Mel Brooks regular] Dom Deluise."[21] Moreover, in all fairness to Brooks, it should be stated that a number of the director's regulars match his comments on the parody actor being best when he or she is most serious. There is no better example of this than gifted performer Kenneth Mars' seminal Nazi playwright in *The Producers* (1968), or his inventive Inspector Kemp from *Young Frankenstein*. While spending some time with Mars at a 1994 conference celebrating the art of Buster Keaton, he entertainingly revealed that although Brooks might expect an actor to play it straight, off-camera the director was often not up to the same task. Brooks had a propensity to ruin takes with his laughter. Indeed, as a comic acknowledgment of this problem, he once left a set and phoned in the director's all-important "cut," ending the scene and saving the take.

Irrespective of these parody styles, the genre had a special 1960s turning point. Spoof historians Nick Smurthwaite and Paul Gelder suggest that "not until the sixties was it generally accepted that the American cinema is made up of genres."[22] This was the decade when film study became a mainstream part of university classwork, catering to a student clientele weaned on the movie crash course made possible by 1950s television. After all, the 1960s has been called the "fourth American era" of movies (after the silents, the studio years, and the post–World War II period of transition), a time when a more educated and movie-conscious public began to constitute the bulk of the film audience.[23]

Five other factors, however, deserve at least brief attention in these 1960s parody developments. First was the late 1950s and 1960s influence of the French New Wave cinema movement. The innovative development of directors such as Francois Truffaut and Jean-Luc Godard had a major influence on American film. Ironically, it was the French homage to an earlier American cinema that helped this country both recognize the significance of its movie heritage and fuel the interest in its movie past. The result was the mushrooming of parody films. One might note that Godard's celebrated first film, *Breathless* (1959, story by Truffaut) is a romanticized French gangster tale with Jean-Paul Belmondo sometimes aping his movie tough-guy idol Bogart. (Previous to this, pioneer American rock 'n roll star Jerry Lee Lewis had also recorded the critically and commercially successful hit song "Breathless," more French homage to American pop culture.) Though the film is not really a spoof, it often plays like a parody of reaffirmation, with a range that extends from Belmondo comically trying to emulate a Bogart movie poster, to his death from betrayal in the streets, which certainly influenced the violent betrayal close of *Bonnie and Clyde*.

The French New Wave films frequently also had fun with the self-consciousness of the filmmaking process. For instance, in Godard's classic *Weekend* (1967), which moves from an epic traffic jam (reminiscent of Laurel & Hardy's *Two Tars*, 1928) to the do's and don'ts of joining a guerrilla band, there is a comic sequence in which revolutionaries are moving through the jungle with a pulsating rock score seemingly on the soundtrack. But then the guerrillas walk by the rock-producing band itself, incongruously playing in a jungle setting. Certainly this scene influenced the similar but more well-known Mel Brooks gag in *Blazing Saddles* in which Gucci-attired Bart (Cleavon Little) is riding majestically through the time-honored expanses of the great American West with the standard swelling musical accompaniment of the genre, only to come upon Count Basie and his orchestra as the source of the music.

Second, the 1960s also found the controversial American arrival of the auteur theory. Although American film critic Andrew Sarris was the English language father/messenger of this critical perspective, credit again goes to Truffaut and other New Wave directors who, before they entered film production, were influential young critics for the journal *Cahiers du Cinéma*, from whose 1950s pages auteurism was born. And obviously, like the general recognition of genre patterns in the 1960s, the appreciation of recurring auteur structures increased interest in, and production of, parodies.

Third, the 1960s represented an early blossoming of several important parody artists also connected to a common 1950s phenomenon—something called *Your Show of Shows* (1950–54). This American television program was for the future parody what the 1970s edition of *Saturday Night Live* might someday represent for dark comedy film. Like *Saturday Night Live*, *Your Show of Shows* was a ninety-minute live comedy-variety program. Starring Sid Caesar and Imogene Coca and featuring Carl Reiner, *Your Show of Shows* included Mel Brooks, Neil Simon, and Woody Allen among its writing staff. Not surprisingly, one of its ongoing features was film parody sketches. As with Sennett, the spirit of such parody was often captured in the titles—*From Here to Obscurity, A Trolley Car Named Desire*, and in comic honor of the drowning in *A Place in the Sun*, the spoof *A Place at the Bottom of the Lake*. Because Caesar was a superb pantomimist, spoofs of silent films were also common. Fittingly, the best thing about Brooks' later parody *Silent Movie* (1976) was the comedy of co-star Caesar. *The* film tribute to *Your Show of Shows* is the movingly imaginative parody of reaffirmation *My Favorite Year* (1982), which affectionately spoofs both the show and an Errol Flynn–like matinee idol Alan Swann (Peter O'Toole) making a guest appearance on the program.

Future film reviews of Brooks' work would sometimes even make reference to *Your Show of Shows*. For example, *Newsweek* critic Paul D. Zimmerman noted in his *Blazing Saddles* critique, "Four men share the screenwriting credit with Brooks, suggesting that the script was put together in the television brainstorming tradition of *Your Show of Shows*."[24] In a later Brooks interview, he revealed that this had been the case: "I wanted to write it [*Blazing Saddles*] the way we wrote *Your Show of Shows*—lock a bunch of weirdoes up together and come out with a great script."[25]

As a side note on the further influence of *Your Show of Shows*, the program added an additional educational twist to parody's "creative criticism": These [Caesar] parodies probably did more to sell the foreign art film to American audiences than any sober ad campaign could have done . . . they introduced in a light and palatable way the fact of a foreign cinema, its characteristic themes and styles, and—most important—the sense there could be an alternative to the familiar American models.[26]

Although the future film spoofs of Brooks, Allen, and Simon would be most fully realized in the 1970s, with Reiner as a parodist coming into his own in the 1980s, the spoofing presence of the central duo (Brooks and Allen) was making itself known in the 1960s. Based upon the huge commercial success (the top-grossing comedy in screen history to that point) of the sexual satire *What's New, Pussycat* (1965, which Allen wrote and starred in), this stand-up comedian was able to make a parody transition to the big screen.

The following year, *What's Up, Tiger Lily?* (1966) appeared, Allen's comic redubbing of a 1964 Japanese secret agent film. It was an outrageous parody of the James Bond craze, which had taken off with the popularity of *Dr. No* (1962). *What's Up, Tiger Lily?*, which has to be *heard* to be believed, might best be summarized by simply stating that this left-field skewering of Bond is based in a plot line about recovering the missing recipe for the world's best egg salad. The next year Allen more directly addressed Bond parody in *Casino Royale* (1967), an overblown and uneven comic spoof of 007 in which the comedian appeared, and for which he did some uncredited writing. Suggested by a novel from Bond creator Ian Fleming himself, Allen appears as little Jimmy Bond, the less-than-capable nephew of the secret agent. (The film's close, with Allen's delightfully surprising emergence as the mastermind of evil, provides the film's only sustained moments of high-quality comedy.) From this three-film foundation Allen launched his often parody-oriented filming-directing career, with *Take the Money and Run* appearing in 1969.

Parody of Bond also figures prominently in the 1960s evolution of Brooks. He and Buck Henry developed and scripted the pilot for television's greatest comic undermining of the secret agent, *Get Smart* (1965–70). The show followed the exploits of Maxwell Smart, Agent 86 (Don Adams) and his beautiful assistant, Agent 99 (Barbara Feldon), with Smart comically bumbling his way through constant spy dangers, frequently using what became a nationwide catchphrase—"Would you believe?"—whenever he launched into one of his zany spy fabrications. Through the years, *Get Smart* has remained popular in syndication, eventually spawning a feature film version, *The Nude Bomb* (1980), in which the world is threatened by a villain whose bombs will destroy all clothing. (On television it has been shown as *The Return of Maxwell Smart*.)

Brooks' 1960 film work is limited to two Oscar-winning properties, *The Critic* (1962, an animated short subject), and *The Producers* (1967). Both films favor satire over parody, but abundant examples of spoofing remain. *The Critic* is a collection of abstract Norman McLaren–like images from which Brooks, with a voice-over attitude similar to that of his stand-up comedy persona, the 2,000-year-old man, attempts to make sense. (McLaren was an award-winning filmmaker whose favorite method—drawing directly on celluloid—resulted in mesmerizing dancing, slashing lines of color.) Brooks' commentary is reminiscent of the comic axiom of vagabond poet Sadakichi Hartman: "If you think vaudeville is dead, look at modern art."[27] Besides satirizing both abstract art and attempts made to analyze it, *The Critic* is a spoof of the art film genre, and more specifically, an affectionate parody of McLaren. *The Producers*, with a story line focusing on the accidentally successful Broadway play *Springtime for Hitler* (a musical comedy about the führer), is ultimately a satire on the absurd values, or lack of values, of a dark modern world. Because *The Producers* was also an unlikely success (winning an Oscar for best original screenplay after being initially panned by most critics), Brooks' satirical point is doubly underlined. Satire aside, *Springtime for Hitler* is a rich parody of the musical, from specific scenes—a spoof of Busby Berkeley's patented overhead shot (in this case the pattern formed by the dancing girls is a giant swastika)—to the general comic irony of trying for a failure in a genre so strongly associated with the "let's put on a show!" positive mindset of anything for a success.

Fourth, the 1960s represented a watershed of antiestablishment activity—fertile ground indeed for a genre (parody) based on the comic dismantling of what is often a long-standing entertainment structure. Moreover, the fact that the antiestablishment 1960s spawned the mainstream birth of black comedy had an even more direct impact on the spoof film. Because of the shared comic disregard each of these genres has for standard norms, there is a natural tendency for dark comedy to appear in parody.

Conversely, a number of darkly comic post-1960s films, such as *All That Jazz* (1979) and *An American Werewolf in London* (1981), also have an equal number of parody parts. Besides reflecting the increasingly macabre humor of the times (see my book *American Dark Comedy: Beyond Satire*, 1996), what more cuttingly direct way is there to parody a traditionally upbeat genre like the musical than the *All That Jazz* conclusion? The big show never gets put on, and the dead director is zipped into a body bag while the sound track blasts out the powerful voice of that exuberant theatre personality Ethel Merman singing the happy anthem "Hooray for Hollywood." In 1984 the Coen Brothers (Joel directs, Ethan produces, and both share script credit) burst onto the film scene with the critically acclaimed dark comedy film noir parody *Blood Simple*. The Coens are best described as dark comedy artists, with films like *Raising Arizona* (1987) *Barton Fink* (1991), and *Fargo* (1996). Sometimes, however, as in the film noir trappings of *Blood Simple* or the gangster foundation of *Miller's Crossing* (1990), parody receives equal status with dark comedy.

Though Brooks' affectionate parody is 180 degrees away from the Coen variety, his discussion of comedy often has a black comedy hue to it: "Gogol [acclaimed nineteenth-century Russian dark comedy writer] said that life is so tragic, so stupendously sad that we'd better laugh a lot and enjoy ourselves. You either get a sense of humor going or you go under."[28] And though rare, Brooks has on occasion revealed a much darker worldview. Before noting the following quote it is important to know that a Mel Brooks interview is generally an invitation for a comedy performance. This is not to say the reader does not learn from the comments, but Brooks is generally "on" during an interview. Just as he wanted to constantly wow his family as a child, he wants to entertain the interviewer, to please. Consequently, when Brooks was asked if he disliked Germans, since his films make fun of them, his reply was shockingly out of character for the artist and his work: "Me? Not like Germans? Why should I not like Germans? Just because they're arrogant and have fat necks and do anything they're told so long as it's cruel, and killed millions of Jews in concentration camps and made soap out of their bodies and lamp shades out of their skins? Is that any reason to hate their fucking guts?"[29]

The fifth reason the 1960s is significant to parody is the ongoing success since 1962 of the Bond films. It has proven to be one of the most popular A-production series in the history of cinema, with the unique popularity of 007 generating a tidal wave of secret-agent parodies, from the aforementioned Brooks and Allen examples to the delightful Pink Panther–Inspector Clouseau collaboration of writer/director Blake Edwards and Peter Sellers, starting in 1964. (Sellers, of course, was also one of the Bond impersonators in *Casino Royale*, in which he could not be passed off as a "double" agent, because he had a hard enough time being accepted as a "single" agent.) And as Mike Myers's outrageously wonderful *Austin Powers* demonstrates (1997, where a "groovy" English secret agent put on ice in the '60s is defrosted in the '90s), Bond continues to be a major spoof target. He was also at the heart of the unfortunately mediocre 1998 *Avengers*, from the popular early 1960s British television series of the same name (on the American small screen, 1966–69). The basic mission of secret agents Jonathan Steed and Emma Peel, both on television and in the movies, was to out–James-Bond James Bond. But as significant as the Bond film has been in encouraging parody, especially during the pivotal 1960s when spoofs started to generate special attention, an additional factor frequently goes unnoticed.

The Bond films were (and continue to be) very close to being parodies themselves, walking a thin line between action adventure and spy spoof (especially with the many sexy women and off-the-wall gadgets), a parody line that grew progressively thinner in later years when Roger Moore became the first in a series of Sean Connery replacements as Bond. Thus, one might even make a case for defining the 007 films as parodies of reaffirmation. This tendency to want it both ways is more apparent in two short-lived film serials born of the Bond craze. James Coburn starred in the 007 spoof *Our Man Flint* (1966), which was followed by *In Like Flint* (1967). And the still underrated comic actor/singer Dean Martin was a campy poor man's Bond (with song) in the Matt Helm secret-agent series also starting in 1966. The first film, *The Silencers*, was easily the best of the four Martin-as-Helm features made. Thus, a crucial 1960s parody legacy of Bond (beyond the obvious spoofs) was the incitement to play even the straight drama with tongue firmly in cheek.

Celebrated film critic Pauline Kael expressed concern with this tendency during the mid-1960s, though her irritation was precipitated not by Bond but by the Western parody *Cat Ballou* (1965). Her complaint was that "spoofing has become the safety net for those who are unsure of their [straight dramatic] footing. Unlike satire, spoofing has no serious objectives."[30] Yet Kael carries a safety net all her own when she closes her piece with the sudden, vague announcement that *Cat Ballou* is not really of a parody nature. (Normally the terms *parody* and *spoofing* are used inter-changeably.) Within the context of this chapter, Kael's attack on spoofing would seem to be directed at the ambiguous parody of reaffirmation. Yet *Cat Ballou*, although not without comic-dramatic duality, is hardly subtle with most of its Western parody, be it the genre's symbol of civilization (schoolmarm Jane Fonda) becoming an outlaw, or a bad man (Lee Marvin) so coldly ruthless he has an artificial silver nose. Moreover, when noting an obvious 1960s parody of reaffirmation, such as *Bonnie and Clyde*, Kael is full of praise. More ironic still is the fact that her almost singular critical support of *Bonnie and Clyde*, at a time when most critics initially found the movie dangerously flippant about violence, helped establish her position as a pivotal American film critic.

It is important to dwell on this mid-1960s Pauline Kael–*Cat Ballou* con-troversy for four reasons. First, by its mere existence the more visible par-ody presence of the 1960s is underlined. This is especially true since Lee Marvin's double role as twin brothers (a likable drunken hired gun, whose horse also has a drinking problem, and the archvillain) was later rewarded with a film establishment Oscar for best actor, and the movie itself was a major commercial success. Second, Kael's acknowledgment and examina-tion of a popular 1960s film tendency best labeled parody of reaffirmation is an indirect period example of the reality of a more sophisticated audience better able to recognize and enjoy subtle nuances in their parody. This is consistent with today's view of the audience metamorphosis then taking place. Kael and the subject of more film-literate audiences also brings to mind her early 1960s battle with Andrew Sarris over the merits of auteur-ism (which is dependent upon a viewer having seen several films by the same director). Kael found auteurism more redundant than artistic. And as in her later complaint with reaffirmation parodies, she essentially felt the filmmaker had not taken enough of a creative risk. Third, one might label Kael's critical flip-flop on this type of parody (from *Cat Ballou* to *Bonnie and Clyde*) as an additional example of her "convenient pluralism." (For more on this, see criticism historian Edward Murray.[31]) However, another explanation is simply that the nature of reaffirmation parody was making the subject all the more complex to analyze, even for the influential critic. Certainly, Kael's semantic ambiguity over the terms *spoof* and *parody* rep-resents more evidence of this. Fourth, besides encouraging further 1960s spoofs of the Western, the fact that *Cat Ballou* both generated so much Kael attention and is a milestone of sorts in the analysis of reaffirmation parody highlights again the importance of the Western in the history of film spoofs.

Parody developments since the watershed 1960s, especially when coupled with the video revolution, continue to encourage the ever-greater film awareness of the general audience. And in the following pages, with this chapter's seven basic parody characteristics as a foundation, a pivotal collection of films from the genre (and their auteurs) are accorded a thorough examination. But the bottom line remains the same—this is an ongoing comic celebration of everything called parody.

NOTES

1. Brad Darrach, "*Playboy* Interview: Mel Brooks," *Playboy*, February 1975, p. 49.

2. Gerald Mast, *The Comic Mind: Comedy and the Movies*, 2d ed. (Chicago: University of Chicago Press, 1979), p. 47.

3. Joe Lee Davis, "Criticism and Parody," *Thought*, Summer 1951, p. 180.

4. Ibid., p. 185.

5. Tony Mauro, "Parody Hits Right Note with the Court," *USA Today*, March 8, 1994, p. 1-A.

6. David Kiremidjian, *A Study of Modern Parody* (New York: Garland Publishing, 1985), p. 18.

7. Oscar Wilde, "The Decay of Lying," in *Criticism: The Major Texts*, ed. W. J. Bate (Chicago: Harcourt Brace Jovanovich, 1970), p. 642.

8. Maurice Yacowar, *Methods in Madness* (New York: St. Martin's Press, 1981), p. 115.

9. Joseph A. Dane, "Parody and Satire: A Theoretical Model," *Genre*, Summer 1980, p. 153.

10. Linda Hutcheon, *A Theory of Parody* (New York: Methuen, 1985), p. 43.

11. Wes Gehring correspondence with William Goldman, October 5, 1980, p. 1.

12. Ibid., p. 2.

13. Mast, *The Comic Mind*, p. 308.

14. William F. Nolan, *John Huston: King Rebel* (Los Angeles: Sherbourne Press, 1965), p. 124.

15. Colin McArthur, *Underworld USA* (New York: Viking Press, 1972), p. 24.

16. Leslie Nielsen and David Fisher, *The Naked Truth* (New York: Pocket Books, 1993), p. 9.

17. Ibid., p. 207.

18. Pauline Kael, review of *Blazing Saddles*, *The New Yorker*, February 18, 1974, p. 100.

19. Margaret A. Rose, *Parody II Meta-Fiction* (London: Croom Helm, 1979), pp. 25–26.

20. Yacowar, *Methods in Madness*, p. viii.

21. Colin L. Westerbeck, Jr., "Flying High and at Bargain Rates," *Commonweal*, September 12, 1980, p. 502.

22. Nick Smurthwaite and Paul Gelder, *Mel Brooks and the Spoof Movie* (New York: Proteus Books, 1982), p. 7.

23. Gerald Mast, *A Short History of the Movies*, 2nd ed. (Indianapolis: Bobbs-Merrill, 1976), pp. 475–503.

24. Paul D. Zimmerman, "Wild, Wild West," *Newsweek*, February 18, 1974, p. 104.

25. Darrach, "*Playboy* Interview," p. 64.

26. Yacowar, *Methods in Madness*, p. 31.

27. Gene Fowler, *Minutes of the Last Meeting* (New York: Viking Press, 1954), p. 95.

28. Darrach, "*Playboy* Interview," p. 61.

29. Ibid., p. 54.

30. Pauline Kael, "Spoofing: *Cat Ballou*" (1965), in *Kiss Kiss Bang Bang* (Boston: Little, Brown, 1968), p. 28.

31. Edward Murray, "Chapter 6, Pauline Kael and the Pluralist, Aesthetic Criticism," in *Nine American Film Critics* (New York: Frederick Ungar, 1975), pp. 110–140.

2

Everyone's Going West

When Stan Laurel (as himself) is asked in *Way Out West* (1937) if a particular character is dead, he replies, "Well, we hope he is; they buried him!"

When W. C. Fields' huckster gambler Cuthbert J. Twillie is asked in *My Little Chickadee* (1940) if this is a game of chance, he answers, "Not the way I play it."

In *Go West* (1940) Groucho's con man philosophy is, "I'm not in business for love, you know. I was in love once and I got the business."

BACKGROUND

Though B-Westerns were very popular during the 1930s and 1940s, it was director John Ford's critical and commercial classic *Stagecoach* (March 1939) that returned the genre to A-productions, as well as making a star out of John Wayne. While history has declared *Stagecoach* that era's watershed Western, it was not created in a vacuum. Other major sagebrush sagas to surface in the first half of 1939 included: *Jesse James* (starring Tyrone Power and Henry Fonda), *The Oklahoma Kid* (with the unlikely Western duo of James Cagney and Humphrey Bogart), *Dodge City* (Errol Flynn), and *Union Pacific* (Joel McCrea). In the fall of 1939, the parody of reaffirmation *Destry Rides Again* further established the Western's comeback, as well as jump-starting the career of Marlene Dietrich. Needless to say, the success of these two films and the resurfacing of first-run Westerns in general were a major catalyst for both the Fields and Mae West parody *My Little Chickadee* and the Marx Brothers's spoof *Go West*. In fact, the former film, which was released in early 1940, even had particular story and character ties to *Stagecoach*; these will be examined shortly.

Given the film comedian significance of W. C. Fields, Mae West, and the Marx Brothers, these are the pivotal but hardly the only comic players to jump on this period Western parody film bandwagon. For instance, in 1940 radio and movie comedian Jack Benny did a still very entertaining spoof, *Buck Benny Rides Again*. But what is most interesting about this movement is that among the major movie comic personalities, Laurel & Hardy pre-dated the trend by two years, as well as making the most amusing of the bunch—*Way Out West*. Indeed, with the exception of their *Sons of the Desert* (1933), it is easily Laurel & Hardy's greatest feature.

The Fields/West and Marx Brothers vehicles are diverting but not their best work. Coming relatively late in their film careers, the movies are in-triguing, in part because they turned to broad parody. This is not normally associated with their earlier films, though there are always exceptions, such as the back-burner spoofing of the gangster genre in the Marx Brothers film *Monkey Business* (1931).

This chapter will examine *Way Out West, My Little Chickadee, Go West*, and that nonconventional parody *Destry Rides Again*. In the latter case, reaffirmation spoofing ties will also be made with the later *Butch Cassidy and the Sundance Kid* (1969).

WAY OUT WEST

Although most major American film comedians eventually get to a par-ody of the Western, Laurel & Hardy's *Way Out West* came twelve years after the last full-scale comic personality attack on the genre—Buster Kea-ton's *Go West* (1925). In the years that have followed Laurel & Hardy's spoof, the Western has yet to know such a long respite from comedy.

Besides the fundamental parody contrast of *Way Out West*—placing comic antiheroes Laurel & Hardy in Western macho land—the film, like all good spoofs, represents a funny, insightful dissecting of a target genre structure. Moreover, the team avoids the standard parody shtick of dressing as cowboys and assuming colorful Western names, such as Mae West's Flower Belle Lee in *My Little Chickadee*. Instead, there is a refreshing charm in their appearing in garb similar to what they might wear in a modern picture, including the all-important derbies. *Variety's* review even made special note of this: "They wear their usual costumes, despite the cowboy-western surroundings."[1] And fittingly, they continue to be Stan and Ollie to all they encounter. Consequently, it is as if they have just exited a comedy time machine and are doing parody fieldwork.

In otherwise keeping to a broadly Western terrain familiar to most viewers, however, *Way Out West* is more of an integrated feature than is often the Laurel & Hardy norm. Thus, the comedy duo find themselves heading to Brushwood Gulch to deliver a gold mine to the now-orphaned Mary Roberts (Rosina Lawrence), so virtuously portrayed as to be a send-up of the traditional sickeningly sweet Western heroine. Like Mark Twain's own Western spoof, *Roughing It* (1872), Stan & Ollie find plenty of painfully comic diversions along the way, from hitching a stagecoach ride to confronting the traditional crooked saloon owner Mickey Finn (played by longtime team nemesis James Finlayson). Naturally, good triumphs in the end, though true to comic antihero form, Stan's and Ollie's lives never become any easier.

The film begins when Hardy is victimized by a shallow stream sinkhole: Laurel safely and obliviously walks across. The movie closes on Ollie once again taking another "bath" in the stream. For those interested in comic genealogy, Laurel & Hardy style, the sinkhole is no doubt the forefather of all those wonderful bottomless mud puddles that often turn up in the team's modern setting films.

The beginning and ending symmetry of the sinkhole material makes it all the more artistically satisfying. Moreover, *Way Out West* is generally devoid of the padding that often mars other Laurel & Hardy features, and the two carry the film nicely without needing a romantic subplot—often considered a period necessity, regardless of the comedy stars. Any extra footage merely enriches the parody; for instance, most spoofs add additional targets beyond the focus genre or auteur under attack. Consequently, there is the delightful way in which Stan gets the stagecoach to stop for the duo in the middle of the wilderness.

Playing upon the phenomenal 1934 critical and commercial success of director Frank Capra's screwball comedy *It Happened One Night*, Laurel borrows from the conclusion of that film's famous hitchhiking scene. In Capra's movie, Clark Gable's character has exhausted his supply of hitchhiking hand gestures, and lovely co-star Claudette Colbert offers to give him a "hand," or more precisely, a leg. She pulls up her skirt to expose one of the beautiful limbs for which she was famous on Broadway. Naturally, a car immediately screeches to a halt, with an editing cut to a braking tire for added comedy effect. In *Way Out West*, Laurel & Hardy also find themselves hitchhiking, and when it looks as though the stagecoach is going to pass them by, Stan, in the spirit of Colbert, pulls up his pant leg and—amazingly—stops the coach. Laurel, ever conscious of details (he produced the film, too), also has a cut to the braking stagecoach wheel.

Though without the comedy buildup of *It Happened One Night* (Gable

initially fails at numerous hitchhiking techniques and then pooh-poohs novice Colbert's offer of assistance), Stan's exposure of a less-than-lovely limb
works for six reasons. First, it is a parody of the earlier film, with the
comedy contrast of Colbert's limb and Stan's. Second, there is the comic
surprise that anyone would *stop* for such a sight. Would not the driver be
more inclined to brandish a whip and speed up the horses? Third, it is a
spoof of male sexuality. This is neither something a man would normally
do, nor something another male (especially in the macho Old West) would
stop for. (Thus, one does not have to be in on the specific parody reference
to find it amusing.)

Fourth, it is also, in part, a takeoff on Laurel's screen character, since
any sexual awareness (regardless of gender) invariably seems alien to him.
Fifth, Stan's feminine action (exposing his leg) is, however, comically consistent with the couplelike nature so often associated with the team, in
which the bossy Ollie is sometimes seen as the "man" and the often-
submissive Stan is the stereotypical "woman." Sixth, Laurel's success at
stopping the stagecoach is a comic affront to Hardy not unlike the one
Colbert administered to Gable. An ongoing Laurel & Hardy premise has
always been that despite the general comic incompetence of both their
screen characters, the seemingly more-dense Stan frequently betters his
partner. And all in all, when one returns to the *It Happened One Night*
scene that inspired this parody, it seems to have Laurel & Hardy written
all over it—because the car that Colbert's sexy gam brings to a stop-on-a-
dime halt is a rickety Model-T Ford, the antiheroic car of cars so often
associated with Laurel & Hardy's modern stories.

It is not necessary, though, to expound at length about brief scenes to
praise the film. Its comedic richness varies from sexy saloon girl Sharon
Lynne's comic seductive stalking of Stan (she eventually tickles a deed out
of his possession while reducing him to an audience-contagious laughing
fit), to the Stan & Ollie musical interludes, which also vary from a soft-
shoe number to their crooning "In the Blue Ridge Mountains of Virginia."
They are interludes, however, only in the sense of a Chico Marx piano
number; they are entertainingly comic in and of themselves, as well as
representing more parody—undercutting the period popularity of B-
Western singing cowboys.

Laurel's laughing fit scene is also an excellent example of how the team
could take a standard bit of their shtick (routines involving uncontrollable
laughter surface in several Laurel & Hardy movies) and fashion it into a
spoof of something distinctively Western. That is, the saloon girl à la prostitute who uses her natural talents to assist the greasy villain is a Western
given, whether it is the Marlene Dietrich model examined later in the *Destry Rides Again* portion of this chapter, or Madeline Kahn's send-up of the
type (and of Dietrich) in the *Blazing Saddles* section of Chapter 4. Though
this is fast company, *Way Out West*'s Sharon Lynne holds her own. In

Laurel & Hardy, Sharon Lynne, and James Finlayson make like fumble recovery time in football as they go after a loose gold mine deed in *Way Out West* (1937).

truth, with the possible exception of a young Jean Harlow walk-through in Laurel & Hardy's 1929 short subject *Double Whoopee*, Lynne provides the sexiest turn of any actress in the team's filmography.

Now it is up to Lynne's saloon girl to get the deed from Laurel's person. Played straight, she would use her "charm" to distract Stan and get the document. But the thin one is essentially asexual and/or childlike presexual. Therefore, when she chases him into her bedroom, locks the door, and tries to undress him to get at the deed hidden on his person, he is not turned on, but rather, tickled. However, for the viewer, the humor comes generously laced with a sexual tension of almost erotic proportions. What a wonderful spoof of the genre's bad girl and the voyeuristic feelings of the male viewer. To paraphrase Mae West, "When women go bad, men usually go right after them." And the beauty of this "ticklish" scene is that Laurel manages to top it with more sexual innuendo. That is, for a brief time Lynne's character gets the document . . . only to have Stan reclaim it and again slip it down his front—he wants to be tickled some more. But it implies what would obviously be a real world/West desire for more sex. Stan continues to laugh even after losing the deed, often with charming direct looks at the camera, as if to ask, Who's acting?

In contrast, *Way Out West* also has a modestly unique slant not found in any other personality comedian Western parody examined in the text: Laurel adds a bit of fantasy to his persona. His character has the ability to ignite his thumb like a lighter in *Way Out West*. In Laurel & Hardy literature this is referred to as "white magic," a variation of which later occurs in *Block-Heads* (1938). In my 1990 critical biography of the duo (Greenwood Press), I expressed reservations about this development. That is, although amusing, such "white magic" is inconsistent with the delightfully dumb persona of Stan. If he really has such skills, there is no reason for his comic suffering through all the team's problems; Laurel could solve everything with just a little hocus-pocus.

Such fantasy characteristics would be perfectly in keeping with the mischievous Pan-like persona of Laurel contemporary Harpo Marx, whose surrealistic antics, not to mention his surrealistic pockets, frequently seem otherworldly. One might better demonstrate the more typical difference between Harpo and Laurel's screen characters by contrasting the manner in which they respond to the same comedy setup. In *Horse Feathers* (1932), Groucho admonishes Harpo, "Young man, you'll find as you grow older you can't burn the candle at both ends." But Harpo triumphs by producing a candle doing just that—one of the most pleasant examples of the pocket wizardry that is Harpo's ongoing wardrobe. In *Them Thar Hills* (1934) the Laurel & Hardy stock company figure Billy Gilbert tells Stan, "You can't burn a candle at both ends." The skinny one replies, "We don't. We burn electric lights." In each case the response is consistent with the viewer's comedy expectations for the character—the inspired stupidity of Stan, and the otherworldly sorcery of Harpo. Moreover, a key principle in Laurel & Hardy comedy, as defined by both director Leo McCarey (who teamed and helped mold the duo) and Laurel (the dominant creative player of the team) was to keep the action close to reality.

With these reservations noted, however, three factors now seem to make Laurel's magic in *Way Out West* less bothersome. First, as noted earlier, because the two maintain their names and make minimal costume changes, there is already a certain outlandish, time-tripper quality in their surfacing in sagebrush land anyway. Giving Stan a touch of fantasy power is not inconsistent with this. Second, one could conceivably link it to Laurel's screen persona by arguing, "Stan is so dumb he doesn't even know one can't do that." Coupled with this is another explanation: Hardy fails and/or quickly withdraws from "white magic" because he knows it should not work. In *Way Out West*, Ollie continually tries to emulate Stan's thumb-lighting abilities. When it finally happens, *he gets burned* (also a nice metaphor for his relationship with Stan), and once more the allegedly brighter one finishes second to the dunce in the derby. Third, Stan's initial foray into magic is to light their pipes. And smoking is such a manly thing in Westerns; witness the proverbial rolling of a cigarette. In fact, if I had been

"White magic" proves comically scary for Ollie as Stanley attempts to help out in *Way Out West* (1937).

writing *Way Out West*, I would have had the normally antiheroic Laurel fumbling through just such a task. But be that as it may, having Laurel & Hardy puffing away like two cracker-barrel philosophers down at the general store is bizarre enough that a thumb-lighting catalyst does not seem that strange.

For all the rich visual humor expected of the team and found here, including breaking into the second floor of the saloon using a pulley system (causing Hardy's crater-making crash landing and later, launching a donkey tied to Ollie's substantial girth), the film also has its verbal moments. For instance, there is the gem that opens the chapter and when fully fleshed out reads like this—Sharon Lynne's saloon girl, posing as the rightful owner of the gold mine, asks Laurel & Hardy, "Tell me, tell me about my dear, dear daddy [from whom the inheritance came]. Is it true he's dead?" Stan replies, "Well, we hope he is; they buried him!" And shortly after this, before the duo realize their delivery error, Laurel (in true comic wise fool tradition) tells Lynne's hustling character, "Now that you've got the mine, I bet you'll be a swell gold digger."

A verbal slant also necessitates a footnote to the team's marvelous song and dance abilities. Laurel & Hardy author Charles Barr, after calling this their most musical picture, has insightfully observed, "Considering how good are Ollie's singing voice [their joint harmonizing] and both men's dancing . . . they could easily have made a musical number into as much of a trademark as Stan's cry."[2] I would suggest that this is their most musical film because they *are* out West. But it goes beyond the B-Western singing cowboy perspective noted earlier. Though this is part of it, the traditional Western is often peppered with populism—people interacting easily and equally with others on an "everyman" level. And once past the crooked saloon owner and his dance hall wife, this cowboy spirit is nicely represented by the singing troupe the Avalon Boys, the starting point (either together, or in part) for two of the movie's three Laurel & Hardy musical interludes.

In fitting populist tradition, in each case the team *joins* a number already in progress. And although Hardy has the superior voice, Laurel is comically game either to milk the lyrics with special intonations or lip-sync to wildly incongruous voices (both during their rendition of "In the Blue Ridge Mountains of Virginia"). With regard to comic voices, Stan first pretends to have a rich baritone. Dominant Ollie, always prepared to act when something is amiss, then procures a mallet from the bartender and pops Laurel on the noodle. But instead of being knocked out, Stan's musical gearbox shifts (more surrealism) to a woman's high-pitched falsetto. The final comic topper occurs at the song's close when Laurel collapses . . . his screen persona being so vacuous that it took that long for a pain wave (trickle?) to tell his brains lights out. (As with many classic routines, it is a set of three—baritone, falsetto, and knockout.)

Before closing on Laurel & Hardy and music, three observations merit attention. First, even with "sound" comedy the team finds a way to return to their specialty—visual and/or physical comedy, whether by dancing or the well-placed smack from a mallet. Second, the populism slant need not be limited to their music bits. In fact, the duo could be used as poster boys for this "ism." *Way Out West* never reveals just how or why the team has come to be delivering the mine deed. It is just a given they are acting out of inherent goodness, neither tempted to steal the property, nor even expecting compensation for their efforts. Third, beyond populism, the musical numbers are an excellent microcosm of Laurel & Hardy's inherently child-like nature. They are similar to kids with minimal attention spans, and the songs represent how easily the two can be distracted. Moreover, the readiness to join in (singing and dancing) can also be chalked up to the unselfconscious nature of children. And one need not see this as an alternative "reading" to the populism slant previously addressed. Cynics often see populism's trusting camaraderie as childish. Regardless of how the viewer integrates the *Way Out West* musical interludes, they remain an essential and charming part of this spoof.

Unlike some classics, that initially go unappreciated (Buster Keaton's 1927 parody of reaffirmation *The General* most readily comes to mind), *Way Out West* garnered to-die-for reviews. Laurel & Hardy aficionados might haggle over just which feature film is their greatest (with 1933's *Sons of the Desert* probably the nominal winner), but *Way Out West* wins the critiquing sweepstakes.

Surprisingly, many reviews did not focus on the team's masterful spoofing of the Western. But enough did to make one ponder why Laurel & Hardy's future work did not embrace a parody approach more often. Regardless, *New York Daily Mirror* critic Blaud Johaueson called the film "a hilarious burlesque of the heroic westerns," with Stan & Ollie nicely described as "two knights [the mythic metaphor for cowboys] . . . sadly addicted to blunders."[3] Later she observed, "Their story aptly matches the creative works of the great authors who think up western plots."[4]

New York American reviewer Robert Garland said, "They [Laurel & Hardy] manage to make a merry mix-up of the average cowboy contribution to the talkies that look[s] like a silent."[5] Garland's statement is perceptive because it implies, in a casually elegant manner, that despite the ease with which they derail B-Western singing cowboys, Stan & Ollie's silent comedy remains their métier, or "do it visually," as their mentor Leo McCarey would say. And while this *New York American* critic is definitely referring to the duo's ongoingly effective presound style, the student of the Western might interpret the reference to silents more ambiguously. The inference is that this is a great, largely silent film that spoofs a genre whose last great movies were made in the silent era, such as *Tumbleweeds* (1925), with Western star William S. Hart or genre-defining director John Ford's *Three Bad Men* (1926).

Period reviewer William Boehnel uses the team's Western setting as a punning defense for a slapstick style not fully appreciated in the 1930s, calling them "the last frontier" for a "low humor" that "may not be as slick and smart as its more refined counterpart, but it is usually eminently more enjoyable and certainly more eternal."[6] Years later, *Village Voice* critic William Paul, in one of the most insightful essays ever done on Laurel & Hardy, would more than validate Boehnel's defense by observing, "*Way Out West* is a rarity: in its consistency of pacing and inventiveness it is one of the few classic slapstick films of the sound era."[7] Stan & Ollie are as simple and straightforward as the alphabet but with just as many possibilities.

Way Out West is such an entertaining and integrated Laurel & Hardy feature, I am reminded of *New York Times* reviewer Frank S. Nugent's amusing opening to his rave critique of the movie: "Too many books are being written on the anatomy of humor and none on the humor of anatomy."[8] I do not normally quote disparaging remarks on the subject of comedy theory, unless humor is involved; laughter *and* learning should go hand in hand. Nugent's piece is so unabashedly affectionate about these "anatomical funny men," at a time (1937) when many serious critics would never admit to such Laurel & Hardy comedy pleasures, that his insightful criticism merits recognition at any celebration of the film.

The phenomenally positive audience response to this film sometimes becomes a lead-in for the reviews—a fascinating sociological slant . . . invaluable pieces of time recorded. Even if a critique had little else to say, such descriptions of riotous joy merit preserving, since they bring a period to life. For example, Dorothy Masters's *New York Daily News* review says one will be "privileged" to see the duo, "if the floorboards hold out under standing-room-only weight and the rafters survive the Vesuvius-rivaling bellows of audience lung power."[9] Indeed, the critique's title says it all: "Laurel-Hardy Comedy Jeopardizes Theatre."

Reviewer Archer Winston was so moved by the *Way Out West* audience response that he opens his piece by focusing on a specific family: "A child got completely out of control . . . [and] I noticed that the hysterical abandon was hereditary. Papa had it, too."[10] Winston is so taken with the incident, that like some film scientist, he records one of the comedy bits that was so convulsing viewers. Stan overhears a saloon patron complain about a piece of meat being "tougher than shoe leather." A light goes on in Stan's muddle-headed mind—he places the meat in his shoe, nicely covering a hole in the sole. Again the review title says it all: "Laurel and Hardy Panic Rialto [Theatre] With Their Act."

Winston's documentation of the audience response is all the more impressive given his confession, "You can't pass off that sort of thing lightly even if you fail to share the merriment."[11] Moreover, his critique later showcases a scientific given of comedy research—the influence of a group on an individual response. "Your reviewer, who is most assuredly not susceptible [to slapstick], found himself betrayed into . . . [the fun] on several occasions."[12] And whereas Winston is sharing what today's critiquing community often label their "guilty pleasures," the reviewer/duo fan Robert Garland merely seems embarrassed that he so enjoyed *Way Out West* with a "packed" audience who "whoop it up, with Stan and Oliver."[13]

Before closing the book on these *Way Out West* reviews, it bears noting that two of the most euphoric critiques were penned by women (Blaud Johaueson and Dorothy Masters), the sex often alienated by Laurel & Hardy's frequent run-ins with domineering wives. (And this scenario is central to the team's aforementioned classic, *Sons of the Desert.*) This is not to say Stan & Ollie are limited to a male audience, but men are decidedly in the majority.

Interestingly enough, Laurel & Hardy's key 1930s personality comedian contemporaries, W. C. Fields and the Marx Brothers, also enjoy a largely male audience. Like Stan & Ollie, the antiheroic Fields often suffers through screen marriages to heavy-handed wives (especially Kathleen Howard). In contrast, the Marxes, or more precisely, Groucho, is best known for his comic verbal attacks on stuffy society matron Margaret Dumont. The movie heyday (1930s) for all these comedians coincided with a major male-threatened era, the Great Depression, a period when many saw "the husbands' increasing dependence upon their wives to provide additional or even primary income for the family . . . [as] a rapid deterioration of the father's status."[14]

Regardless, if women critics were to rave about any of Laurel & Hardy's features, it is fitting that Johaueson and Masters should rate *Way Out West* so highly. There is not a frying pan in sight, and Sharon Lynne's comic saloon girl temptress Lola Marcel is an inspiredly fun bad girl. As Johaueson observes, Lynne is a "first rate siren."[15] As if Johaueson and Masters were balancing their praise of the film's two central female roles, Masters singles out Rosina Lawrence, the unknowing heiress Mary Roberts, who slaves for Lola and James Finlayson's "Mickey Finn." (This moniker puns the actor's real nickname, Finn, and the knockout drink—a Mickey Finn.) Laurel & Hardy's rescue of Mary from her Cinderella-like drudgery would also no doubt qualify as an action sympathetic to a women's audience. Moreover, as critic William Paul states, again consistent with a stereotypical feminist slant, *Way Out West* is "one of the gentlest comedies Laurel & Hardy made."[16]

As an offbeat footnote, Johaueson's unofficial symbol for this parody is the boys' partner in funniness, Dinah the burro, who has a vital role in Stan & Ollie's misguided attempt to break into Finlayson's saloon. With tongue firmly in cheek, one might even count the role as another (though highly unconventional) woman's role. Certainly, it would not be inconsistent with Johaueson's attention to Dinah, who also received billing in the credits and managed eventually to get the better of the team.

The bottom line, however, is that the team, or as Laurel liked to describe them, "two minds without a single thought," were a perfect fit (or, is that misfit?) for the West . . . what in this case the *Brooklyn Daily Eagle* called the "horse-laugh opera."[17] And seldom has parody been better served, even with a genre so heavily trafficked with spoofs because of its fundamental association with all things American.

MY LITTLE CHICKADEE

Stan Laurel's second wife, Virginia Ruth, first suggested Laurel & Hardy make a parody Western but history has not provided students of comedy with a ready name to credit for the birth of the W. C. Fields/Mae West vehicle *My Little Chickadee* (1940). The catalyst for the film is invariably more broadly attributed to the studio that produced it (Universal), though one West biography gives recognition to the picture's executive producer, Lester Cowan.[18]

Laurel & Hardy and friend on the set of *Way Out West* (1937).

The Universal focus, however, merits special attention for several reasons. Universal was an A-studio, but just barely, and in the late 1930s it was attempting to be more of a major player, though still with an eye on economizing. The studio's approach was to take a star who had slipped somewhat at the box office and team him/her with someone who had had more recent success. The thinking was that the viewer would be drawn to this two-for-one attraction.

Two 1939 Universal examples of this approach have ties to *My Little Chickadee*. Early in the year Fields' screen career was given a jump start when he was teamed with radio comedy star Edgar Bergen (and dummy Charlie McCarthy) in *You Can't Cheat an Honest Man*. There is a certain irony here, because Bergen's monster success on radio, *The Chase & Sanborn Hour* (starting May 9, 1937) had Fields as an early regular. And although he left the program after five months (continuing to make guest appearances), radio historian John Dunning notes, "Much of the credit for the early [strong] showing goes to W. C. Fields, who started an immediate feud with Charlie McCarthy and kept the show moving at a fast pace."[19] The key to this successful comic rivalry was based in Fields' long-established film premise that he hated children. Charlie McCarthy was just a Baby LeRoy (an earlier Fields film nemesis) grown into a smart aleck, albeit one made of wood.

Though Fields would receive top billing in *You Can't Cheat an Honest Man*, Bergen and McCarthy's *Chase & Sanborn Hour* was leading the radio ratings, so it is not surprising that *Variety* suggested they, instead of Fields, would be the key to the film's box office.[20] Regardless, the film was a critical and commercial success. *Newsweek*'s closing commentary suggested the veteran had stolen the show. "In giving one of the funniest performances of his career, Fields allows plenty of footage to Edgar Bergen, who handles the romantic assignment as well as Charlie McCarthy and Mortimer Snerd [a country fool and Bergen's newest dummy]—Charlie's rival for Bergen's knee."[21]

Universal's formula of mixing old and new generated an even bigger hit in late 1939 with the release of *Destry Rides Again*. The movie revived the career of Marlene Dietrich, and up-and-coming star Jimmy Stewart (further boosted by *Mr. Smith Goes to Washington* opening shortly before *Destry*) saw his film stock go through the roof. Though neither Fields nor West had direct ties to *Destry*, this parody of the reaffirmation Western was such a success that it inspired Universal (Lester Cowan?) to think in terms of a horse opera spoof for the revitalized Fields and the newly signed West. And it was a connection some period critics would later make note of. For instance, *New York Daily News* reviewer Kate Cameron even titled her critique, "Mae West and Fields Give *Destry* a Ride."[22]

Like Dietrich, West's career had been in eclipse, neither sex symbol having made a film since 1937. But Universal's formula teaming paid off again when *Chickadee* proved to be a major commercial hit. It outgrossed *You Can't Cheat an Honest Man* and Fields' later hit Universal films *The Bank Dick* (1940) and *Never Give a Sucker an Even Break* (1941).

This spoof was effective for three reasons. First, it was timely, coming out early in 1940, after the 1939 revival of A-Westerns. Second, as film historian William Everson has suggested, the movie's opening scenes closely resemble the outset of John Ford's 1939 Western classic *Stagecoach*, which was released shortly before the Fields/West film began shooting.[23]

Both movies start with prostitute figures (Claire Trevor and Mae West) being driven from town by bluenosed women's groups. In each case the "loose" woman's journey brings her in romantic contact with another outcast of society (John Wayne and Fields). Both movies also feature milquetoast character actor Donald Meek as a figure mistaken for a minister. In fact, he performs the comic fake marriage of Fields and West in *Chickadee*. (Really a gambler, he begins the impromptu ceremony, "Of course, you're both acquainted with the rules of the game. I mean . . .") And both films include an epic running battle (from a stagecoach and train, respectively) with a seemingly endless supply of Indians. Thus, *Chickadee* actually parodies several key scenes from what is now often considered the archetypal Western.

Third, the teaming of West and Fields in a Western spoof drew upon several natural strengths. For starters, as the *Boston Herald* noted, it "unites for the first time the two most unusual comic talents in the world of comedy."[24] *Time* magazine went several praiseworthy steps further, calling it "an inspired coupling . . . of America's leading mental strip-teaser (West) with the comic talents of one of the funniest men on earth (Fields)."[25] Beyond that, each had humor personae (and costumes) strongly linked with the late nineteenth century—well within the time frame of the genre. Their screen characters were equally tied to satire, especially of the hypocritical small-town woman's club variety, an unofficial ruling clique often associated with the Western—especially those of John Ford.

Taking the West persona a step further, it was very appropriate for her to be in a parody, since her campy character was an ongoing spoof of sexuality, from the hourglass dresses, to her provocative looks, gestures, and lines. A *Chickadee* crack such as, "I generally avoid temptation, unless I can't resist it," represents Mae's mission to deromanticize romance and undermine sentimentalized womanhood. That the core of her character parodied sexuality, giving it a certain ambiguity, also explained her longtime appeal to gay men—"a female female impersonator, presenting sex largely as a matter of style."[26]

As West spoofs sex, the booze-guzzling Fields persona forever parodies bravery, such as his recurring *Mississippi* (1935) yarn about his days as an Indian fighter, when he took down his old bowie knife and "cut a path through a wall of living flesh." Fields, especially in period pieces, robustly embraces the American Southwest's tall tale. He utilizes a variation of his *Mississippi* "bravery" in *Chickadee* by assuming credit for thwarting the Indian attack on the train, when in fact his sole retaliation is a comic misfiring of a slingshot.

Fields' *Chickadee* slant as Cuthbert J. Twillie, whom the film picks up in midyarn, has him claiming, "I reached down into my boots and drew two more six-shooters. Bang! Bang!" When a captivated but questioning listener asks how he could shoot three guns at once, Twillie responds, "I had one in my teeth. Bang! Bang! Shoo! Shoo! [blowing the smoke from his imaginary gun barrels] Three Indians bit the dust. The slaughter I wreaked upon the poor savages was devastating." (In reality, the shots by West's Flower Belle Lee saved the day.)

The fallout from Twillie's yarn has two interesting ties with film parody history, past and future. First, it leads to his being appointed sheriff of Greasewood City by the crooked saloon owner who runs the town, Jeff Badger (Joseph Calleia). This apes the hiring of the town drunk (Charles Winninger) by another dishonest saloon power broker (Brian Donlevy) in *Destry*. In the latter case, Jimmy Stewart's title character will eventually become a deputy to Winninger's sheriff, and initially be seen as harmless in that position (thus the appointment) as Winninger and, later, Fields. Second, having the woman be the sharpshooter while the antihero receives the credit was undoubtedly the model for a similar situation in the Bob Hope Western spoof *The Paleface* (1948; see the following chapter).

In *Chickadee*, moreover, in the spirit of a parody film, both Fields and West take time (they co-scripted the picture) to burlesque their characters. This is best realized at the close, when they exchange trademark lines. First, Fields observes in his best Mae West intonation, "You must come up and see me sometime." West answers with Fields's patented drawl, "Ah yeah, yeah, I'll do that, my little chickadee." As a topper, The End sign is then superimposed over West's keister. These are merely the most obvious examples. Another bit of self-parody occurs when Twillie briefly hides his identity from Flower Belle with a mask. West quickly figures things out, though, by zeroing in on that Fields "proboscis"—his favorite term for a famous entertainment nose second only to Jimmy Durante's "schnozzola."

Interestingly enough, a period newspaper comic strip that also affectionately spoofed Fields had an influence on *Chickadee*. The comedian was the inspiration for the Great Gusto, a prominent character in the strip "Big Chief Wahoo" (1936).[27] Wahoo played the stooge to Gusto, who had a medicine show—the classic con man setting for Fields since his success as a medicine show huckster in the Broadway production of *Poppy* (1923). In fact, Fields starred in his second film adaptation of *Poppy* (the first being in 1925) the same year "Big Chief Wahoo" debuted—1936.

Fields was a fan of the strip, and its creators Allen Saunders and Elmer Woggon were eventually feted by the comedian in Hollywood.[28] "Wahoo" undoubtedly influenced *Chickadee*, in which huckster Twillie also has an Indian sidekick who functions as a stooge, Clarence (Fields friend George Moran). Fields' character is first seen in *Chickadee* as he naps in comfort on a litter behind Clarence's horse. One of the film's most celebrated comic exchanges comes later between Twillie and Clarence:

Twillie: My brave—go upstairs and park your stoical presence outside the tepee of Mrs. Twillie. Number eight [the hotel room of Flower Belle]. I'll proceed to the local gin mill and absorb a beaker of firewater.

Clarence: Big Chief gottum new squaw?

Twillie: New is right. She hasn't been unwrapped yet.

As a footnote to the final line, this was considered a sexually provocative crack at the time. *Life* magazine, which selected *Chickadee* as their Movie of the Week for February 19, 1940, included Fields' observation in a section titled "Hays' Office [the film industry's censorship department] lines that got by."[29] The article's other two examples were Mae West bits. One

A "Godfrey Daniel" (a.k.a. "God damn") moment in W. C. Fields' *My Little Chickadee* (1940), with George Moran.

was her response to a suitor wondering what kind of woman she was: "Too bad I can't give out samples." The other was her take on spring being the time for love: "What's the matter with the rest of the year?"

Besides the comic pleasure, I include the West lines to address the fact that although *Chickadee* was a commercial hit, it did not revive her career, à la Dietrich. Her films had been hurt by the implementation of the censorship code in 1934, a development her cinematic sexual innuendo had helped bring about. But a key point that seems to have been missed is that by 1940, provocative language, as exemplified by *Chickadee*, was no longer holding her back, at least not to the degree of the mid-1930s. *New York Daily Mirror* critic Lee Mortimer called the laughs "lusty," adding, "if you want to be legalistic about it, there's a plenitude of blue material in *My Little Chickadee*."[30]

Indeed, *Life* could have picked some much racier examples from the film, such as, "I see you're a man with ideals. I guess I better be going while you've still got them." But even more fun are her comments when briefly filling in as a substitute teacher. When asked for a definition of subtraction, she answers, "A man has $100 and you leave him with $2. That's subtraction." Or, after reading a lesson on the board, "I am a good boy. I am a good man. I am a good girl," she makes the aside, "What is this, prop- aganda?" Although the censors had hurt her movie career earlier, by 1940 even a racy West had become passé. *Chickadee* represented more of a "nice to have you back" swan song than a revival of her future in film. That *Chickadee* is a broad parody encourages this passé position, because we laugh at what was once a standard West love scene (such as her *Chickadee* relationship with a masked bandit). Moreover, when one reads her later autobiography, *Goodness Had Nothing to Do With It*, there is a sense that at least some of the apparent parody she meant to be taken straight.[31]

Luckily, Fields never took anything straight, other than possibly his liq- uor, and he is considered to have won the battle of *My Little Chickadee* wits, as the Fieldsian jargon for a title suggests. Or, as the period reviewer for the *Brooklyn Daily Eagle* put it in such flourishing Fields language, "the lakuacious W. C. is the chief laugh-provoker."[32] More than one critic has labeled Fields' best scene as the one in which he relates his epic struggle with Chicago Molly, who tried to break up a New York saloon where Twillie was tending bar.[33]

Fittingly, Twillie shares the misadventure while bartending in a Grease- wood saloon, telling a customer how he had to knock Chicago Molly down after she targeted him, for no reason, with an assortment of food from the lunch counter—a "melange" consisting of "succotash, asparagus with may- onnaise and Philadelphia cream cheese." When his fellow bartender (Fields crony James Conlin) claims credit for decking Molly, Twillie replies yes— but he was the one who started kicking her. Then he tops the black comedy effect of this admission (as well as further spoofing what a traditional hero would *not* do) by going into detail about the kicking experience: "So I starts kicking her in the midriff. Did you ever kick a woman in the midriff that had a pair of corsets on?" The customer replies (amusing in its own right), "No, I just can't recall any such incident right now." Twillie con- tinues, "Why, I almost broke my great toe. I never had such a painful experience."

Unlike Laurel & Hardy's foray into Western parody, where they avoid the sometime misogynistic nature of their comedy, the Chicago Molly seg- ment demonstrates that Fields, to use an appropriate pun, was pulling no punches in his standard battle of the sexes. He does, however, defuse his comic violence by eventually revealing that Molly and an elderly gray- haired woman returned to beat up both Fields' character and his fellow bartender.

One would not say the real Fields performed cowardly acts, but his meth- ods could be dangerously eccentric. Probably the most famous case in point was the night he was doing his pool routine in the Ziegfeld Follies (years before his Molly yarn) and found the laughs were not coming at the right times. Eventually he discovered a mugging Ed Wynn under the table. Fields was not amused, and he promised fatal consequences if it happened again.

It happened again. This time Fields brained Wynn with his pool stick during the routine, knocking him unconscious. The audience thought it was a set piece and loved it. Fields continued his popular pool bit, which received additional laughs when Wynn uttered unconscious moans. Fields later offered to incorporate the whole routine into his act, but Wynn declined.

With Fields and West sharing the screenplay credit on *Chickadee*, the film fluctuates between their separate scenes with an even more pronounced division than the Fields versus Bergen-McCarthy scenes in *You Can't Cheat an Honest Man*. As when the film came out, the consensus today is that Fields fared better in *Chickadee*, a view shared by George Eells and Stanley Musgrove in their biography of West.[34] Their book also provides an interesting overview of the behind-the-screen maneuvering on the script, with West charming her co-star into being a surprising ally for much of the actress's writing—a more volatile situation having been expected. (The script also included uncredited material by writer Grover Jones and *Chickadee* producer Lester Cowan.)

Although the two stars' screen time is fairly balanced, they share few scenes, and West's character is both the first seen and the dominant one early in the film. She is a passenger on a stagecoach robbed by a Zorro-like outlaw. Liking what he sees, he takes her as well as the gold. The masked bandit, later revealed to be the crooked saloon owner (Joseph Calleia), eventually returns Flower Belle to town. But he cannot stay away, and her good name (probably a misnomer for a West character) is ruined, resulting in her being run out of town. With the leader of this pioneer Moral Majority being played by Margaret Hamilton, now forever immortalized by *The Wizard of Oz* (1939) as the Wicked Witch of the West, modern screenings of *Chickadee* often find her upstaging Flower Belle. This represents an ongoing distraction, since Hamilton's Mrs. Gideon (as in the Gideon Bible?) dogs the forced exit of West's character (fittingly by rail, à la "*rail*roading"), her apparent mission in life to warn do-gooders en route that the sinful Flower Belle best not be allowed to disembark. Hamilton has literally become a wicked witch of the *West*.

Appropriately for someone who steals the picture from West, once W. C. Fields makes his appearance, he immediately gets the better of Mrs. Gideon. His Twillie asks about Flower Belle. When Gideon says she cannot say anything good about her, his comeback is, "I can see what's good; tell me the rest." Fields and Hamilton are so entertaining, one wonders what might have happened had he played the Wizard of Oz, as had been planned.

Fields' entry into the picture, which just precedes the exchange with Hamilton, is equally memorable. His horseback-riding Indian companion Clarence, dragging a litter behind him upon which Twillie is sleeping, has stopped on the tracks, bringing a halt to the train. Awakened by the commotion, Fields' character spoofs the accommodations one would expect on such a Western vehicle by asking, "Have you any private car on this train? Ah, Roman bath with exclusive bar?" Following the predictable "No!" comes his patented "Drat!" But he decides to board the train anyway, sending Clarence on ahead to Greasewood City. It is a funny entry into the picture—literally a show (train) stopper, made all the more unique by its delayed anticipation.

Whether by coincidence or design, it is interesting that Twillie should first appear upon a litter. In Laurel & Hardy's *Way Out West*, their initial surfacing finds Oliver being pulled on a litter behind a donkey led by Stan. Moreover, as in *Chickadee*, where Flower Belle owns the opening moments, much of *Chickadee*'s start focuses on Sharon Lynne's sexy dance hall girl. In each case the viewer eagerly awaits the appearance of the male comedians. That Fields "borrows" a joke from *Way Out West* suggests the litter parallel was not mere chance. The recycled material appears just prior to Twillie's Chicago Molly yarn. A customer asks him about having buried his wife a few years ago. Fields' bartender replies, "Ah, yes, I had to; she died." (For a comparison, see the Laurel quote that opens the chapter.)

In Fields' defense with regard to the litter, he uses it for a comedy agenda different from Hardy's. That is, each situation mirrors the persona of the player involved. Fields is a flamboyantly wordy huckster forever out for himself. That he should sleep while a largely silent sidekick does his navigating is fitting for Twillie the opportunist. It is funny both because they represent an odd pair and because despite this spoof of leisurely Western travel, Fields' character wants so much more, à la his requests when stopping the train.

Hardy is also taking advantage of an often silent, servantlike partner. But as noted in the *Way Out West* portion of the chapter, Oliver is invariably made to comically pay for his superior attitude toward Stan. Consequently, vacuous Laurel innocently leads the donkey-powered litter upon which Hardy is sleeping over bumps in the road and through a stream. Though both Fields and Hardy know antiheroic moments in their Western travails, the litter portion of the films contrasts a wet and bruised Oliver with a bargain basement huckster (Fields) making the most of a modest situation not unlike the Mississippi con artists King and Duke on the raft in Twain's *Adventures of Huckleberry Finn* (1885).

Twillie eventually finds himself sitting with Flower Belle on the train. The first of only a handful of scenes together, it is probably the most entertaining, with Fields's character getting the upper hand purely by accident. Flower Belle thinks he has a bag full of cash, whereas it is really advertising "currency," a paper money facsimile on one side of countless bills, with a Twillie sales pitch on the flip side. Thus, the scene is an effective spoof of the Western gold digger, especially since the actress' persona, on-screen and off, was that of the original "material girl."

Flower Belle is not, however, totally shut out. The money "marriage"

Ollie is "chauffeured" in *Way Out West* (1937), as Stanley looks on.

she orchestrates is false—no binding ties for her, even with the promise of cash. (Only West's character and Donald Meek's pretend preacher know the ceremony is a sham.) Plus, the apparent wedding highlights hyprocrisy in a Western setting by instantly vaporizing all of Flower Belle's past transgressions. Suddenly Margaret Hamilton's comic avenging angel is acting like the Welcome Wagon lady, and Mae West's character is now invited to stay at the next stop.

The plot line—and one should be aware that the term is used loosely—meanders into more stock W. C. Fields and Mae West territory as the couple disembark in Greasewood City. Fittingly, this involves shtick at home in the Western. For Twillie, it is a matter of finding a place to drink and gamble—a double fantasy readily available in the genre's ever-present saloon. Like a good cowboy, he likes nothing better than the camaraderie of male drinking companions, especially when they also play audience to his yarns. Amongst such revelers in *Chickadee* he comically speaks of alcohol's special nature: "During one of my trips through Afghanistan we lost our corkscrew and were compelled to live on food and water for several days."

As with everything Fieldsian, in or out of cinema, drink is a panacea. After he is roughed up (off-camera) for cheating at poker in Badger's saloon, he is quick to accept the owner's apologies when they include a free tab at the bar . . . to which he gravitates posthaste. Twillie is not unaware

W. C. Fields does not quite get out of town quickly enough in *My Little Chickadee* (1940).

of Badger's interest in his wife (the reason for the crooked power broker's sudden turnaround), but the clown with the potato nose has his priorities. I am reminded of a famous line by acclaimed author and Fields contemporary Rudyard Kipling, another sometimes misogynous artist, and how W. C. would have rewritten it. Kipling's observation, from his "The Betrothed"—"A woman is only a woman but a good cigar is a smoke"—most certainly would have become, "A woman is only a woman but a good bottle is a drink."

After all, this was a comedian who downed prodigious amounts of alcohol throughout his life. During normal film work, Fields' only cover-up for his martini cocktail shaker habit was to claim that it was full of pineapple juice—a hoax generously accepted by most, though pranksters once filled it with real pineapple juice, causing him to boom, "Somebody's been putting pineapple juice in my pineapple juice."[35]

For Fields, *normal film work* could not be equated with nondrinker Mae West. She even had a clause inserted in her contract stipulating that if Fields showed up tipsy, he would be asked to leave, something she claims was invoked once during the production of *Chickadee*. Still, in her autobiography she implied he kept drinking, relating how he once complained, "Someone has stolen the cork out of my lunch!"[36] Quite possibly their minimal number of scenes together, generally explained as comic competition, was an outgrowth of her attitude toward alcohol. After all, she had observed of Fields, "I'm sensitive to liquor fumes, especially when breathed over me at close range."[37]

While Twillie's time in Greasewood is taken up with drinking, gambling, and the occasional attempt at a foray into Flower Belle's boudoir, West's character continues her standard manhunting ways. Besides the attention she receives from Joseph Calleia's saloon owner/masked bandit, Belle has also stolen the heart of the local crusading newspaper editor Wayne Carter (Dick Foran). As in some earlier West films, the romantic dichotomy juxtaposes an adoring crook with an idealistic "john" bent on reforming her. When Twillie is added to the picture, one has still another West romantic triangle—the comic fool (Fields) she does not take seriously and the upstanding handsome one (Foran) who wants to save her (presumably with a fair share of lovemaking—not *sex*—thrown in).

It is a given, of course, that West operates winningly in all settings, from keeping Twillie at bay in the hotel (separate rooms) and belting out a sexy rendition of the song "Willie of the Valley" in Badger's saloon, to playing an unorthodox but effective teacher in the school sponsored by editor Carter. Like the story, neither Badger nor Carter are going anywhere fast with Belle. The comic catalyst for an entertaining wrap-up is provided by Twillie's attempt to get some affection from that bride who "hasn't been unwrapped yet." He manages to steal a kiss when he enters her bedroom dressed as the masked bandit, resembling a lumpy Zorro with a large proboscis. In a huckster send-up of the honest Western hero, when Flower Belle calls him a "cheat" for getting a smooch under false pretenses he replies, "Anything worth having is worth cheating for."

Unfortunately for this mismatched duo, Margaret Hamilton's one-woman defamation league spots what appears to be the bandit visiting Mae West's character. Her Mrs. Gideon alerts the authorities, and the couple is jailed. Belle manages to escape, intent on saving her "husband" from this false charge. Haste is of the utmost importance, because *Chickadee* soon introduces a sometimes Western theme of normally frightening proportions—the vigilante violence of a lynch mob.

Films of the 1930s (Westerns as well as other genres) had also touched on the subject as an indirect commentary on the shocking frequency with which Americans had taken the law into their own hands since the end of World War I (1918). Variations on this tendency range from celebrated German director Fritz Lang's first American movie, the contemporary *Fury* (1936, in which a mob burns down a jail when they cannot hang a falsely accused prisoner), to John Ford's frontier classic *Young Mr. Lincoln* (1939, with the future president saving two young men from a lynch mob).

Of course, *the* period example of the terror and tragedy of such vigilante violence had not yet appeared—the much-praised William Wellman–directed Western *The Ox-Bow Incident* (1943, in which three innocent men are hanged despite the protests of some levelheaded onlookers).

With all this said, *Chickadee*, or more specifically, W. C. Fields, manages to spoof this dark theme in, ironically, the most American of genres—the Western. For instance, when Twillie, with his neck already in a noose, is asked if he has any last wish, he calmly observes, "I'd like to see Paris before I die." When the hangman acts disgusted and turns away, Fields' character adds, "Philadelphia will do." As he is left alone to hang, he drawls, "Vote for Cuthbert J. Twillie for sheriff."

This comic moxie is unique for several reasons. First, it parodies the fearful demeanor one would expect in such a situation. Second, it pushes the envelope into absurdity. A misguided mob is hanging him, yet he is using the situation as a platform to begin his election campaign. Third, Twillie has no reason for this comic bravado. Normally, when an antihero type acts cavalier in a parody film tough spot, he has some secret assurance of safety. For instance, Woody Allen's *Love and Death* (1975) character is supposed to be executed, but an angel earlier told him he would be saved. Consequently, when the appointed time approaches he is entertainingly casual about death. Unfortunately for this Allen shlemazel, the angel lied and the firing squad does its job, though off-camera.

Unlike Allen's future figure of frustration, Twillie is rescued. Dead-eye Belle, her aim already established earlier in the Indian attack scene, shoots the hangman's rope in two. (One is reminded of the future spaghetti Western, *The Good, The Bad, and The Ugly*, 1967, in which Clint Eastwood's Good frequently shoots the necktie party rope of Eli Wallach's Ugly.) After Twillie's close call the real masked bandit rides by and throws down the stolen bags of gold. By then Belle is on the scene, holding the mob at gunpoint while she both reiterates Twillie's innocence (proven by the bandit's resurfacing) and tells them to check the contents of the bags. When she feels the mob danger has passed and the bandit has had time to escape, she leaves the mob to their own devices.

From this point on the negligible story quickly wraps. Since the gold has been returned, the censorship code did not necessitate Joseph Calleia's Badger as bandit paying for his crimes. And with the revelation that Belle is not married, Badger and Foran's editor are falling all over each other for her exclusive attention. But Mae's persona, forever true to a philosophy of not being true to any one man, tells them she cannot, at this time, make a commitment to either of them. She does, however, add a provocative come-on: "Anytime you've got nothing to do and lots of time to do it, come up." Belle and Twillie then spoof their signature lines and the film closes.

Although *Chickadee* was a major commercial success, its critical reception has been misrepresented through the years. For instance, the comedian's grandson, Ronald J. Fields, writes in the otherwise insightful *W. C. Fields: A Life on Film* (1984), "The movie in general received terrible notices."[38] But a survey of period reviews (some already noted) finds this is just not the case. Where does this misconception come from? The late 1930s anticipation of teaming W. C. Fields and Mae West in a Western spoof could never live up to the hype, and numerous reviews reflected this. Yet most of these critiques found the parody well worth seeing. For instance, the *New York Post* said: "Even if *My Little Chickadee* isn't the explosion of saucy mirth you'd expect from a team of Mae West and W. C. Fields, it's a right merry movie, and the Roxy's [theater] audiences are liking it to the extent of drowning out a good portion of the dialogue."[39] *Newsweek* said the same thing, only more succinctly: "The war of temperaments [Fields versus West] failed to come off, and if *My Little Chickadee* isn't the comedy riot it promised to be, it is hilarious enough."[40]

Besides these qualified hosannas, there were many reviews of singularly high praise. The entertainment bible, *Variety,* called the duo a "hefty package of lusty humor that will click with general audiences."[41] The *New York Daily Mirror* critic said, "The welding of their professional talents . . . results in a film that should entertain great numbers of people."[42] And as noted earlier, *Time* magazine's reviewer called the coupling "inspired." Although *Chickadee* was not without detractors, as are most movies (*The New York Times* labeled it "strained"[43]), the preponderance of period literature in its camp easily pushes the film into the critical success category.

GO WEST

Go West (1940) comes late in the Marx Brothers' film career. They would officially retire as a movie team after their next picture, *The Big Store,* just one year later. Two additional movies, *A Night in Casablanca* (1946) and *Love Happy* (1950), were done more to help pay Chico's gambling debts than as a team comeback. Moreover, the latter film is primarily a Harpo/Chico vehicle, with Groucho merely putting in a few brief appearances, though one of them involves a walk-on by a young Marilyn Monroe in only her third screen appearance.

Consequently, *Go West* does not rate with either the team's classic early work at Paramount, such as *Monkey Business* (1931) and *Duck Soup* (1933), or their first two pictures at MGM, *A Night at the Opera* (1935) and *A Day at the Races* (1937). Still, *Go West* is the best of their final pictures, especially after the disappointing *Room Service* (1938) and *At the Circus* (1939). Indeed, its late 1940 opening (with a broad release in March 1941) received rave reviews. No small part of this was riding the period's Western parody craze, which earlier in 1940 had included *Chickadee* and Jack Benny's *Buck Benny Rides Again.*

Variety was so impressed with their Western spoof, the pivotal publi-

Groucho, Harpo, and Chico ponder sagebrush land in *Go West* (1940).

cation compared it to the team's glory days: "The three Marx Bros. ride a merry trail of laughs and broad burlesque [parody] in a speedy adventure through the sagebrush country . . . [being] reminiscent of the early Marx picture hits under the Paramount banner several years ago."[44] *New York Mirror* critic Edith Werner said, "The mad Marxes, equipped with 10-gallon hats, fit beautifully in this burlesque of the West in 1870."[45] Her punning article title was a capsule review plug all on its own: "For Laughter, Go West With the Marx Brothers." The *Hollywood Reporter* called it "screamingly funny," and *Showman's Trade Review* labeled it "among the tops in entertainment."[46] And the *New York Daily News* declared: "Somewhere between the gags that come in such rapid succession that you hardly have time to catch your breath in the interim is the old Western formula, so distorted to fit the occasion that you have to look twice to recognize it."[47]

Several reviewers related the team's Western antics to the madcap movie comedy of Mack Sennett's pioneering Keystone films. The *New York World Telegram* critic said, "The new Marx Brothers' picture at the Capitol [theater], which is a slapstick à la Keystone, is about as good an entertainment as you will find anywhere these days."[48] The Keystone connection is most blatant when linked to the celebrated runaway train sequence near the movie's close. But critic Rose Pelswick, after calling *Go West* "an amusing burlesque of the standard horse opera," was one of the rare period critics to zero in on this Keystone chase analogy: "The trio dashes through an assortment of wild-eyed gags, the best of which is a Keystone type chase aboard a train."[49] Fittingly, however, the period's most gifted film reviewer, the *New Republic*'s Otis Ferguson, whose writing merits the attention given the later pioneering movie critic James Agee, was the most poetic in his Marx Brothers/Keystone connection: "Many things are as before, but in general, here for the first time in years is a picture that goes right back to Keystone, not just because everything is blowing up or breaking down, as God knows it seems to be, but because it was made with an infectious crazy exuberance and a constant flow of invention, and it is done in motion."[50]

New York Times critic Bosley Crowther would later include the *Go West* train segment "along with such classics as the eating of the shoe from [Chaplin's] *The Gold Rush*," in his list of the ten greatest sequences ever filmed.[51] The segment was so popular that it was later made available to home movie audiences as a short subject (for purchase or rent), independent of the feature film.

Go West has several parallels with Laurel & Hardy's Western spoof. In both films the teams have in their possession a valuable deed that needs to be turned over to a young heroine. But in each case they let it fall into the hands of a crooked saloon owner. Consequently, as in *Way Out West*, the Marxes find it necessary to crack a saloon safe under cover of darkness. The humorously insightful Marx Brothers critic Joe Adamson, whose watershed study carried the winsome title *Groucho, Harpo, Chico and Sometimes Zeppo* (1973), was bothered by the Stan & Ollie connection.[52] Adamson was not taking an elitist position. He had nothing against Laurel & Hardy. It is just that their antiheroic personae invites *being* bullied, whereas the Marx Brothers at their best *attack* bullies. Thus, Adamson is right to be upset when saloon owner Red Baxter (Robert Barrat) initially gets the best of Groucho's novice cowboy S. Quentin Quale, including tripping him down a flight of steps.

This is not, however, a new situational development. The downside of their move to MGM years before was that studio's attempt to broaden their appeal by homogenizing their personae. Most specifically this meant making Groucho more vulnerable, giving him pathos, which went against the nothing-sacred comic aggression of the Paramount years. Even the celebrated *Night at the Opera* has Groucho being booted down three flights of stairs by a minor character. In MGM's defense, the total comic anarchy of *Duck Soup* had found neither critical nor commercial success, although it now is considered the team's greatest film. And until MGM picked up their option (after they were released by Paramount because of the failure of *Duck Soup*), the Marxes' film future was iffy.

MGM rescued the team's movie career at a certain artistic price. And although it is normal for Adamson to desire a more comically confrontational Groucho, *Go West* might be the only post–*Duck Soup* film in which an argument can be made for Groucho's initial failure at the hands of a villain such as Red Baxter. One of the most basic of Western plotlines is the revenge story. A key component of this scenario is an early ritualistic humiliation of the hero, a development that has been around since the silent cowboy film days of William S. Hart. It is probably most synonymous, however, with the later 1950s work of director Anthony Mann and Jimmy Stewart—a collaboration that helped both revitalize and give new direction to the actor's post–World War II film career.

In *Go West*, the humiliation of Groucho's character makes the later success of his appropriately named Quale and accompanying team all the more comically effective. Besides, their ultimate defeat of the evil saloon owner differs from Laurel & Hardy's *Way Out West* victory. Stan & Ollie's success minimizes any confrontation. They simply (actually, nothing is simple for them) steal back the deed, with their escape doubling as the film's close. In contrast, the Marxes go head-to-head with the Red Baxter gang both when they are retrieving the deed and later when they commandeer a train.

At the very close, moreover (with the bad guys vanquished), the Marxes have returned to their earlier antiestablishment form. Finding themselves at the historic 1869 golden spike ceremony that marked the completion of the first American transcontinental railroad, they amusingly mock and disrupt the solemn occasion. First, Groucho's figure takes it upon himself to act as a comic master of ceremonies: "And now, ladies and gentlemen, the Prez of the New York and Western Railroad will cut the tape, drive the spike, and bank the eight ball in the corner pocket. Take it away, Prez!" But fittingly, the most physically comedy-prone of the Marxes (Harpo) then manages to wield the sledgehammer and drives the "Prez" instead of the stake into the ground. And with that blow the Marxes have quite literally buried all things serious as they spoof this real piece of Western history.

There is also a sense in *Go West* that Groucho is merely slumming in sagebrush and cactus land. From that vantage point, the humiliation scene can be "read" as merely the mustached one's indifference to playing cowboy. Consistent with this is the comment he makes as he struggles with his hat, holster, guns . . . , shortly before first meeting Baxter: "How they handle all this [cowboy stuff] and ride a horse at the same time is beyond me." Also in harmony with this position is that his sexual innuendo surpasses even the entertaining bluntness of the pre-censorship code Paramount years. For instance, his first observation upon entering Red's saloon is to tell the sexy dance hall girl, Lulubelle (June MacCloy), "I didn't recognize you standing up." One is reminded of critic James Agee's later crack about writer/director Preston Sturges' 1944 *Miracle of Morgan's Creek*: "The Hays office [censorship board] has been either hypnotized into a liberality for which it should be thanked, or has been raped in its sleep."[53] The raciness of Groucho's dialogue is consistent with comments made earlier on the provocative *Chickadee* chitchat of W. C. Fields and Mae West.

Just as *Go West* closes strongly, it has a potent opening reminiscent of earlier classic Marx Brothers routines. And paradoxically here, the comic humiliation of Groucho's character is acceptable. That is, in the wild and crazy earlier world of these men from "Marx," Groucho dominated everyone . . . except his brothers. By studying the comedy duos within the Marx team (especially Groucho and Chico), one sees the normally comic "King Leer" in continuous comic defeat. Prime examples would include Chico's inability to stop at merely pump-priming bids in*The Cocoanuts* (1929), ruining Groucho's Florida land auction; Harpo forever leaving Groucho behind in the ongoing motorcycle-sidecar gag of *Duck Soup*; and the tootsie-fruitsie ice cream scene in *A Day at the Races*, in which Chico sells Groucho a "library" of unnecessary betting books.

The most otherworldly illustration appropriately draws upon eccentric Harpo. In *Duck Soup*'s inspired mirror scene, Harpo, comically disguised as Groucho in his nightgown and cap, magically passes as his brother's reflection. It is funny and somehow fitting that the early invincible huckster Groucho should be vulnerable only to his brothers—like a "Superman" comedian who is just one of the boys among the Kryptonite crowd. Groucho is the ultimate example of how one can never get too self-important among family.

With this long-established "all in the family" derailing of Groucho in mind, *Go West* opens with S. Quentin Quale at a train depot ten dollars short of the seventy-dollar ticket west. In come the Panella brothers, Chico's Joseph and Harpo's Rusty. The latter has the same sagebrush destination in mind, but he has only ten dollars. Groucho's huckster, sensing two suckers, moves in for a financial kill. His con man angle is that Rusty would be in danger out West dressed in Eastern garb (never mind that his Quentin character is wearing top hat and tails). Cowboy toughs supposedly would pick on Rusty as a tenderfoot.

Quentin's appeal to Chico's Joseph on his brother's behalf produces one of the film's best lines. "You love your brother, don't you?" he asks. Joseph answers, "No, but I'm used to him." Letting this pass, Groucho's character begins his clothing con with a beaver cap—"the 1870 model." Despite wanting to make a sale, he cannot avoid the Groucho insult, suggesting that with Rusty's mug the tail of the cap should be worn in front.

Quentin's asking price is ten dollars, because "This is the last hat of its kind, the beavers have stopped making them; they're all out playing football." But Joseph claims they can afford only a dollar. Groucho's character agrees in perfect huckster fashion, "Well, I'll take it, but I'm only making a buck on it." Being out West, Harpo's Rusty does not have his standard issue trench coat with the magic pockets from which to draw the money, or the surreal object. But he still produces comedy by literally fishing his on-a-string coin purse from well down in his pants.

It is deep enough to cause Quentin to ask, "What floor was that on?" Eventually Rusty hands over a ten-dollar bill that Groucho's con man naturally attempts to pocket. Joseph is quick, however, to demand, "Nine dollars change, please." Quentin pretends the omission is an accident but under his breath shares his true feelings about people who expect their rightful change: "Money lover." It turns out Groucho's wise guy is more on target with his comment than he imagined—Rusty has more than just his purse on a string. The ten spot Quentin has just pocketed is reeled in by Harpo's figure at the same time Joseph is getting the change from Quentin.

The pattern is now established for the financial draining of another Groucho huckster by his brothers. A number of one-dollar transactions take place, always paid for with the same mobile ten spot and forever closing with Joseph's comic refrain, "Nine dollars change, please." As in earlier film examples of the mustached one being taken by his brothers, part of the fun is that Groucho knows something is suspicious, but he is powerless to stop it. Or, as his Quentin observes, "There's something corrupt going on around my pants and I just can't seem to locate it."

The scam gets so good that Chico's Joseph eventually offers Quentin just a dollar, as sales tax. But Groucho's character wisely observes, "I couldn't afford it." When Joseph convinces him the tax must be paid, Quentin momentarily gets the best of the brothers. Though pocketing the dollar, he continues to hold on to the elusive ten-dollar bill, and Rusty breaks his string trying to retrieve it. However, Harpo's ever-resourceful silent one produces a pair of scissors (a favorite tool of his) and methodically cuts his way into Quentin's pants pocket while Joseph verbally distracts Groucho's huckster. Once again the busy ten-dollar bill is Rusty's. Then Harpo's character administers the financial coup de grâce by switching hats with Quentin, the place where Groucho's figure keeps the rest of his money.

The reversal of a Groucho scam in this Western spoof is significant for four reasons. First, though I demonstrated in my book *Groucho & W. C. Fields: Huckster Comedians* (University Press of Mississippi, 1994) that the con is never out of fashion in American film comedy, one of its most natural settings is the Old West. Literary historian Susan Kuhlmann nicely describes the era's con artist as the "individualization of [Westward] manifest destiny . . . the belief that a free man may be whatever he claims he is, may have whatever his skills can win."[54] Kuhlmann goes on to suggest that the characteristics of those who "opened" our country—resourcefulness, adaptability, nomadic tendencies, and a desire to get ahead—also describe the con man. Significantly, the beginning of the film has the Marxes heeding nineteenth-century journalist Horace Greeley's suggestion to "Go West," thus, the title of the movie. Although most cultures, past and present, have no doubt had confidence men, there is recognition even outside this country of nineteenth-century America's special affinity for the type.

Indeed, in 1855 French commentator Charles Baudelaire linked this country's fascination with and fondness for the con man with the fact that "Americans love to be fooled."[55] That might seem a strange claim to the contemporary reader, but literary historian Stephen Matterson bolsters the position by citing the great period success and popularity of America's greatest real-life huckster, P. T. Barnum. Barnum's autobiography, *Struggles and Triumphs*, which first appeared in 1855 and was revised and updated throughout the showman's long life, is generally considered one of the most widely read books in America (after the Bible) during the second half of the nineteenth century.

His biography represents a blueprint for success based on an affectionate suckering of the public. Fittingly, one of Barnum's most famous cons had a Western scenario, when he got 24,000 people to turn out for a "grand buffalo hunt" that actually featured only a very modest herd of yearling buffaloes.[56] The thrust of the book, as huckster historian Gary Lindberg suggests, finds the public "paying to be entertained [by the con]."[57]

Groucho acting the huckster is invariably amusing. But his greater and more fundamental entertainment value here is that he is showcased in *the* huckster period—the Old West. The conning of con man Groucho by his brothers is also usually funny. However, the scene's second special slant is that just as *Go West* parodies one's Western expectations, Joseph and Rusty's taking of Quentin represents a spoof of a normal huckster situation (Groucho's character is not normally hoodwinked).

Third, moving beyond the Western parody foundation, the scene has an added fun factor by way of including all three brothers. The typical in-family thwarting of the mustached one is usually done by a single sibling. By Chico and Harpo acting together, this odd Western duo gives the viewer the visual surrealism of the latter, and the former's talent for both putting an entertaining dialect spin on the English language, and milking a line such as, "Nine dollars change, please."

Fourth, though a lesser Marx Brothers movie, this scene is arguably (after *Duck Soup*'s mirror sequence), the best comic sidewiping of Groucho by his brothers. No small part of this is the comic lines, some of which have already been quoted. Another is the inspired Quentin crack that opens the chapter: "I'm not in business for love, you know. I was in love once and I got the business."

The Marxes' eventual decline at MGM has sometimes been equated with the studio's reluctance to spend top dollar for writers, as they once did, such as bringing Broadway hit maker George S. Kaufman to Hollywood to co-script the classic *A Night at the Opera*. It is a valid point, and *Go West* scripter Irving Brecher, who also wrote the lesser *At The Circus*, is not in a class with Kaufman. But the journeyman Brecher had his moments, and a lot of them occurred in *Go West*. In addition, denigrating Brecher does not take into account that some period critics praised his Western parody writing. For example, the *Hollywood Reporter* titled their *Go West* review "[Director] Buzzell, Brecher Set Up Big Laugh Fest."[58]

There is no easy explanation for why this scene, or the film in general, should have jelled for the team and Brecher, especially coming as it did in an otherwise mediocre winding down of the Marx Brothers' film career. But if forced to get hypothetical, I would credit the inherent richness of doing a Western parody. It is the only spoof among the team's late work, and so much of the inventive material dovetails back into a Western time frame. For instance, one of the biggest period laughs is generated by a telephone reference. Groucho's character observes, "This is 1870; Don Ameche hasn't invented the telephone yet." (The year prior to *Go West*'s release, 1939, Ameche had played the title role in the popular film *The Story of Alexander Graham Bell*.)

Though the suckering of Groucho's character by his brothers, and the closing train sequence (to be further examined shortly) generate most of the *Go West* critical attention, there are other winning parody scenes, including purloining the deed from the safe. While Harpo's character works at this task, his cowboy companions in the next room try to distract three pretty saloon girls from blowing the whistle on them. Naturally, given Groucho's and Chico's film personae's obsession with women (the latter's name is even based on this—chasing chicks, a.k.a. girls), their characters are the distracted ones, besides getting drunk in the bargain.

Incapacitating the boys with liquor is a saloon girls' ploy that both spoofs the standard stereotypical cowboy's ability to handle massive quantities of booze, and sets up a passing parody of *Gone With The Wind* (1939), which was finally (late 1940) going into general release after an unprecedented long road show engagement. Consequently, the women serve mint juleps and constantly have the boys toast the South, particularly the girls' home states—South Carolina, Mississippi, and Louisiana. Like the earlier comic tag line, "Nine dollars change, please," toasting the three states became another amusingly effective bit of repetitive patter (with both brothers standing and bowing to each other, sitting, then repeating the process with the mention of the next state).

Chico's character, after a few drinking salutes through this three-state ritual, wonders aloud about the varied geography, given that the women are sisters. The reply by Groucho's figure is especially funny because it spoofs the pedestal status of the Southern belle—"They are [sisters] but their mother lived in a trailer." Eventually, when the mustached one is well soused, *Gone With The Wind* is more directly parodied. Turning to a saloon girl, he drunkenly observes, "You know something else, Scarlet, Dixie wouldn't be Dixie without Dixie."

Marx Brothers author Allen Eyles, although not overly taken with the film, is fond of another parody dimension of this mint julep scene. He enjoys the sexual physical posturing of Groucho, which is just another way of spoofing the ladies' man persona of the comedian—"Groucho's way of stretching out on a couch with one of the girls, in which he has one leg stuck naturally half-way up into the air, the kind of reclining position that goes quite logically with somebody of his strange upright shape [the crouching walk of a dirty old man]."[59]

Groucho's self-deprecatingly sexually over-the-top physical maneuvering here is a spoofing of sexiness that can be linked with his "King Leer" eyes and active eyebrows. Of course, he is equally famous for the numerous verbal variations that parody his character's sexual nature. For example, in a scene from *Monkey Business* (which spoofed another genre—the gangster film), he asks, "Do you think girls think less of a boy if he lets himself be kissed? I mean, don't you think, although girls go out with [easy] boys like me, they always marry the other kind?"

A final parody element that closes the mint julep scene, playing on a standard Western stereotype, is the alternate waves (six in total) of good guys and bad guys who keep coming and forcing the others to reach for the proverbial sky. The winner for most outrageous weapon appropriately goes to Harpo's surreal cowboy, who produces a small cannon. Naturally, the Marx Brothers crew ultimately gets the upper hand, as well as the deed.

The next day there will be a battle over who gets control of the train east to negotiate directly with the railroad company about right-of-way land privileges. But that night the boys find it necessary, fleeing as they are from the heavies, to stay in an Indian village. Besides allowing them one more traditional Western scenario (cowboys and Indians) off which to bounce parody, WASP America's inherent racism proves to be a catalyst for satire. Although the scene obviously cannot approach the scope of Mel Brooks' indictment of Western racism in *Blazing Saddles* (1974, see Chapter 4), it reminds the viewer that of all genres subjected to parody, the Western is the most likely to be vulnerable to the satirical message. The racism card works against the normal affectionate undercutting of a genre and/or auteur that one calls parody (see the opening of Chapter 1).

The best take on this *Go West* satire occurs when Groucho's character tries to make friends with the chief. After the Indian seems to rebuff him, the mustached one goes on a comic offensive. But even though his voice inflection is that of self-righteous indignation, the verbal bullets he is firing ironically run counter to his position. And in each case, Chico's figure will accent that irony:

Groucho: Are you [the chief] insinuating that the white man is *not* the Indian's friend? Huh! Who swindled you out of Manhattan for $24?
Chico: White man.

Groucho: Who turned you [Indians] into wood and stood you in front of a cigar store?

Chico: White man.

Groucho: Who put your head on a nickel, and then took the nickel away?

Chico: Slot machine.

Granted, the final comment of Chico's character is not politically correct, but then, political correctness has never been a Marx Brothers priority. More to the comedy point, the dialogue adheres to the humor rule of three—the viewer is comically surprised that the expected response, "White man," is not forthcoming on the third Chico response. But credit the Marxes for at least a brief sympathetic slant on the plight of the Indian at a time when such things were rare. And this positive spin on the race card continues when Harpo's Rusty performs a musical duet with the chief (harp and pipe) that eventually becomes a solo by the nontalking Marx Brother. Unlike the much more elaborate and ambitious Harpo musical interlude of *A Day At The Races*, in which he plays Pied Piper to a large cast of singing and dancing blacks, the minority music of *Go West* does not succumb to period racial stereotypes. Harpo's number on his namesake instrument ends the film's Indian segment, and one never sees the tepee sleeping arrangements of the three men from Marx, though earlier Harpo is strongly encouraged by the chief to stay away from a particularly attractive Indian maiden.

The next scene is the train depot of a neighboring town the following morning. The evil Red Baxter and his cohorts are already on board, with other gang members posted about the train yard on the lookout for the team and the picture's romantic duo, Terry Turner (John Carroll) and Eve Wilson (Diana Lewis). Turner and Wilson will ride ahead and board the train at a later point. But the Marxes manage to overwhelm the engineer and the fireman and now must figure out how to operate a train. This is called comic fun.

The highly praised train sequence that follows (see this segment's opening pages) is a smorgasbord of comedy bits, from the bad guys chasing the Marxes through and on top of the passenger cars, to a derailment that slows down neither the engine nor the comic action. Ironically, the eclectic nature has also, on occasion, been used to detract, not from the comedy, but rather its Marx Brothers uniqueness. For instance, "The climax . . . is quite amusing but the trouble is that it would be just about as amusing if it featured Abbott and Costello or Martin and Lewis."[60]

Granted, there is some truth to this, but all comedy, or entertainment in general, builds upon certain traditions. And in comedy, there is nothing older than the chase, the foundation of the *Go West* climax. That is why so much of the aforementioned praise of this sequence is footnoted with

Homage to the Marx Brothers' zany train finale in *Go West* (1940).

references to Sennett's Keystone period—the beginning of the comic chase phenomenon in American cinema. Still, there are enough rifts of a "Marxist" nature to give it a team stamp. For example, although many comedians have used direct address through the years, the device is most often associated with the pun-loving Groucho. Thus, one of the picture's biggest laughs occurs after he asks the train's bound and gagged engineer a question. Obviously, receiving an answer necessitates momentarily removing the gag. Once information is obtained and the engineer's mouth covered again, Groucho's character turns to the camera and enthusiastically puns, "You know, this is the best gag in the picture."

Groucho is also known for making common lines memorable when delivered in uncommon situations. For instance, when a sexy Thelma Todd finds him in her *Monkey Business* closet and asks what he is doing, Groucho nonchalantly replies, "Nothing; come on in." A nonsexual variation of this common/uncommon mind-set occurs in *Go West* shortly after the train has jumped the tracks. It immediately plows into a small house, which becomes lodged over the engine (without slowing down the train) while a man on the building's roof obliviously continues to shingle. At this point Groucho's character casually leans out a house window (from the engine lodged inside) and invitingly calls to the roofer, "Hey, come on down. There's a lovely fire in the living room."

The Marx world is nothing if not surreal, and this prolonged cannonball run is full of such imagery, from the engine suddenly becoming a "mobile" home, to an earlier point in the derailment when the train finds itself briefly going in a circle and making like a merry-go-round, with an orchestration of "Here We Go Around the Mulberry Bush" on the soundtrack. But the team's tour de silly of surrealism occurs at the chase's conclusion. To keep the engine fired after the fuel supply was jettisoned, Harpo's Rusty has turned into a railroad Paul Bunyan, chopping the passenger cars into so much kindling. One's last comic image of the train is that of nearly flatbed cars, whose only remaining wall remnants resemble the jaggedly surreal bottom teeth of a jack-o'-lantern at Halloween, a holiday the team's comic appearance always brings to mind.

Rusty, who in an earlier portion of the chase has pulled a standard Harpo object metamorphosis—sharpening his ax on a speeding train wheel as if it were a revolving grindstone—is the ultimate hero of the railroad sequence. He provides kindling when the heavies abandon what is briefly a fuel-less train. Thus, the team gets East first and the negotiations go in the romantic duo's favor. Making Rusty a kindling king is an imaginative use of the most chaos-producing Marx Brother. His patented comic gift of destruction is normally an entertainment end in itself, such as his war on clothing in *Duck Soup*—ruining a suit belonging to Ambassador Trentino (Louis Calhern), cutting Zeppo's hat in two, snipping the plumes off the army helmets. . . . Indeed, Harpo puts his *Go West* ax to more traditional destructive use earlier in the film when he chops a deck of cards in half, having overheard a poker dealer request that someone "cut" the cards. This also reinforces a basic Marx Brother credo that things, especially the language, are not always what they seem to be.

The railroad sequence seems to have been loosely inspired by Buster Keaton's parody film of reaffirmation, *The General* (1927), which is almost a feature-length train chase. Tragically, by this point in his career Keaton had been reduced to a low-paid MGM gag man. Still, it was an uncredited Keaton who came up with one of the Marx Brothers' most applauded sketches—the packed-like-sardines stateroom scene of *A Night At The Opera*, in which everyone comes tumbling out when team regular Margaret Dumont eventually opens the door. Consequently, it seems fitting that there is a Keaton connection in the best of *Go West*. But the material has become so "Marxist" in nature by 1940 that Groucho even takes time out of his busy train chase schedule to make a pass at saloon girl Lulubelle, who is a passenger. Naturally, the modest Keaton persona works nothing like this, even though his sweetheart joins him on board during *The General*'s finale.

All in all, *Go West* is a generally agreeable outing that would have made a much stronger retirement film than *The Big Store*. And as suggested before, if one needs a comedy Rosetta Stone for deciphering its success, it is undoubtedly the parody factor. Indeed, the Western premise was so rich that it also seemed to generate more genre-related, on-the-set comedy. For example, director Buzzell told Harpo that when he was spoofing a saloon shoot-out with Red Baxter, "you're not stalking slowly enough." Harpo *spoke* back, "But I'm a silent actor—not a stalking one."[61] Even the chronically pessimistic Groucho, who was privately less than positive before shooting started, later wrote to a friend, "We're about through with 'Go West.' I haven't seen it hooked up [the final print edited together] but I imagine it's pretty good."[62] Just as parody has helped many comedians enter features, it could prove a boon to those who had nearly done it all on screen and needed a late career recharge.

DESTRY RIDES AGAIN

The broad personality comedian spoofs examined thus far in the chapter—*Way Out West* (1937), *My Little Chickadee* (1940), and *Go West* (1940)—represent an important *obvious* sagebrush parody trilogy at a time when the Western genre was resurfacing in A-pictures. An analysis of *Destry* has been delayed until now (despite its 1939 release) because it is a nontraditional burlesque—the aforementioned parody of reaffirmation, a mixing of the serious and the comic. This duality, coupled with *Destry*'s huge critical and commercial success, placed the film in the unique situation of both helping fuel a period fascination with the Western *and* having fun spoofing the form (its genre structure).

The subjectivity of all art, comic or otherwise, does not lend itself to ranking works, though critic and connoisseur alike are wont to play the game. Thus, while I would never place the reaffirmation parody ahead of the broad spoof, the former approach sometimes embraces a mesmerizingly complex array of entertainment options. Such is the case with the enchanting *Destry*.

The film works on so many levels, one is challenged with the cliché "where to begin." But the logical starting point would be to address the film's unique, for that time, mixing of traditional Western drama with comedy. In a 1997 biography of *Destry*'s star and title character, Jimmy Stewart, the film is mistakenly called "the first comic western."[63] Although there are numerous earlier "comic Westerns," from Laurel & Hardy's *Way Out West* to Buster Keaton's *The Frozen North* (1922, see Chapter 1), the biographer was not far wrong in suggesting *Destry* was a pioneering Western parody—*if* one means A-features starring nonpersonality comedians. And the comic ante was upped further by casting surprise leads never before associated with the genre. Or, as the 1939 *New York Times* critic observed, "What sets this one off from its fellows [other Westerns], converts it into a jaunty and amusing chronicle, is the novelty of finding a [Marlene] Dietrich and a Stewart in it and playing it . . . as though their names were Mr. and Mrs. Hoot Gibson [earlier Western screen star]."[64]

Though there is no denying the film's humor, period critics were especially taken with its mix of the comic *and* the serious, which still qualifies it as a watershed reaffirmation parody. Reviewer William Boehnel credited *Destry* with taking "a lot of the staple elements of Western melodrama" and creating"a racy, exciting, forthright 90 minutes of thrills and humor which you simply cannot afford to miss."[65] *New York Daily Mirror* critic Robert Coleman seconded Boehnel with the more succinct *Destry* label— "comedy thriller."[66]

Reviewer Elizabeth Copeland's rave *Destry* critique still found the writer confessing, "The tale changes mood so frequently that one is never quite sure whether he is expected to regard it as a comedy or a tragedy."[67] Critic Archer Winston had similar thoughts about the title character: "James Stewart, [whose screen persona is] honest as always, skips from comedy to tragedy."[68]

Mass-market *Newsweek* was more generic in its overview (no mention of tragedy) but was still aware of the film's entertainment diversity: "This cowboy comedy-drama packs enough action and gusty humor to satisfy the most crotchety of moviegoers."[69] Broad-based *Variety* was equally generalized in its praise of *Destry*'s infinite variety, calling it "primed with action and laughs and human sentiment . . . [ingratiating itself] heartily all the way up and down the family age line."[70]

Besides this multifaceted, compound genre onslaught, *Destry* works on several additional parody levels. First, and most front and center, is Dietrich's immoral-but-with-a-heart-of-gold saloon girl Frenchy. She is the hostess/singer at likeable bad guy Kent's (Brian Donlevy) Last Chance Saloon, where she also doubles as his girlfriend. In the beginning she is not averse to helping him cheat local ranchers out of their land. Kent's goal is to obtain the rights to a broad strip of property to demand a toll on cattlemen driving their stock north. He will stop at nothing, including murder, to reach these ends.

Dietrich's involvement in the picture garnered the most press space. Indeed, as the title of *New York Daily News* critic Kate Cameron's review implied, the film might better have been called *Dietrich Rides Again*.[71] This comeback picture was the result of a provocative parody development. For much of the 1930s Dietrich had been ossified into a beautiful, brittle icon, more pretty picture than performer. This was the result of the actress's longtime collaboration with mentor/director/lover Joseph von Sternberg. Critic and later documentary producer John Grierson would coin a famous description of von Sternberg's slide into a static style with Dietrich: "When a director dies he becomes a photographer."

Reviewer Copeland said of this *Destry* metamorphosis, "Dietrich is the greatest surprise of the picture . . . [she] becomes more human, more amicable and more alive than she ever has been on the screen."[72] The significance of the transition merited underlining in Copeland's critique title,

"Human Marlene Revealed in Rowdy Destry." *Commonweal* critic Philip T. Hartung added, "If Dietrich had shown in her last few pictures half the vigor that she exhibits in *Destry*, perhaps she would have been working [in film] during the past two years."[73]

Although entertainment "vigor" is generally to be encouraged, normally there is no direct correlation between the phenomenon and parody. But such is not the case here. *The* scene in the movie is a knockdown, drag-out brawl. Seemingly, nothing new. It is, after all, a Western, and short of a shoot-out, what is more typical of the genre than fisticuffs? This is the parody beauty of *Destry*'s donnybrook: it is between two women. Talk about a spoofing broadside of a traditionally macho genre. In mainstream movies of the time, a physical fight between women was groundbreaking. And the parody topper was that the woman with the most "vigor" was Dietrich. As one review punned, the former bloodless beauty was "switching from clotheshorse to horse opera [action] in mid-career."[74]

The period press christened the bout between Frenchy and Lilly Belle Callahan (Una Merkel) "the best slug-fest since [heavyweight boxers] Tunney and Dempsey." (The fight is precipitated by Lilly Belle feeling Frenchy has gotten too personal with her husband.) Dietrich's then-teenage daughter would later write of the fight: "I had never seen so much press crowding a movie set. *Life, Look*, all the wire services and fan magazines, photographers everywhere. Dietrich doing a Western had sparked excitement in the first place; now she was fanning the flames, playing it raucous and rowdy all the way—no holds barred."[75] Insightful Dietrich biographer Steven Bach would call her squaring off with Merkel's character "the champion catfight in all of film history."[76] Fittingly, even at the time *Destry*'s director (George Marshall) and producer (Joe Pasternak) "promised [Dietrich and Merkel] that this sequence alone would make movie history."[77] More specifically, it is one of movie parody's most memorable moments. And the consensus at the time was that the publicity it generated was the best single marketing ploy in the film's huge commercial success.

Like the majority of great cinema scenes, there is some debate about just how it came to pass, from Dietrich begging Marshall to be part of the scene (versus depending entirely upon stuntwomen), to a laid-back director curious to see what kind of film footage Dietrich and Merkel might produce. The latter scenario sounds the most logical, since Marshall's underrated filmmaking status dated back to the more casual silents, in which he, appropriately enough for someone directing a Western, had begun his career as an actor playing Indians. Fight participant Merkel offered strong support for the latter position: "Marshall said, 'There'll be no rehearsal. You [and Dietrich] just go in and do whatever you can. Try it! And we'll keep shooting as long as you can keep up the fight! If it gets to be too much for you we can get the stunt girls in and they can finish the rest of it.' "[78]

Let me hasten to add, however, that *all* accounts document a Dietrich

Marlene Dietrich and Una Merkel spoof their battle royal scene in *Destry Rides Again* (1939).

and Merkel eager to give the scene their all. Dietrich's daughter has recorded that the actress whispered to Merkel just before the fight, "Una, don't hold back—kick me, hit me, tear my hair. You can punch me too—because I am going to punch you!"[79] In another text, Merkel remembered, "Neither one of us knew what we were doing, but we just plunged in and punched and slapped and kicked for all we were worth."[80] The comic conclusion of the fight has Jimmy Stewart's title character, the new deputy, dumping a bucket of water over the two women. Merkel comically observed, "He did it in a long shot and then he had to do it over for close-ups, and then *Life* magazine wanted pictures so they did it over again! He dumped water on us for *hours*."[81]

History has not recorded any added incentives Merkel might have brought to the making of a parody Western. But a period article with the amusing title of "Reite Ihn, Cowboy!" reveals that both Dietrich and her producer were childhood fans of German author Karl May, who wrote entertaining (though often inaccurate) Western novels. Pasternak reminisced, "When I read [May's] *The Black Mustang* I was worse [more addicted to Westerns] than the kids now with [a fascination for the Lone Ranger's] 'Hi-yo, Silver.' I wanted to take the first boat over here and be a cowboy.''[82] An equally enthusiastic Dietrich added, "So did I. And here I am in a Western at last."

The Dietrich-Merkel donnybrook is also a harbinger of another pivotal parody scene: late in the film the women of the town march on a shoot-out between Kent's men and Jimmy Stewart's. Though not without drama, ultimately including Frenchy's death, women breaking up a Western's standard gunplay is another derailing of one's genre expectation.

Destry's status as Dietrich's comeback film merits an additional note only the more astute period critics recognized—her Frenchy is not unlike the cabaret entertainer (Lola-Lola) she plays in *The Blue Angel* (1930, Germany), which made her an international star. One of these attentive reviewers was the *New York Sun*'s Eileen Creelman: "She returns to her old self, the laughing, singing, fiery Dietrich of *The Blue Angel*."[83] *Newsweek* was even more to the point: "The Berlin-born actress merely returns to the tough and painted husky-throated *femme fatale* that first brought her screen popularity in *The Blue Angel*."[84]

What neither of these critics addressed, nor any other period writers of whom I am aware, is that despite the *Blue Angel* connections, Frenchy is also a spoof of this earlier character. Decades prior to Madeline Kahn's combination send-up of Frenchy and Lola-Lola in *Blazing Saddles* (1974, see Chapter 4), Dietrich was laying the parody groundwork in *Destry*. Although Frenchy is a tough saloon hostess, she also has a sense of humor and vulnerability (ultimately she gives her life for the love of Stewart's character) that are completely alien to Lola-Lola. The latter is a figure who destroys men (particularly Emil Jannings's tragic professor), rather than save them. Frenchy's wisecracking humor *was* new to Dietrich's screen world and that made all the difference . . . both to the actress' career and the richness of the parody.

Besides the pluralistic parody richness of Dietrich's role, a second major spoofing dimension involves Stewart's Destry. He has been hired by the sheriff of Bottleneck—Charles Winninger's former town drunk Washington Dimsdale. Years before, a sober Dimsdale had been deputy to Destry's famous lawman father. Now appointed marshal by a crooked mayor, because nothing is expected of a comic drunk, Dimsdale is on a mission to prove himself by cleaning up Bottleneck. With the elder Destry dead, Dimsdale wires for assistance from the legend's son. But the young man (Stewart) who arrives is hardly what he expected, and therein begins the parody.

Stewart's Thomas Jefferson Destry does not believe in guns—the ultimate spoofing of a Western's six-gun–toting hero. Moreover, when he arrives in town by stage, he helps a lady passenger disembark, so that Bottleneck's first view of him is of someone holding a parasol and a parakeet cage. The scene is a parody emasculation of the first order, since Dimsdale's buildup of Stewart's character ("Destry will ride again!") has a curious town turning out en masse. And later when he meets Brian Donlevy's resident badman Kent, Destry's defense of not carrying a gun ("One of us might have got hurt and it might have been me. I wouldn't like that—*would I?*") pushes the spoofing envelope into apparent comic cowardice. As the saloon crowd laughs, Frenchy ups the humor quotient by providing Destry with a mop and a pail of water, suggesting this is the only way he will be able to "clean up the town." Besides being funny, it is also an effective plot device to get the bucket of water into the setting for the forthcoming Frenchy/Lilly Belle fight. And the fact that an implied sissy (Destry) both breaks up the donnybrook and uses a prop originally used to comically mock him further adds to the humor.

A second parody spin of Stewart's Destry is that the character represents a gentle spoofing of what is known in American humor as the crackerbarrel philosopher. This rural or small-town man of the people uses a wisdom based on a lifetime of experience to defend and protect the rights of the underdog. Often an older figure, *the* period example was the celebrated Will Rogers. With Rogers' untimely 1935 death, populist director Frank Capra had taken up the cracker-barrel tradition (only with younger heroes), starting with quintessential American actor Gary Cooper playing the title character in *Mr. Deeds Goes to Town* (1936).

Interestingly enough, Capra's arguably best exploration of the populist crackerbarrel is *Mr. Smith Goes to Washington* (1939), with Jimmy Stewart in the lead. Though not yet released when *Destry* went into production, the Hollywood buzz (which proved true) was that Capra had a monster hit on his hands. Indeed, the behind-the-camera talent of *Destry* was well aware of Stewart's *Mr. Smith*'s activity, because they delayed the shooting of the parody Western until he was available. Moreover, a number of *Mr. Smith* connections surface in *Destry*.

Crackerbarrel populist films often key upon corrupt politics. In each movie a crooked machine has appointed an apparent patsy to finish an unexpired term of office. *Mr. Smith* has Stewart's naive boy/man becoming a United States senator. *Destry*'s aforementioned drunk is made marshal. In both cases the bad guys have underestimated these appointments.

As a counterweight to dishonest politicians, crackerbarrel populist films often refer to real-life American heroes. In the Capra film, Stewart's character is named *Jefferson* Smith, and he makes time to visit Washington, D.C., memorials to Lincoln and Jefferson. In *Destry*, Stewart's figure is *Thomas Jefferson* Destry, and the sheriff who hires him is *Washington* Dimsdale. Plus, populist heroes, whether real figures from American history or products of the screenwriter, are individuals of idealism, sacrifice, and strong family ties. Fittingly, Stewart's character in both movies has had a crusading-for-justice-type father who was murdered (each, as was the case with Lincoln, shot from behind). And though both these abhorrent actions take place prior to the start of the films, the legacy of the fathers is a strong, ongoing presence in both pictures.

How does Stewart's Destry spoof this paternalistic (be it father and/or forefather) genre and its crackerbarrel figure? He affectionately plays his character with a much older mindset than the very youthful individual (Stewart was then a boyish thirty-one) who arrives in Bottleneck. His chief bit of shtick along these lines is an endless supply of stories to fit every situation. Traditional crackerbarrel philosophers are most famous for their entertainingly folksy axioms of horse sense. Probably the greatest artist at this was Kin Hubbard (1868–1930); his status was frequently endorsed by no less a crackerbarrel giant than Will Rogers. Hubbard's populist figure Abe Martin made insightful comic observations as, "It's purty hard t' underpay a city official," and "Two can live cheaper than one—but not as long."[85]

Destry's take on homespun humor with a message is of a much more long-winded nature, and therein lies part of the parody. No succinct axioms here. To use a popular crackerbarrel maxim for wordiness, Destry enjoys "taking the long way around the barn." Though his stories are not in a league with the rambling of W. C. Fields or Mark Twain's famous "The Story of the Old Ram," which originally appeared as part of the humorist's Western *Roughing It*, Stewart's Destry makes the act of telling the tale as amusing as the message.

This affectionate spoofing of the all-wise crackerbarrel philosopher is heightened further by Destry claiming at the onset of every story that what follows happened to a friend. Besides being an amusing device based in repetitive shtick—"Reminds me of a friend of mine," or, "I had a friend once"—it further burlesques the crackerbarrel figure by suggesting that Destry's wisdom drawn on experience includes *everyone else's* experiences, too. Destry could be called a parody derailment of Will Rogers' signature line, "I never met a man I didn't like." That is, not only has Destry seemingly never met a man he didn't like, he appears to have befriended every one of them, and elicited from each a suitable-for-philosophizing story!

The best Destry tale occurs after the character's less-than-manly introduction to Bottleneck. Dimsdale is in a comic lather about the town's first impression of Stewart's character. Destry observes:

You know, what you were just saying there reminds me of a friend of mine. He woke up in the middle of the night and he thought he saw a great big white hand coming up at him [Dimsdale interrupts with a "Yeah?"] over the edge of the bed. [Destry's delayed reply now follows "Yeah."] So he got his gun out from under his pillow, and he aimed and he shot a great big hole right through his own foot. [Dimsdale again interrupts with "No!" and this time Destry immediately answers, "Yeah."] Now, he shouldn't have gone by that first impression, should he? Heh? [chuckling from Dimsdale].

Besides being a beguiling parody of the crackerbarrel figure, this example is especially diverting for several additional reasons. First, it is a well written and funny story in and of itself, and Stewart's normal, slow, and methodical speech is a natural for the delivery of a folksy story. Second, though the tale simultaneously spoofs and amuses, it still delivers the all-important crackerbarrel philosopher wisdom—that first impressions often are misleading. Third, although not targeted directly, the fact that a pistol is readily available for the unfortunate "ventilating" of the foot reinforces Destry's antigun position. The fourth factor comes full circle back to parody. One cannot make the *Destry/Mr. Smith* connection without adding the qualifier that, just as Stewart's Western figure spoofs the cracker-barrel philosopher in general, it specifically burlesques the actor's earlier Capra character. That is, both figures sometimes seem to act the fool, but Smith does so out of naive innocence, whereas spoofing Destry can also be "read" as assuming a pose—that of *wise* fool.

Moving beyond the multifaceted entertainment of the foot-shooting tale, Destry's stories serve a wide range of other purposes. When "Wash" (Dimsdale's Washington) is dying, he requests the comfort of a Destry story by asking, "I bet you knew a fellow . . ." There is legitimate poignancy here, since Destry's past yarns have always proved a laughing release for the easily excitable Wash. And now, near death, he logically wishes for one last entertaining distraction. If there had been any threat of pathos becoming bathos, it is jettisoned with Wash's affectionately dark comedy line, "This [story] better be good."

Destry's yarns also fulfill a purpose similar to John Ford's use of comedy in *Young Mr. Lincoln* (June 1939). Ford's direction of Henry Fonda's Lincoln, borrowing from Carl Sandburg's mythic biography of the cracker-barrel president, has humor working as a safety valve—buying time for mob mentality tempers to cool and Lincoln to think. Destry's ancedotes serve the same purpose, whether it is dealing with Brian Donlevy's trigger-happy villain or Jack Carson's equally loose-cannon good guy.

In addition to these functions, the Destry story phenomenon is integral to the film's happy ending. His character tells the town's lovely schoolmarm type, Janice Tyndall (Irene Hervey), "You know, speaking of marriage . . ." She immediately interrupts with an attentive, "Yes, Tom?" And he responds, "I had a friend once . . ." At this point the soundtrack music comes up, the Destry monologue fades out, and the closing credits appear. The viewer, however, preconditioned on what to expect from a Destry story, need hear no more than, "I had a friend once." Life will go on as usual, only with Janice eventually, one assumes, getting him to a church. Of course, a devil's advocate might question whether Destry could get through a whole wedding without derailing the process by being reminded of a friend. Regardless, the storytelling close meshes nicely with the film's archetypal comedy ending—the promise of a wedding and the upbeat new beginnings associated with this ceremony.

A final way in which Destry's roundabout ancedotes embellish the movie concerns their relationship to Dietrich's Frenchy. Two factors merit attention. First, the unflappable Destry stories (which are at the heart of this demeanor) are a wonderful comedy catalyst for setting off the easily volatile Frenchy. This is a component Stewart biographer Allen Eyles could add to his insightful comparison of the *Destry* stars—"Dietrich and he were a well-balanced pair: she exotically foreign and sexy, he homespun and ultra-American."[86] Second, just when the viewer thinks Dietrich's Fraulein-goes-West character (her "Frenchy" nickname notwithstanding) is locked into being the mirror opposite of Destry, she entertainingly spoofs his storytelling habit with a "friend"-related anecdote of her own. Indeed, she even breaks in on Destry as he attempts to spin another yarn for her and the crooked mayor (Samual S. Hinds). Frenchy observes:

Frenchy: I had a friend in Louisiana like that [addictive personality]. Only every time he came to town he went to the nearest oyster house. [He'd] eat a hundred oysters. I'm sorry, I interrupted you.

Destry: Well, I don't think there's much point to my story. Hundred oysters?

Frenchy: And everyone told this friend of mine not to eat oysters in July. He wouldn't listen. [The mayor asks, "What's the point to that?"] He found a pearl that big. [Frenchy forms a circle with her thumb and index finger. And the mayor says, "Oh, that's good."] No, it was bad, the oyster I mean. [pause] Killed him. [There is another pause, and Destry asks, "Who got the pearl?" She looks at him as if he were a Neanderthal.]

Destry: "I did."

Dietrich steals every *Destry* scene she is in. But her tongue-in-cheek "friend" story is Frenchy's slickest bit of larceny. Besides spoofing Stewart's character, she outpitches him (no simple task) in the yarn-telling department. This comic superiority comes across in several ways. First, she easily wins the most entertainingly meandering title. Second, despite her roundabout storytelling, no audience is more transfixed than Destry and the mayor. The cliché of "hanging on every word" has never been more apt. Third, Dietrich presents her piece while showcasing a wonderfully Western pastiche, from her cowboy garb to the cigarette she is rolling. Thus, the viewer simultaneously revels in the parody while still enjoying the Western ambience.

As with most spoof films, *Destry* does not limit itself to kidding one or two genres. Although the Western and populism are the central targets, the film also does a burlesque number on screwball comedy. The time and setting for the latter genre is usually a contemporary look at a wealthy matriarchal ruling household of zanies, such as the pivotal *My Man Godfrey* (1936, see my book, *Screwball Comedy: A Genre of Madcap Romance*[87]). *Godfrey* was the first example of the genre to be labeled "screwball" by period critics. And the movie has a special link to *Destry*.

Una Merkel gets the attention of screen husband Mischa Auer in *Destry Rides Again* (1939).

Both films showcase the talents of Mischa Auer, who plays Una Merkel's second husband in *Destry*. But his comedy career was established with an Oscar-nominated supporting actor turn as the eccentric boy toy of a rich dowager in *Godfrey*.

He reprises a variation of this role in *Destry* by being very much under the thumb of Merkel's Lilly Belle. And although they do not live in a "crazy" mansion, his wife's boardinghouse, complete with marital battles royal and funny lodgers such as Billy Gilbert (of Laurel & Hardy fame), goes a long way toward being a screwball comedy dwelling out West. Having these components surface in sagebrush land is an automatic jump start to parody. But it is not without a period precedent. In 1935 Laurel & Hardy mentor Leo McCarey, who would later orchestrate such significant screwball comedies as *The Awful Truth* (1937, winning a directing Oscar) and *My Favorite Wife* (1940), brought a semblance of the genre to the West in *Ruggles of Red Gap*.

As implied earlier, screwball comedy is also about a reversal of stereotypical sex roles, sometimes to the point of symbolic emasculation. One need not be a psychology student to see this *Destry* supporting player tendency reinforced by the initial relationship of Dietrich dominating Stewart's character. And though he eventually asserts himself, his longtime refusal to carry a gun in a Western is standard textbook symbolism for being less than manly. The comic antihero relationship of Auer's Boris to both Frenchy and Merkel's Lilly Belle is even more overt. He loses his pants to Frenchy in a game of stud poker. Moreover, whenever Boris attempts to assert himself and/or simply escape, Lilly Belle rules by waving around a large phalliclike shotgun. Billy Gilbert's barkeeper will also find himself pantless in this Western world that sometimes spoofs at screwball comedy. (Less than two months after the release of *Destry*, Gilbert played his brightest feature film role—another antiheroic male in the screwball comedy masterwork *His Girl Friday*, 1940.)

Boris, who can never measure up to Lilly Belle's late great first husband (his picture hangs over their bed!), aspires to be a cowboy. And the comic enthusiasm this transplanted Russian (with the endearing accent) brings to his sagebrush goal makes for an importantly diverting supportive character. Happily, by the picture's close, Auer's Boris has both become a cowboy and usurped the position of his dead rival.

The latter development is also consistent with screwball comedy's tendency to vanquish symbols of death for the promise of *lively* romance. The example of this occurs in the archetypal screwball comedy *Bringing Up Baby* (1938), with Cary Grant as an absentminded professor/scientist and Katharine Hepburn a daffy Connecticut socialite. Grant's professor has spent his professional life assembling the giant skeleton of a brontosaurus, symbolizing the lifeless future he faces as an academic engaged to a suffocating woman aptly named Swallow. The bottom line in this genre, besides the la-de-da escapism (especially big during an economic depression), is that the male is saved from a life of rigidity. Fittingly, *Baby* ends with Grant realizing he loves Hepburn just after she has caused his symbolic, *rigid* dinosaur skeleton to collapse. Consistent with that, one's last image of Boris finds him destroying the picture of Lilly Belle's dead first husband and hanging his own cowboy portrait over their bed. For all its comedy, the scene is not without sexual overtones. (As an amusing footnote to the *Bringing Up Baby* connection, the second billed B-picture supporting *Destry*'s long initial Los Angeles theatrical run was the antiheroic Dagwood and Blondie film *Blondie Brings Up Baby*, 1939.)

As the preceeding pages have demonstrated, *Destry* creatively pushes the horizon of expectations for a spoof film, especially in its mix of the serious and comic, à la a parody of reaffirmation. But the film's innovation within the boundaries of burlesque convention go further. Historical critic Nina Nichols noted: "By combining the setting, characters, and tensions of the western with elements of both the musical [Dietrich's saloon songs] and screwball comedies, the film participates in the tendency toward cinematic self-reflection common in the late Thirties and early Forties."[88] This was addressed earlier, in part, when examining both *Destry*'s screwball connections and the revival of Dietrich's film career, a metamorphosis that meant breaking some previous cinema stereotypes of the actress while reaffirming others. Moreover, Dietrich's songs were immensely popular with the public, especially "See What the Boys in the Back Room Will Have," rivaling the status of her previous signature tune, "Falling in Love Again."

Further self-reflection might address, however briefly, the Western itself. At the A-feature level this genre, which honors traditional American ideals, was largely a no-show for much of the 1930s. This is only natural historically, as "a [depression] society marked by a mood of despair finds little comfort in mythic celebration of its origins."[89] But by the late 1939 release of *Destry*, the worst of the Depression was past and America was even feeling somewhat nationalistic—both phenomena tied in part to the war already in progress in Europe. Though the majority of Americans wanted no part of the conflict, "be prepared" munitions-related industries were already putting many people back to work. Thus, it is fitting that this somewhat jingoistic genre should stage a major comeback at this time.

Even more appropriate is that an "on the fence" America should embrace a law officer (Destry) who avoids violence (guns) until the eleventh hour. An insightful explanation for those who would question the consistency of Stewart's pacifist eventually strapping on six-guns comes in historian Robert B. Ray's provocative *A Certain Tendency of the Hollywood Cinema, 1930–1980*. Ray's position is that conflicting patterns in American mainstream film are consistently overcome by a reconciliation in a single character "magically embodying diametrically opposite traits."[90] Ray's examples of conflicting societal dichotomies played out in a single figure include a gangster becoming a coward because he was brave (*Angels With Dirty Faces*, 1938), and a sensitive violinist doubling as a tough boxer (*Golden Boy*, 1939).[91]

The viewer accepts Destry's pacifism, because early in the film he demonstrates he is both tough and proficient with a gun. We are not going to root for a pacifist who is simply a putz and/or a coward. Using Ray's model, in light of America's eventual involvement in World War II, one might argue Destry is a precursor for *Sergeant York* (1941), in which a pacifist eventually becomes a highly decorated war hero.

Going hand in hand with this tendency toward self-reflection is the fact that *Destry* surfaced in the watershed year (1939) of America's golden age of film production. This studio era culmination has been so widely acknowledged that fifty years later (1989) an organization as incongruously connected to movies as the U.S. Postal Service issued a commemorative sheet of stamps honoring four especially memorable 1939 movies. Significantly for this chapter, one of these films was the significant Western *Stagecoach*, and a second was the Western-like parody of reaffirmation *Gunga Din*. (The other two movies were *Gone With The Wind* and *The Wizard of Oz*.)

As this portion of the book has demonstrated, studying *Destry* and the spoof films of several acclaimed personality comedians, the late 1930s (through 1940) also found a great deal of cinema self-reflection (parody style) focusing on the most inherently American genre—the Western. Naturally, in the years since then this genre has continued to be a magnet for parody filmmakers. Yet this chapter documents both the most saturated spoofing period (of a specific genre) and the greatest array of comedy talent doing the job. To paraphrase the title of this chapter, "Everyone was going West."

A WESTERN EPILOGUE

If *Destry* were not accorded the status of greatest Western parody of reaffirmation, *Butch Cassidy* (1969) would be the odds-on favorite for that honor. The first and only comic Western to be nominated for a best picture Oscar, it merits further commentary in conjunction with both *Destry* and another key film from noteworthy 1939, *Gunga Din*.

As briefly chronicled in Chapter 1, the winsome duo (Paul Newman and Robert Redford) of *Butch Cassidy* made their way by comically avoiding shoot-outs, with screenwriter William Goldman patterning their breezy banter on the amusing wordplay of *Gunga Din*'s Cary Grant, Victor McLaglen, and Douglas Fairbanks, Jr. But before one explores on the *Gunga Din* connection, *Butch Cassidy*'s lineage to *Destry* deserves attention.

The latter movie became a model for the A-picture Western parody of reaffirmation. And although its title character is a lawman, versus the outlaw team of *Butch Cassidy*, the heart of each film's humor is the incongruity of cowboys avoiding gunplay. Goldman would later amusingly recount the difficulty he had convincing studio people to keep the portion of the script where Butch and Sundance avoid a "super posse" by leaving the country for Bolivia: "The criticism was 'Get rid of that South American shit.' And I would answer, 'But they *did* it. It happened.' And they would say, 'We don't care if it happened. [Western icon] John Wayne doesn't run away. You can't have your hero run away.' "[92]

As with Stewart's Destry, Newman's Butch is also a comically entertaining talker. Both men represent a skewering of the crackerbarrel-type figure. But Destry concentrates on "friend" stories, whereas Butch is forever pitching adventuresome travel scenarios, from starting over in the Spanish-American War, to robbery plans in assorted countries. Butch is also much less modest than Destry, telling Sundance early in their saga, "I got vision and the rest of the world wears bifocals." Still, both are at their best spinning yarns, or as Sundance is wont to say (also applicable to Destry): "You just keep thinking [and talking], Butch; that's what you're good at."

Newman's character also puts together a poignant verbal pipe dream as he and Redford's Sundance knowingly face death at the film's close. Even award-winning Goldman, the most modest of writers and always self-deprecating about his work, is fond of the scene anchored in the observation: " 'I got a great idea about where we should go next'—I can look at that and say, 'Yes, I am proud of that scene.' They are dying and they don't mention they're dying."[93]

The tragic deaths of Butch and Sundance also have a parody of reaffirmation precedent in *Destry*—Dietrich's Frenchy taking the bullet meant for Stewart's title character. Though maybe not as moving as the demise of Newman and Redford's characters (few scenes are), the death of Dietrich's kindred spirit is still memorable. And the film manages to milk her exit, too, because shortly after she succumbs in Destry's arms, a minor character reintroduces one of her songs, "Little Joe." A fun, raucous number (also associated with Charles Winninger's sweet, murdered sheriff Wash Dimsdale), it now rings bittersweet as one is reminded of the lively Frenchy.

In shifting to the *Gunga Din/Butch Cassidy* connection, Goldman merits intuitive points for picking up on a Western subtext rarely addressed in the former film. But it was almost as if the rebirth of A-Westerns in the late 1930s (à la *Stagecoach, Destry* and the personality comedian spoofs addressed in this chapter) were inundating even the most unlikely of subjects—*Gunga Din*, a screen adaptation of Rudyard Kipling's heroic poem about British soldiers putting down an uprising in India.

Few were the period critics, however, who recognized this *Gunga Din/* Western link. One exception was the *New York Herald-Tribune*'s Lucius Beebe: "It is my suspicion that Mr. Stevens must have directed Westerns at some time in his career. If he didn't, he found out why they still constitute the most popular form of cinematic entertainment produced."[94] Fittingly, Beebe's take on the Western anticipated a later observation by *Destry* director George Marshall: "Westerns have more elements of audience appeal than any other type of motion pictures."[95]

Though there might be debate on that point today, the Western's ascendancy at the close of the 1930s can hardly be questioned. Indeed, the business-related title of the article from which the Marshall quote was culled said it all: "Westerns Aid Film Industry." This genre's hold on both the country and Hollywood was so strong that when I perused the January 1940 issues of *The Los Angeles Examiner* for related articles on the late 1939 release of *Destry*, I found a plethora of material on that film and Westerns in general. For instance, although *Destry* had already been reviewed in the *Examiner* (a November 1939 rave that starts with a sagebrush-inspired "Yippee-e-e-e-e-e"[96]), the newspaper gave the picture a second enthusiastically full-blown critique in January: "Here it is, folks, the rip-roaringest, dang busted Western to hit the screen in many a day."[97]

Along related lines, *Destry*'s excellent supporting cast had garnered praise in most period reviews. And no one was more rhapsodized over than Sam Hinds's likable crooked mayor/judge. The character actor had been best known prior to this for his amateur fireworks maker in Frank Capra's

Oscar-winning *You Can't Take It With You* (1938). Thus, the *Examiner* did a special piece on him, opening the article with: "Hollywood began talking about" him soon after *Destry*'s release: " 'Have you ever seen anyone as clever as Sam Hinds in the role of the tobacco-chewing judge in that picture?' they asked one another."[98]

When the January issues of the *Examiner* were not running expanding coverage of *Destry*, their writers were fervent in their attention to the burgeoning popularity of the Western. This is best demonstrated by the late January same-page coverage of two memorable events for the genre—a special preview of W. C. Fields and Mae West's *My Little Chickadee* and a premiere in which cowboy star Gene Autry's *South of the Border* was "deliberately smashing a local precedent" that had formerly kept B-Westerns out of first-run theaters in Hollywood and Los Angeles.[99]

It is hardly surprising, then, that in critic Lucius Beebe's Western "reading" of *Gunga Din*, he should reiterate late in the review the uniqueness of what the film's director had done: "Mr. Stevens saw to it that a splendid Western emerged on the screen, even if the action was set in India."[100] In Beebe's analysis he pondered whether Stevens had had any Western production experience. Though the director would later make one of the genre's greatest epics, *Shane* (1953), his pre–*Gunga Din* film experience was almost entirely comic.

Given William Goldman's fascination with *Gunga Din*'s frequent humor slant, a brief foray into Stevens' early Hollywood years is especially pertinent. Most pivotal is his first significant industry job—working with Leo McCarey as a cameraman on the silent films of Laurel & Hardy. Besides helping to explain the broad comic performance of another McCarey alum, Cary Grant (whose *Gunga Din* comedy shtick was not without Stan & Ollie overtones), the Laurel & Hardy/McCarey connection is important for two reasons.

First, it again points up the antiheroic factor previously noted in other parody films. Second, it provides a celebrated duo as a starting point for the comic male bonding of *Gunga Din*, *Butch Cassidy*, and to a lesser extent, *Destry* (Boris' willingness to do anything for Stewart's character, if it leads to his becoming a cowboy). As in a Laurel & Hardy film, the male camaraderie is more important than any entanglement with a woman. In fact, a key thrust of the *Gunga Din* humor involves Cary Grant and Victor McLaglen's soldiers playing every trick possible to keep their fellow reveler, Douglas Fairbanks, Jr., from leaving them to get married.

In contrast, the schoolmarm Etta Place's (Katharine Ross) relationship with Butch and Sundance is both more complex and tragic, with her eventually leaving the two men rather than see them die. Still, her position is definitely secondary to the Butch/Sundance duo. For instance, listen to the tone of Sundance's invitation for her to join them on their move to Bolivia: "You speak it [Spanish] good. And it'd be good cover for us going with a

Cary Grant and Victor McLaglen share a Laurel & Hardy moment from *Gunga Din* (1939).

woman—no one expects it—we can travel safer. So what I'm saying is, if you want to come with us, I won't stop you, but the minute you start to whine or make a nuisance, I don't care where we are, I'm dumping you flat." The scene is so patently unromantic that Butch's immediate comment invariably generates a big audience laugh: "Don't sugarcoat it like that, Sundance—tell her straight." Regardless, I find it meaningful that in correspondence with Goldman, he noted male camaraderie first when underlining *Gunga Din*'s "great influence" on *Butch Cassidy*: "The camaraderie, the sadness of good men dying, the joy of what film can do . . . nothing has ever moved me as much as a kid as *Gunga Din*. It is, still, my favorite [film]."[101]

In a second Goldman letter, the screenwriter shared why he gave a certain comic flair to Sundance, too, despite the laughter factor normally being solely associated with Butch: "The humor was present because Cassidy was such a charming historical figure. . . . People just plain liked him. And from that I suppose I deduced that the kid had to have some humor about him also, or why would Cassidy have befriended him."[102] Consequently, although Laurel & Hardy do not come to mind, as is the case with *Gunga Din*, there is definitely a comic male bonding *team* flavor to Butch and

Sundance. Or, as the *New York Daily News*' Wanda Hale phrased it, the two actors "make like a comedy team, playing their roles for laughs to the bitter end."[103] Also, the film is not without the slow deliberate pacing of Stan & Ollie, though Goldman connects it more to the style of another comedy legend: "The [*Butch Cassidy*] humor was Jack Benny–like, slow and amiable."[104] (Coincidentally, as mentioned earlier, Benny had done his own Western spoof, *Buck Benny Rides Again*, the year after *Gunga Din*.)

Both *Butch Cassidy* and *Gunga Din* generated reviews one associates with parodies of reaffirmation—the registering of several genres, with comedy in the forefront. For instance, Eileen Creelman's *New York Sun* review of *Gunga Din* used "Smashing Good Melodrama" in its title, but she went on to write: "There were thrills, but there were laughs, too. The action was more slapstick than serious, probably the funniest [battle scene] slaughter in history. All the hairbreadth escapes were in a comedy mood."[105] Blaud Johaueson's *New York Daily Mirror* critique told much the same story, with a title that could serve as a summary—"Thrills, Tears, Comedy Make *Gunga Din* a Great Show."[106]

Though most *Butch Cassidy* reviews compared the duo to an all-male version of Arthur Penn's antigangster parody of reaffirmation, *Bonnie and Clyde* (see *Newsweek*, October 13, 1969), *Cue* magazine was most on target with the comment that *Butch Cassidy* veered "between parody and a serious action saga."[107] While *Motion Picture Daily*'s Richard Gertner also mapped out the picture's "shifting emotional moods," his take was a provocative attempt to key on the laughter: farce as exemplified by "their use of too much dynamite to blow up a railroad car containing a safe," the satire of having a "teacher instruct them in Spanish phrases so they can stage holdups in Bolivian banks," and broad physical comedy as Newman's Butch "does a vaudevillian turn on a bicycle to impress his friend's girl."[108]

Vincent Canby's *New York Times* review was most direct in addressing the various entertainment strains in *Butch Cassidy*. Goldman and director George Roy Hill "have consciously mixed their genres . . . behind gags and effects that may remind you of everything from [Francois Truffaut's] *Jules and Jim* to *Bonnie and Clyde* and [Sam Peckinpah's] *The Wild Bunch*."[109]

Before the film was finished, director Hill provided another slant on *Butch Cassidy*: "Ours is more than even an 'adult' Western; it's not a Western at all. It's a character study."[110] But as Hill explained what he meant by this, his examples constantly embraced a spoof of the Western badman stereotype, such as Butch "rode away from a train robbery when it became apparent that bloodshed would be unavoidable."[111]

Of course, one cannot close the book on *Butch Cassidy* and parody of reaffirmation without touching on Goldman's fairy tale *The Princess Bride*, which is allegedly the "good parts" version abridgment of S. Morgenstern's adventure tale of the same name. (Like an act from his hucksterish Butch, Goldman's Morgenstern would seem to be a fabrication. There is no mention of the latter author in the "World Cat[log]" computer database, which notes writers and texts as early as the twelfth century.) In my correspondence with Goldman, he recommended I read *The Princess Bride* for further *Butch Cassidy* background. His reputedly edited version of the Morgenstern adventure also involves the addition of a contemporary comic commentary. And early in the text Goldman notes that the most talked-about *Butch Cassidy* scene is the jump off the cliff: "When I wrote that, I remember thinking that those cliffs they were jumping off . . . were the Cliffs of Insanity that everyone tries to climb in *The Princess Bride* . . . [with a] death that was lurking right behind."[112]

Although there is also a cliff-jumping scene in *Gunga Din*, the "Insanity" slant of *The Princess Bride* seems to be footnoted in Goldman's winning cliff dialogue for *Butch Cassidy*. It takes Butch some time to convince Sundance to jump, despite being surrounded by a "super posse." Eventually, Sundance reveals the reason behind his reluctance: he cannot swim. With this, Butch is convulsed with laughter, eventually replying, "You stupid fool, the fall'll probably kill you." With this bit of illogic, they jump.

When one thinks of the wonderful moments of comic absurdity in Goldman's *Princess Bride*, as personified by the Cliffs of Insanity another reason for the rich canvas that is *Butch Cassidy* is revealed. Despite the success of any film capturing period detail (especially their brief New York interlude on the way to Bolivia), most popular culture entertainment ultimately pleases with some contemporary signature. Just as *Destry*'s antiviolence subtext probably had more than a little to do with a period reluctance to become involved in yet another European war, *Butch Cassidy*'s breezy moments of antiestablishment antics had direct ties with the helter-skelter absurdity of America in the counterculture 1960s.

Butch Cassidy's very beginning sets the tone for the modern mind-set of things not being what they seem. Sundance has been accused of cheating at cards, and a fast-draw shoot-out is in the making. But when the accuser realizes whom he is up against, he panics. What to do? Butch provides the perfect honor-through-absurdity formula: "What would you think about inviting us to stick around? ["What?"] You don't have to mean it or anything—but if you'd just please invite us to stick around, I promise you we'll go." The frightened cowboy invites Butch and Sundance to stay, they go, and the eccentric tone for all that follows is set.

Ultimately, *The Princess Bride* does two things beyond its delightful ability to entertain. First, despite being a fairy tale, it reminds us life is not fair and sometimes the wrong people die. As Goldman comically phrases it, "This isn't *Curious George Uses the Potty*."[113] Second, despite this warning, it gives us a happy ending by bringing its hero back from death, as if to imply, enjoy it here because you are not going to get this in reality. Thus, along similar lines, though the viewer knows Butch and Sundance die at the film's close, by making a freeze-frame of their final action image

Butch, Etta, and Sundance go to the movies, the deleted film theatre scene in *Butch Cassidy and the Sundance Kid* (1969).

(with the color then drained to resemble an antiquated Western sepia still), they live on as legends—part of a genre that is as close as America gets to native fairy tales. This ending is also consistent with Hill's decision to drop an earlier poignant but somewhat heavy-handed scene in which the film's three principal players visit a nickelodeon and see an early Western film in which Butch and Sundance die.

Consequently, *Butch Cassidy* is both an extension of the rich Western parody tradition examined extensively in this chapter, and a peek ahead at the increasingly layered, multifaceted spoof movie of modern cinema (since 1960), regardless of target genre or auteur. Obviously, *Butch Cassidy* has much in common with the 1960s revisionist Western work of Peckinpah and spaghetti Western auteur Sergio Leone (see Chapter 4), not to mention the French New Wave work of Truffaut, especially the freeze-frame conclusion of his *400 Blows* (1959). Indeed, the *Butch Cassidy/Bonnie and Clyde* ties are largely by way of Truffaut, since Arthur Penn was greatly influenced by the French film movement. But once these modern links are acknowledged, as well as the moments of 1960s absurdity, *Butch Cassidy* has just as much or more in common with the parody work of the *Destry* era. Plus, *Butch Cassidy* is largely devoid of the violence and cynicism that define the world of Peckinpah, Leone, and Penn's *Bonnie and Clyde*.

Maybe it is as simple as coming back to Goldman's comments about people just liking Butch, and by extension, anyone with him. The film is about an innate comic humanity that is not that far from the spirit of *Destry*, in which even a crooked judge can be a crowd pleaser. Robert Redford said it best in his foreword to Lula Parker Betenson's *Butch Cassidy, My Brother*. Describing her happiness with the movie, the actor wrote: "She felt the picture had captured a quality long missed in . . . accounts of the West . . . [that many of the] "badmen" were, in fact, kids who never grew up or high spirited men whose sense of fun and pranks couldn't be contained by the law. This was the way we interpreted the legend in our film."[114] Like most great works, *Butch Cassidy*'s roots are many. And at its most fundamental entertainment level, one finds in Newman's Butch the spoofing goodwill that was Jimmy Stewart's title character in *Destry*—even if they are on opposite sides of the law.

NOTES

1. *Way Out West* review, *Variety*, May 5, 1937, p. 16.

2. Charles Barr, *Laurel & Hardy* (1968; reprint, Los Angeles: University of California Press, 1974), p. 101.

3. Blaud Johaueson, "*Way Out West*: Laurel & Hardy Go Western," *New York Daily Mirror*, May 4, 1937. In the *Way Out West* file, Billy Rose Theatre Collection, New York Public Library at Lincoln Center.

4. Ibid.

5. Robert Garland, "Laurel & Hardy Hit New High in Hilarity With *Way Out West*," *New York American*, May 4, 1937. In the *Way Out West* file, Billy Rose Theatre Collection.

6. William Boehnel, "Laurel & Hardy in Lively Comedy," *New York World-Telegram*, May 4, 1937. In the *Way Out West* file, Billy Rose Theatre Collection.

7. William Paul, "Film: *Way Out West*," *Village Voice*, January 29, 1970, p. 58.

8. Frank S. Nugent, *Way Out West* review, *New York Times*, May 4, 1937, p. 29.

9. Dorothy Masters, "Laurel-Hardy Comedy Jeopardizes Theatre," *New York Daily News*, May 4, 1937. In the *Way Out West* file, Billy Rose Theatre Collection.

10. Archer Winston, "Laurel and Hardy Panic Rialto With Their Act," *New York Post*, May 4, 1937. In the *Way Out West* file, Billy Rose Theatre Collection.

11. Ibid.

12. Ibid.

13. Garland, "Laurel & Hardy Hit New High in Hilarity With *Way Out West*."

14. Henry Jenkins, *What Made Pistachio Nuts? Early Sound Comedy and the Vaudeville Aesthetic* (New York: Columbia University Press, 1992), p. 255.

15. Johaueson, "*Way Out West*: Laurel & Hardy Go Western."

16. Paul, "Film: *Way Out West*."

17. Winston Burdett, *Way Out West* review, *Brooklyn Daily Eagle*, May 4, 1937. In the *Way Out West* file, Billy Rose Theatre Collection.

18. George Eells and Stanley Musgrove, *Mae West: A Biography* (New York: William Morrow, 1982), p. 195.

19. John Dunning, *Tune In Yesterday: The Ultimate Encyclopedia of Old-Time Radio, 1925–1976* (Englewood Cliffs, NJ: Prentice-Hall, 1976), p. 126.

20. Dunning, p. 126; *You Can't Cheat an Honest Man* review, *Variety*, February 22, 1939, p. 12.

21. *You Can't Cheat an Honest Man* review, *Newsweek*, February 27, 1939, p. 25.

22. Kate Cameron, "Mae West and Fields Give *Destry* a Ride," *New York Daily News*, March 16, 1940, in the *My Little Chickadee* file, Billy Rose Theatre Collection, New York Public Library at Lincoln Center.

23. William K. Everson, *The Art of W. C. Fields* (New York: Bonanza Books, 1967), p. 177.

24. Keith Memorial, *My Little Chickadee* review, *Boston Herald*, March 11, 1940, in the *My Little Chickadee* file, Billy Rose Theatre Collection.

25. *My Little Chickadee* review, *Time*, February 26, 1940, p. 66.

26. Kathleen Rowe, *The Unruly Woman: Gender and the Genres of Laughter* (Austin: University of Texas Press, 1995), p. 123.

27. Maurice Horn, ed. *The World Encyclopedia of Comics* (1976; reprint, New York: Avon Books, 1977), pp. 636–37.

28. Ibid., p. 637.

29. "Movie of the Week: *My Little Chickadee*: Mae West and W. C. Fields Burlesque the Westerns," *Life*, February 19, 1940, pp. 63–65.

30. Lee Mortimer, "Mae West, Fields Cut Up in *Little Chickadee*," *New York Daily Mirror*, March 16, 1940, in the *My Little Chickadee* file, Billy Rose Theatre Collection.

31. Mae West, *Goodness Had Nothing to Do With It* (1959; reprint, New York: Macfadden-Bartell, 1970).

32. Herbert Cahn, "*My Little Chickadee* Pairs Fields, Mae West," *Brooklyn Daily Eagle*, March 16, 1940, in the *My Little Chickadee* file, Billy Rose Theatre Collection.

33. For example, see: William Boehnel's "Mae West and W. C. Fields Co-Star in *My Little Chickadee*," *New York World-Telegram*, March 16, 1940, in the *My Little Chickadee* file, Billy Rose Theatre Collection.

34. Eells and Musgrove, p. 198.

35. Robert Lewis Taylor, *W. C. Fields: His Follies and Fortunes* (Garden City, NY: Doubleday, 1949), p. 242.

36. West, *Goodness Had Nothing to Do With It*, p. 189.

37. Ibid., p. 188.

38. Ronald J. Fields, *W. C. Fields: A Life on Film* (New York: St. Martin's Press, 1984), p. 215.

39. *My Little Chickadee* review, *New York Post*, March 16, 1940, in the *My Little Chickadee* file, Billy Rose Theatre Collection.

40. "Mae and Bill Out West," *Newsweek*, February 26, 1940, p. 30.

41. *My Little Chickadee* review, *Variety*, February 14, 1940, p. 18.

42. Mortimer, "Mae West, Fields Cut Up in *My Little Chickadee*.

43. Frank S. Nugent, *My Little Chickadee* review, *New York Times*, March 16, 1940, p. 8.

44. *Go West* review, *Variety*, December 18, 1940, p. 16.

45. Edith Werner, "For Laughter, *Go West* With the Marx Brothers," *New York Mirror*, February 21, 1941, in the *Go West* file, Billy Rose Theatre Collection.

46. "Buzzell, Brecher Set Up Big Laugh Fest," *Hollywood Reporter*, December 11, 1940, p. 3; *Go West* review, *Showman's Trade Review*, December 14, 1940, in the *Go West* Special Collection file, Margaret Herrick Library, Academy of Motion Picture Arts and Sciences, Beverly Hills, California.

47. Wanda Hale, "Marx Bros. in Stride In Their New Comedy," *New York Daily News*, February 21, 1941, in the *Go West* file, Billy Rose Theatre Collection.

48. *Go West* review, *New York World Telegram*, February 21, 1941, in the *Go West* file, Billy Rose Theatre Collection.

49. Rose Pelswick, "Latest Marx Lunacy," *New York Journal American*, February 21, 1941, in the *Go West* file, Billy Rose Theatre Collection.

50. Otis Ferguson, "Methods of Madness," *New Republic*, January 27, 1941, p. 117.

51. Joe Adamson, *Groucho, Harpo, Chico and Sometimes Zeppo* (New York: Simon and Schuster, 1973), p. 379.

52. Ibid., p. 371.

53. James Curtis, *Between Flops: A Biography of Preston Sturges* (New York: Harcourt Brace Jovanovich, 1982), p. 189.

54. Susan Kuhlmann, *Knave, Fool, and Genius: The Confidence Man as He Appears in Nineteenth Century American Fiction* (Chapel Hill: University of North Carolina Press, 1973), p. 6.

55. F. O. Matthiessen, *American Renaissance: Art and Expression in the Age of Emerson and Whitman* (1941; reprint, New York: Oxford University Press, 1954), p. xviii.

56. P. T. Barnum, *Struggles and Triumphs; Or, Forty Years' Recollections of P. T. Barnum* (1855; reprint, Carl Bode, ed., New York: Penguin Classics, 1987), p. 126.

57. Gary Lindberg, *The Confidence Man in American Literature* (New York: Oxford University Press, 1982), p. 187.

58. "Buzzell, Brecher Set Up Big Laugh Fest," p. 3.

59. Allen Eyles, *The Marx Brothers: Their World of Comedy* (1969; reprint, New York: Paperback Library, 1971), p. 156.

60. Ibid.

61. Edward Buzzell, "Mocked and Marred by the Marxes," *New York Times*, December 15, 1940, p. 6.

62. Groucho Marx, *The Groucho Letters: Letters From and To Groucho Marx* (New York: Simon and Schuster, 1967), p. 26. For a less than positive preshooting take on *Go West*, see pp. 22–24.

63. Frank Sanello, *Jimmy Stewart: A Wonderful Life* (New York: Pinnacle Books, 1997), p. 100.

64. Bosley Crowther, *Destry Rides Again* review, *New York Times*, November 30, 1939, p. 25.

65. William Boehnel, *Destry Rides Again* review, *New York World-Telegram*, November 30, 1939, in the *Destry Rides Again* file, Billy Rose Theatre Collection, New York Public Library at Lincoln Center.

66. Robert Coleman, "Destry Rides Again: Comedy With a Wallop," *New*

York Daily Mirror, November 30, 1939, in the *Destry Rides Again* file, Billy Rose Theatre Collection.

67. Elizabeth Copeland, "Human Marlene Revealed in Rowdy *Destry*," January 12, 1940, in the *Destry Rides Again* file, Billy Rose Theatre Collection.

68. Archer Winston, *Destry Rides Again* review, *New York Post*, November 30, 1939, in the *Destry Rides Again* file, Billy Rose Theatre Collection.

69. "Marlene in Hoss Opera: 'Destry Rides Again' Puts On A Lively Two-Gun Show," *Newsweek*, December 11, 1939, p. 33.

70. *Destry Rides Again* review, *Variety*, December 6, 1939, in the *Destry Rides Again* file, Billy Rose Theatre Collection.

71. Kate Cameron, "Dietrich Rides Again to Screen Triumphs," *New York Daily News*, November 30, 1939, in the *Destry Rides Again* file, Billy Rose Theatre Collection.

72. Copeland, "Human Marlene Revealed in Rowdy *Destry*."

73. Philip T. Hartung, *Destry Rides Again* review, *Commonweal*, December 15, 1939, p. 187.

74. "Marlene in Hoss Opera: 'Destry Rides Again' Puts On A Lively Two-Gun Show."

75. Maria Riva, *Marlene Dietrich By Her Daughter* (New York: Alfred A. Knopf, 1993), p. 494.

76. Steven Bach, *Marlene Dietrich: Life and Legend* (New York: William Morrow, 1992), p. 249.

77. Donald Spoto, *Blue Angel: The Life of Marlene Dietrich* (New York: Doubleday, 1992), p. 152.

78. Charles Higham, *Marlene: The Life of Marlene Dietrich* (W. W. Norton, 1977), p. 192.

79. Riva, *Marlene Dietrich By Her Daughter*, p. 494.

80. Higham, *Marlene: The Life of Marlene Dietrich*, p. 192.

81. Ibid., p. 193.

82. "Reite Ihn, Cowboy!," *New York Times*, December 3, 1939, section 9, p. 8.

83. Eileen Creelman, *Destry Rides Again* review, *New York Sun*, December 1, 1939, in the *Destry Rides Again* file, Billy Rose Theatre Collection.

84. "Marlene in Hoss Opera: 'Destry Rides Again' Puts On A Lively Two-Gun Show."

85. Kin Hubbard, *Abe Martin's Almanack for 1908* (Indianapolis: privately published, 1907), p. 8; Kin Hubbard, *Abe Martin's Brown County Almanack* (Indianapolis: privately published, 1909), p. 104.

86. Allen Eyles, *James Stewart* (1984; reprint, New York: Stein and Day, 1986), p. 58.

87. Wes D. Gehring, *Screwball Comedy: A Genre of Madcap Romance* (Westport, CT: Greenwood Press, 1986).

88. Nina Nichols, "Destry Rides Again," *Cinema Texas Program Notes*, February 4, 1980, p. 79. In the *Destry Rides Again* Special Collections file, Margaret Herrick Library, Academy of Motion Picture Arts and Sciences, Beverly Hills, California.

89. Ibid., p. 78.

90. Robert B. Ray, *A Certain Tendency of the Hollywood Cinema, 1930–1980* (Princeton, NJ: Princeton University Press, 1985), p. 58.

91. Ibid.

92. William Goldman, "William Goldman on the Craft of the Screenwriter," *Esquire Film Quarterly*, October 1981, p. 126.

93. Ibid., p. 129.

94. Lucius Beebe, "Sitting In At The Try-Outs of 'Stars In Your Eyes' [*Gunga Din* review]," *New York Herald-Tribune*, February 5, 1939, p. 2.

95. "Westerns Aid Film Industry," *New York Morning-Telegraph*, June 15, 1941, in the *Destry Rides Again* file, Billy Rose Theatre Collection.

96. Erskine Johnson, " 'Destry Rides Again' Great Entertainment," *Los Angeles Examiner*, November 29, 1939, section 1, p. 17.

97. Sara Hamilton, " 'Destry' Film on Screen at Two Theatres," *Los Angeles Examiner*, January 13, 1940, section 1, p. 8.

98. Sara Hamilton, "Folks, Meet Sam Hinds, That Judge in 'Destry,' " *Los Angeles Examiner*, January 14, 1940, section 5, p. 5.

99. "Premiere Set for Western" and "Preview of W. C. Fields Latest Feb. 6," *Los Angeles Examiner*, January 31, 1940, section 1, p. 11.

100. Beebe, "Sitting In At The Try-Outs," p. 2.

101. Wes Gehring correspondence with William Goldman, October 5, 1980, p. 2.

102. Wes Gehring correspondence with William Goldman, August 28, 1980, p. 1.

103. "Butch Cassidy and the Sundance Kid," *Filmfacts*, vol. 12, no. 15 (1969) p. 338.

104. Goldman, "William on the Craft of the Screenwriter," p. 126.

105. Eileen Creelman, "A Smashing Good Melodrama at the Music Hall, *Gunga Din*," *New York Sun*, January 27, 1939, in the *Gunga Din* file, Billy Rose Theatre Collection.

106. Blaud Johaueson, "Thrills, Tears, Comedy Make *Gunga Din* A Great Show," *New York Daily Mirror*, January 26, 1939, in the *Gunga Din* file, Billy Rose Theatre Collection.

107. "Butch Cassidy and the Sundance Kid,"*Filmfacts*, p. 338.

108. Richard Gertner, *Butch Cassidy and the Sundance Kid* review, *Motion Picture Daily*, September 10, 1969, pp. 1,6.

109. Vincent Canby, *Butch Cassidy and the Sundance Kid* review, *New York Times*, September 25, 1969, p. 54.

110. "Butch Cassidy: Tardy Movie Salute," *Newark Evening News*, December 23, 1968, in the *Butch Cassidy and Sundance Kid* file, Billy Rose Theatre Collection.

111. Ibid.

112. William Goldman, *The Princess Bride* (1973; reprint, New York: Ballantine Books, 1992), p. 12.

113. Ibid., p. 188.

114. Robert Redford, Foreword, in *Butch Cassidy, My Brother*, by Lula Parker Betenson as told to Dora Flack (1975; reprint, New York: Penguin Books), p. xiii.

3

The Pre-Brooks King of Parody:
Bob Hope . . . And Disciple
Woody Allen

Hope's film noir spoof *My Favorite Brunette* (1947) opens with his character, Ronnie Jackson, on San Quentin's death row: "This is the worst
last meal I ever had." And when there is no word from the governor on
commuting his sentence, Jackson adds, "Well, I'll know who to vote for
next time."

Allen's spoof of film noir, fantasy, and romance, *Play It Again, Sam*
(1972), is forever showing the difficulty his character, Allan Felix, has
emulating Bogart. For instance, "I'm red-headed, I'm fair-skinned. I don't
tan, I stroke."

BACKGROUND

One of the most dominant comedians of World War II and the ensuing
Cold War years was Bob Hope, who sometimes teamed with Bing Crosby
in the *Road* pictures. Woody Allen, *the* comedian of the modern age (since
1960) is a longtime disciple of Hope. During the 1970s, the height of Allen's popular success, he was persistent in both his praise of Hope's great-
ness and its influence on his own films. Allen and the Film Society of New
York's Lincoln Center eventually conspired to put on a 1979 Hope film
retrospective. Allen edited and narrated a sixty-three-minute compilation
of clips from seventeen Hope films entitled *My Favorite Comedian*. Hope's
work had inspired him to enter film comedy, or as he observed in the voice-
over of his film salute to Hope, "when my mother took me to see *Road to*

Morocco, I knew exactly what I wanted to do with my life." Revisionist movie critic Jeffrey Couchman, writing for the May 6, 1979, *New York Times*, noted that Hope's "natural comedic asset is his voice, as distinctive in its twang as the voice of either Groucho or W. C. Fields and well suited to his clipped, understated delivery. . . . [T]hese sounds are enhanced by a wonderfully mobile face [including] lips which practically curl around his sloped nose in a sneer of contempt or mock ferocity."[1]

John Lahr's *New Yorker* profile of Hope (December 21, 1998) praised the comic comfort his films brought to a war-weary 1940s audience, "in which cowardice was lovable and danger was without consequence." But as with the Lincoln center salute, Lahr's article was most articulate when it called on Woody Allen. This comedy disciple celebrated Hope's delivery by likening it to Groucho—but "It's more realistic than Groucho, and so his range is much wider . . . Groucho . . . had a sense of deep surrealism or deep suffering. Hope's persona is glib. He's not concerned with suffering but what he is concerned with is very, very amusing."

It was not that Hope's movie work was devoid of previous praise— tributes from period reviews are well documented in the following pages. And it was not that heavyweight critics had previously ignored his films. In 1969 British author and gifted comedy historian/theorist Raymond Durgnat observed, "Hope's characterization is a rich and relevant one. He has spasms of Harold Lloyd's optimism, [Eddie] Cantor's jitteriness, [W. C.] Fields's disillusionment, and a Don Duryea desperation, while his bouts of childlike bluff and hopeful cunning expertly transpose into farcical terms the comic vices of salesmanlike opportunism."[2] It was just that by the late 1970s the full extent of Hope's film legacy was becoming increasingly obvious (his last movie having appeared in 1972). At the same time, his controversial 1960s conservative politics were an ever-lessening distraction from his screen art. Hope was finally being rediscovered.

Like his early idol, Charlie Chaplin, Hope was born in England, christened Leslie Townes Hope. But whereas the creator of the "Little Fellow" came to America as a young adult, Hope's family resettled when he was a child. Perhaps this immigrant bonding helped him become, with the possible exception of Will Rogers, the entertainer most likened to an American ambassador of goodwill, entertaining troops abroad or hobnobbing with presidents. He has maintained this position while managing to entertain the nation for sixty-plus years in vaudeville, radio, television, the movies, and books. This unique position was already acknowledged in the mid-1940s: "The gap left by the death of Will Rogers [1935], as a comedian whose barbs at politics and politicians were particularly appreciated in Washington, has been filled. Bob Hope has stepped into the shoes of Will Rogers in this respect."[3]

More than any other major film comedian, Hope has consistently used parody for the heart of his work—the antihero as fool when trying to copy a real hero. Although exceptions exist, the best and majority of his movies are parody in nature. As noted in Chapter 1, most screen comics tackle *the* American genre sometime in their career but Hope made four send-ups: *The Paleface* (1948), *Fancy Pants* (1950), *Son of Paleface* (1952), and *Alias Jessie James* (1959). The most critically and commercially successful movie of his career was *The Paleface*.[4] In an era (late 1940s and 1950s) still fascinated with a genre whose late 1930s explosion of interest was documented in the previous chapter, Hope was the master of the Western burlesque.

Hope was hardly a slave to the Western, however. He sideswiped an assortment of genres. For example, with Crosby he spoofed Hollywood and the action adventure film in seven *Road* pictures. As a solo, Hope's *My Favorite Blonde* (1942) parodies Hitchcock's *The 39 Steps* (1935), and the comedian's *My Favorite Brunette* (1947) trips up film noir. In period pictures such as *The Princess and the Pirate* (1944), *Monsieur Beaucaire* (1946), and *Casanova's Big Night* (1954), Hope spoofs the swashbuckling costume drama. And this says nothing of the fun he had with the horror genre in such early Hope screen outings as *The Cat and the Canary* (1939) and *Ghost Breakers* (1940).

It is also important to underline that *The Cat and the Canary*, a *parody* thriller, was "the first film tailored to the talents of Bob Hope, [and] was crucial to his career."[5] And as period Hollywood columnist Louella Parsons reported, audiences loved the spoofing style of Hope: "With *The Cat and the Canary* doing exceptional business all over the country, [producer] Arthur Hornblow wasn't long in getting the idea to reunite [stars] Paulette Goddard and Bob Hope in . . . [*The Ghost Breakers*]."[6] According to Hope, with the matching success of the latter film, and the first *Road* picture sandwiched in between, his popularity in the movies was finally established.[7] And the pivotal lesson seemed to be, "Parody's your ticket!"

While the two thriller spoofs generated big box office and great reviews, most unforgettable to Hope was the praise he received from his idol, Chaplin, whose third wife, Paulette Goddard, was Hope's co-star in both films. When the two comedians met during the production of *The Cat and the Canary*, Chaplin said to him, "Young man, I've been watching you in the rushes [film footage shot each day] every night. I want you to know that you are one of the best timers of comedy I have ever seen."[8] With Chaplin still the measuring stick for all things illustrious in comic film, Hope could receive no greater compliment. (The best part of the Dean Martin and Jerry Lewis remake of *Ghost Breakers—Scared Stiff*, 1953, was the Hope and Crosby cameo conclusion.)

Hope's parody work places him among the pantheon of outstanding screen comedians. This chapter will focus on three of Hope's strongest spoof movies: the *Road to Utopia* (1945, the best of the *Road* series), *My Favorite Brunette*, and *The Paleface*. After examining these works, the chapter looks at the quintessential parody *Play It Again, Sam* (1972), by Hope's greatest comedy devotee, Woody Allen.

Broad parody has not remained at the heart of Allen's work since the late 1970s, but it can still surface in his films, such as his clever take on the whodunit in *Manhattan Murder Mystery* (1993). The film reunited him with his frequent 1970s romantic partner in parody, Diane Keaton. As with many comedians, Allen's early forays into film had parody roots. (See Chapter 1 for more on this, especially *What's Up, Tiger Lily?*, 1966, his burlesque redubbing of a Japanese secret agent film.)

Take the Money and Run (1969), the first Allen film he also directed, is an ambitious take off on cinema vérité (literally, cinema truth), documentary, the prison film, and crime pictures in general. Other pivotal 1970s spoofs include having fun with science fiction in *Sleeper* (1973, in which he wakes up 200 years in the future), and derailing the art house movie à la Ingmar Bergman's *The Seventh Seal* (1956) with *Love and Death* (1975, which takes Allen's character back to early nineteenth-century Russia at the time of the Napoleonic wars). But regardless of the time frame or genre under affectionate comedy attack, Allen's screen persona frequently brings to mind Hope.

Allen's *Play It Again, Sam* is a reworking of the artist's most successful play of the same name (1969). Though the Bogart of *Casablanca* (1942) acts as an influential tough guy model/guardian angel throughout the movie, Allen's take on how to play a film noir hero is again pure Hope, with *My Favorite Brunette* frequently coming to mind. Thus, it was most appropriate that Allen should help orchestrate the previously mentioned 1970s tribute to Hope, since at no other time was the younger comedian's work so immersed in the parody world of his idol.

HOPE'S *ROAD TO UTOPIA*

Between 1940 and 1962, Hope and Crosby were teamed in seven *Road* films: *Road to Singapore* (1940), *Road to Zanzibar* (1941), *Road to Morocco* (1942), *Road to Utopia* (1945), *Road to Rio* (1947), *Road to Bali* (1952), and *Road to Hong Kong* (1962). Besides spoofing the action adventure genre, the *Road* pictures are a parody of Hollywood itself. As one might assume, given the celebrated nature of the series, the magic of this parody pairing was immediately recognized. The 1940 *Hollywood Reporter* was probably, however, the most perceptive in its praise of the first *Road* movie: "In pairing Bing Crosby and Bob Hope, Paramount has created one of the greatest comedy teams in film history . . . a demand for more of the same is an unqualified certainty."[9] The immediate critical and commercial success of the Road pictures was not lost on Hope, who used them as one more topic in his stand-up patter on stage and for radio. The subject also surfaced in the first of his numerous comic autobiographies,

An elderly Bing Crosby, Dorothy Lamour, and Bob Hope in the framing device for *The Road to Utopia* (1945).

They Got Me Covered (1941). "I don't know what will happen in our next picture . . . *The Road to Morocco* but anyway, Dorothy, Bing, and I are having a lot of fun . . . besides I'm getting a salary for my performances in these 'Road pictures' . . . which, as one critic pointed out, is a perfect example of highway robbery."

Each successive *Road* outing was stronger, with the team peaking on the *Road to Utopia*. It was originally to be the *Road to Moscow*, but because two then-recent Hollywood films on Russia, *Mission to Moscow* and *North Star* (both 1943), had not been commercial hits, production company Paramount decided it needed a new title. It was also a providential change, since the paranoia about communism that followed World War II resulted in the Hollywood blacklisting of many talented artists, all because they might have "red" interests. Even some people involved in the production of *Mission to Moscow* and *North Star* were later hassled by communist witch-hunters—and this was during a time when the Soviet Union was a U.S. *ally* (1941–45). With the Moscow destination scrapped, Paramount was stuck with winter sets and the need for an appropriate story.

But like most comedies, the *Road* pictures are not married to a script. As the reviewer for *The New Yorker* wrote: "The plot, if you care, has the boys whooping around Alaska in search of a gold mine, and Miss Lamour [the ongoing *Road* show romantic interest] is present as the owner of the property."[10] It is the late 1890s, and gold in the Klondike makes *Utopia* the only period *Road* picture, which might contribute to the film's unique status. And given Hope's great future success with Western parodies, it is also fitting that the best of the team's pairings has a frontier setting. As if to be on the safe side, with this period departure, *Utopia* has a contemporary framing device. Hope and love interest Dorothy Lamour are thus well into their white-haired senior years at the film's opening, with an elderly Crosby joining them at the close, after the story has unfolded in an extended flashback.

All the *Road* pictures spoof the movies, but none as effectively as *Utopia*. And it all begins before the story proper. That is, as *Esquire*'s critic noted, humorist "Robert Benchley 'supplies' another element of [parody] importance; [he's] a prologue without portfolio."[11] Prior to the opening titles, one sees Benchley standing behind the desk he normally used in his award-winning short film subjects. Appropriately, these shorts at their best, such as the Oscar-winning *How to Sleep* (1935), spoof professorial figure presentations. Most acclaimed for his inspired and often-spoofing essays, which helped bring the figure of the comic antihero to a broader audience (starting in the 1920s), Benchley had also found major antiheroic success in film and radio. At the time he was arguably America's best-known funnyman.[12] And apropos for this chapter, Allen credits Benchley as being another key influence. Regardless, with tongue firmly in cheek, Benchley introduces *Utopia*:

The motion picture which you are about to see is not very clear in spots. As a matter of fact it was made to demonstrate how not to make a motion picture and at the same time win an Academy Award. Now someone in what is known as the front office has thought an occasional word from me might help clarify the plot and other vague portions of the film. [chuckling] Personally, I doubt it.

Periodically, Benchley reappears in the corner of the screen and shares bits of comic wisdom, such as, "This is a device known as a flashback," or, "Did you ever stop to think of one of those dog teams? The lead dog is the only one that ever gets a change of scenery." Appropriately enough, the *New York Herald Tribune*'s critic used Benchley as a symbol of the film's parody: "He kids the film as much as it kids itself. His ironic explanations of the screen's flashback or calling attention to a group of people as obvious 'extras' underline the superb humor of the show."[13] And *Esquire* said, "His cheerfully inane ad libs do more than merely compound the confusion. They give the idiotic events on the screen a certain related reality."[14] Years later when Hope was asked about the Benchley comments, as well as other examples of spoofing the movies, he said, "They [audience] love anything that gives them a little mental jerk and they want to be 'with it.' "[15] Neither before *Utopia* nor after would the *Road* pictures have such a supporting comedian as gifted as Benchley.

In addition to Benchley's screen corner appearances, numerous scenes detail what plot exists and shout "movie spoof." For instance, the movie includes a talking fish and a talking bear who feels underappreciated. ("A fine thing. A fish they let talk. Me, they won't give one stinking line.") This is a perfect commentary on the saturation comedy of the *Road* pictures, or parody in general—anything for a laugh. And although there is a loose plot reason for the fish and bear to be there, the comments are hardly expected. Hope does his own animal sound (wolf) when he has a big kissing scene with Dorothy Lamour's character (Sal), adding in direct address to the viewer, "As far as I'm concerned this picture is over right now."

Duke Johnson (Bing Crosby) and Chester Hooten (Bob Hope) even discuss being off on another *Road* picture as they dogsled across the Klondike. Chester then looks off into the distance and observes, "Get a load of that bread and butter." While Duke is mystified, the camera cuts to a snow-covered mountain with stars around it—the logo for Paramount, the studio producing the film. At another point a character dressed like a magician strolls through their scene. When asked if he is in the movie, he answers, "No, I'm taking a shortcut to Stage 10."

The biggest spoof, of course, is having Hope and Crosby posing as two murderers who have stolen a gold mine map belonging to Dorothy Lamour's character. It is a funny premise that plays even funnier when the film's other figures accept the trick for a while. Chester and Duke, hardly two tough guys, have difficulty staying in character. The funniest recovery finds Hope's Chester ordering lemonade in a bar. Immediately recognizing his mistake, he quickly growls to put it "in a dirty glass."

Bing Crosby has said, "The basic ingredient of any *Road* picture is a Rover Boys–type plot, plus music. The plot takes two fellows, throws them into as many jams as possible, then lets them clown their way out."[16] As noted in Chapter 1, the *Road* pictures use travel to get Hope and Crosby into as many comic "jams" as possible.

Crosby, however, has left one ingredient out of his *Road* formula. He does not examine the difference between these "two fellows." Though they are both women-chasing con artists (in *Utopia* they have a huckster game called Ghost-O that involves a magic box increasing however much money is placed inside), Crosby's Duke is in charge of all the team's misadventures, as is the case in all the *Road* pictures. For example, in *The Road to Morocco* (1942) Crosby's character goes so far as to sell Hope's into slavery.

And the romantic Crosby always gets the girl—Dorothy Lamour—except in *Utopia*. But this lone Hope victory must be qualified. When the film closes with a return to its contemporary framing device, an elderly Duke drops in on longtime marrieds Chester and Sal, taking the couple by surprise. Duke had seemed to be a goner at the end of *Utopia*'s flashback. An earthquake had suddenly opened an abyss separating Duke from Chester and Sal, and Crosby's character was last seen with an angry mob bearing down upon him. Still the skirt chaser, Duke arrives at Chester and Sal's with two beautiful young "nieces." The topper to this action has Chester and Sal's only child coming into the scene—he is the spitting image of Duke, and is naturally played by Crosby. Thus, even Hope's one "success" with Dorothy Lamour finds him to have been cuckolded despite help from an earthquake.

Hope's favorite description of his *Road* character came from a 1953 *Saturday Evening Post* article: "Fate is determined to make [him] a jerk. He brags and blusters, but there isn't a child over five who can't outwit him, disarm him or steal his pants."[17] Hope's *Road* character could still be the wise guy, as in his bragging situations. But as Hope observed of these pictures, "We put more emphasis on the 'boob' aspect of his 'Road' character."[18] As a reviewer noted, "Theatre ushers report that spectators all laugh at Hope and identify themselves with Crosby."[19] But Crosby's *Zanzibar* character is most succinct: "Stick with me and if you live, we're going to do all right."

Part of the inspired saturation comedy effect of *Utopia* could be attributed to the fact that it was scripted by two of Hope's former radio gag writers, Norman Panama and Melvin Frank. This talented duo's first screen credit was the story idea for Hope's *My Favorite Blonde*. They would later script his *Monsieur Beaucaire* and the *Road to Hong Kong* (with Frank producing and Panama directing this final Hope and Crosby teaming).

Hope and Crosby did not write and direct their films, but they peppered their scripts with much additional gag material, from themselves and from their radio gag men. (During the 1940s Hope and Crosby had competing radio programs.) Thus, many names might have appeared under script credit. Moreover, like other independent personality comedians mentioned earlier in the text, Hope (the team's designated comedian) was directable *if* he wanted to be. For instance, probably the best director Hope worked with was Frank Tashlin, who co-scripted and directed *Son of Paleface*. Tashlin comically described how Hope would get his way: "His narrowed eyes squinting [anticipating the future look of an angry Clint Eastwood?] at you down the maligned nose, is a withering experience. Your puttees curl and your megaphone sags [these two objects were once considered standard fare for a director]."[20]

In *Road to Utopia*, Hope and Crosby had an especially casual approach to filmmaking, though the production of all the *Road* pictures had an easygoing strategy. Crosby observed, "We had a ball [on the *Road*] pictures. We had directors who let us suit our own schedules."[21]

Although the *Road* films are famous for the comic asides of Hope and Crosby (*Utopia* included), American humor has always placed a high premium on visual/slapstick comedy, whether in the movies or on the printed page. For instance, the beloved James Thurber's greatest book is *My Life and Hard Times* (1933), which is so full of visual comedy (not to mention his delightful drawings) that even his episode titles create cartoon pictures: "The Night the Bed Fell," "The Day the Dam Broke," and "The Dog that Bit People." And film's greatest comedy period has long been considered the silent days of Chaplin, Buster Keaton, Harold Lloyd, Harry Langdan, and Laurel & Hardy.

With this in mind, it is interesting to note that the *New York Herald Tribune*'s critic went so far as to credit the visual side of *Utopia* as the key to its success: "Much of the show is premised on the violently witty asides of Crosby and Hope, but it is not the dialogue which sustains the production. It is at its best when pantomime is the springboard for crazy characterizations and ludicrous scenes."[22] Examples include the pickpocket scenes with Hope and Crosby, their reduction to babies when they find out what they lost by not believing in Santa (Claus, in a cameo appearance, had intended to give them two beautiful girls), and Hope's accidental romancing of a bear.

Though not in *Utopia*, the team's most repeated physical game is their "patty-cake" defense. When villains have the duo in a tight spot, Hope and Crosby's characters start playing patty-cake. At a given moment, instead of the normal "patty" to their partner's hand, each punches out the mystified bad guy on his side. When this defense does not work, as in the *Road to Zanzibar*, their characters observe, "They must have seen the [last *Road*] picture."

The final *Road* film opened in 1962, a full ten years after the last joint adventure of Hope and Crosby. By this time their solo movie careers were in decline and their comedy personae seemed tired, but there is no denying a chemistry still exists. Though not without its moments, as well as new parody directions for the team (a science fiction send-up as the duo became reluctant astronauts), the *Road to Hong Kong* would be their last film teaming. (The best part of their space spoof involves an automatic banana feeding device that "apes" a more comically complex device in Chaplin's *Modern Times*, 1936.)

During the 1960s some critics felt the Hope/Crosby parody pictures, with the exception of *Utopia*, "haven't worn too well."[23] One explanation at the time for the continuing appeal of *Utopia*, from the insightful Raymond Durgnat, is that "it tries hardest for those self-spoofing gags which shatter the storyline."[24] No little part of this was the inspired use of Robert Benchley. One might also posit the previously noted factors that it is the only period *Road* picture, and it has a more pronounced use of physical comedy.

The anarchistic comedy of the Marx Brothers, W. C. Fields, and others also was rediscovered during the politically volatile 1960s. In contrast, the late 1940s and 1950s films of Hope and Crosby, Martin and Lewis, Red Skelton, Danny Kaye, and others were in "the more conservative thematic structure of affirmative [status quo]."[25] Put another way, one reason parody was so big for Hope during the 1950s was that political satire was not safe for an artist or an audience during the McCarthy witch-hunting years, when the alleged threat of communism had everyone paranoid about being labeled a "pinko," accompanied by a ruined career and/or life.

For many in the 1960s, therefore, movies of the recent past did not have the antiestablishment bite of, say, the Marx Brothers. A further factor working against the 1960s reception of the *Road* parodies was Hope's real-life pro–Vietnam War stance at a time when the conflict was becoming increasingly unpopular with the American public.

Now, however, *Utopia* and the other *Road* pictures are appreciated by most students of parody, whether critics or kids. In fact, during the 1970s and '80s the series had acquired such a West Coast cult following that despite Crosby's 1977 death, there was periodic talk of still another *Road* film, with Hope to be teamed with Red Skelton. Nothing came of this, which is probably just as well. But it demonstrates the special status now attributed to these films.

While some parody references, on the *Road* or elsewhere, can be obscured by time, the good spoof picture saturates the screen with so much material one has no time to bemoan the occasional parody reference gone astray. And if the performers in the parody vehicle are memorable stars, such as Hope and Crosby, what might be potentially obscure is anything but. For example, a pivotal source of Hope and Crosby's humor is their continual bickering at each other. The basis for this is a comic "feud" originating in their competing radio programs. No doubt this was inspired by earlier radio feuds between Jack Benny and Fred Allen, or W. C. Fields and Edgar Bergen's Charlie McCarthy. Period fans of the *Road* pictures would have had the added bonus of recognizing this shtick move from radio to screen, but the bickering in and of itself is funny, whether one knows the radio connection or not. Good parody works on the shotgun approach; it peppers a large area of subjects, big and small.

HOPE'S *MY FAVORITE BRUNETTE*

My Favorite Brunette was especially important to Hope. It was the first movie product of Hope Enterprises, Inc., and it was made on a fifty-fifty basis with Paramount studio. The comedian was very happy to be his own boss: "When you're under contract to a certain studio you are obligated to do certain things whether you like it or not. Of course, they will fix it for you, but it is not the way to make pictures today."[26]

The private-eye picture was carefully chosen, possibly influenced by the fact that detective stories were Hope's favorite reading material. He spared no expense, using more than a million dollars of his own funds in the project. This added control paid off; the film was a major critical and commercial success and is invariably noted as one of his best.

Whereas the *Road* pictures spoofed the movies as a whole, *My Favorite Brunette* is primarily a parody of the film noir (literally, black cinema) genre, which was at the height of its popularity in 1947. Film noir is known for its man-in-the-middle detectives, such as novelist Dashiell Hammett's seminal Sam Spade in the 1941 film adaptation of *The Maltese Falcon*, or author Raymond Chandler's equally significant Philip Marlowe in the 1946 movie take on the *Big Sleep*. *Time* magazine's critic immediately thought of the latter novelist when reviewing Hope's picture: "*My Favorite Brunette* is a well-roasted rib [spoof] of the fancy talk and fancy incident served up by Raymond Chandler and other authors of the rough and tough school [often labeled 'tough guy fiction']."[27] And the in-film detective that Hope's character attempts to emulate has Sam for a first name, making one think of Hammett's Sam Spade.

Though there are differences between Sam Spade and Philip Marlowe on the printed page, the deviations are blurred in film noir by Humphrey Bogart essaying both roles in these screen adaptations. Despite other actors playing the characters during the 1940s and since, Bogart now seems to "own" these two figures, as well as being considered the definitive film noir lead. (This is why Bogart is so central to Allen's later film noir parody *Play It Again, Sam*.)

Being a detective is not a film noir requirement, but the genre's central male ends up playing a private-eye type, regardless of his given screen trade. For instance, *Brunette* finds Hope playing a baby photographer who lives to be a detective.

Film noir is dark in story line, with suffering and death the indifferent norm. The fatalism of German Expressionism, as well as its visual style (the city at night, shiny black surfaces everywhere, unusual camera angles) had a great influence on film noir. The genre represents corruption mixed with healthy doses of sex and psychotic violence.

Film noir, which flourished from the middle 1940s until the early 1950s, was the result of several post–World War II developments. First was the cynical worldview born of revelations about the Nazi Holocaust, the developing cold war, and the use of the atomic bomb. Second, several Jewish directors who had been active during the period of German Expressionism had fled Nazi-occupied Europe and eventually found themselves in Hollywood. Third, authors ranging from James Cain to Ernest Hemingway, including Hammett and Chandler, had been writing the aforementioned "tough guy fiction" since the 1930s. Although there was still a Hollywood censorship board, 1940s adaptations of these provocative works were allowed to be closer to the original stories (after World War II, people expected more adult fare). Fourth, with so many men serving in the armed forces, women on the home front assumed a lot of jobs previously held by men. When the war was over, there was some tension between returning veterans and the women who had successfully held down the job market. This was no doubt a factor in film noir's having strong, dominating, and dangerous women.

Thematically, this genre undercuts the American dream and success story: people who seem to have achieved success have cheated along the way. The dream is just one more American myth. The genre also undercuts the traditional location of the American paradise—California, be it the 1849 gold rush, or the 1930s migration of Dust Bowl farmers. Thus, film noir invariably takes place in California, often in Los Angeles or San Francisco. Appropriately, the genre sometimes rubs shoulders with the film industry. Indeed, the movies are a metaphor for this negative worldview. That is, films are not what they seem to be, from the false-front buildings to stuntmen for the stars. The dark comedy/noir classic *The Player* (1992) is about a film producer.

Hope's *My Favorite Brunette* appeared in the noir heyday. It would be difficult to highlight a more thorough genre parody. This film is an excellent example of the "creative criticism" mentioned earlier. Wannabe detective Ronnie Jackson (Hope) has his modest studio next to a real detective's office, with film noir star Alan Ladd in a cameo as private eye Sam Mc-Cloud. This is the beginning of a story-long flashback and voiceover narration (both classic noir devices) by Jackson, who is currently awaiting execution on San Quentin's death row.

Besides the immediate comedy contrast between Hope's essentially cowardly figure and his attempts to be a tough guy, the acting styles are blatantly different. Hope is a fully animated, over-the-top comedian. Ladd, like most noir film figures, uses a minimalist style of body movement and dialogue, with the latter both brief and pithy. Noir is an existentialist world in which protecting one's self means personally exposing very little.

Since Hope's Jackson had a hard time even handling his last photography assignment (a two-year-old child who nearly bites off his finger), one would wager Jackson's chances of being a private eye are less than good. But Hope at his best, as he is here, brings such enthusiasm to this detective dream (he has invented a keyhole camera that has already gotten him kicked out of five hotels), that he naturally gets a chance to play the part. A critic observed, "Bob Hope wanders through the show as though he were improvising every incident. Performing such as this is no trick. It is high artistry."[28]

As he sits in Sam McCloud's office while Ladd's tough guy is gone, Hope tries to imitate Sam by downing some whiskey from McCloud's desk. The comic's response might be compared to humorist Robert Benchley's inspired description of strong drink: "In . . . seconds the top of the inhaler's head rises slowly and in a dignified manner until it reaches the ceiling where it floats, bumping gently up and down. The teeth then drop out and arrange themselves on the floor to spell 'Portage High School, 1930' . . . and a strange odor of burning rubbers fills the room."[29] Woody Allen borrows Hope's scene for his *Play It Again, Sam* (1972). Fittingly, Allen's character is also trying to imitate a hard-drinking film noir detective—genre icon Humphrey Bogart.

As in most film noir, the catalyst for the hero's (or in this case, the antihero's) entry into the genre is by way of a beautiful, mysterious woman. The *New York Daily Mirror*'s Jack Thompson described it thus: "Hope with his confusion, double-takes, asides to the audience, and drooling pursuit of the sultry Dorothy Lamour, makes a highly agreeable detective." [30] Mobsters have kidnapped Lamour's scientist uncle, and she desperately wants help from Hope's Jackson, whom she mistakes for Ladd's McCloud.

For the contemporary viewer, *My Favorite Brunette* is a broad takeoff on film noir. This movie seems to have no ties with that more subdued form of spoofing examined in Chapters 1 and 2 known as parody of reaffirmation. Briefly reiterated, this approach has a serious undercurrent that occasionally has the viewer enjoying the burlesque not as parody but as a traditional showcasing of the genre allegedly under affectionate comic attack. Thus, *Brunette* has none of the tragic undertones of *Destry Rides Again*, a reaffirmation parody analyzed at length in the previous chapter.

With this said, it still merits noting that although *Brunette* is obviously broad parody, numerous period reviews include references that at least flirt with the reaffirmation approach. For example: "In addition to being hilariously funny, the picture is a genuine thriller," and it manages to have "suspense and excitement as well as jokes." [31] This was owing in no small part to the casting of two period villains forever linked with the horror genre, Peter Lorre and Lon Chaney, Jr. This observation is made merely to note the enigmatic nature of genre study. Without casting any aspersions on the often-inspired nature of genre criticism, a formula of sorts exists for each type. Yet one must allow for variations to occur over time.

At the risk of sounding blasphemous, even pioneer genre writings by pivotal film critics such as Robert Warshow (on the Western and the gangster film) and James Agee (on comedy) are not without some limitations. Warshow has problems with *My Darling Clementine* (1946), *Kiss of Death* (1947), *High Society* (1956), and *Shane* (1953); Agee has reservations about comedy outside the silent era.[32] (Agee's bias is examined further in this chapter's *Paleface* section.) Genre criticism exists as a guide for the curious mind, highlighting recurring patterns of cultural significance in the arts, and not as a dictator of said patterns. As influential genre author John G. Cawelti has observed, "When genre critics forget that their super texts are critical artifacts and start treating them as prescriptions for artistic cre-

Though a film noir private eye is *not* a Sherlock Holmes type, Bob Hope spoofs that image as Dorothy Lamour plays pretty in *My Favorite Brunette* (1947).

ation, the concept of genre becomes stultifying and limiting."[33] Consequently, *Brunette* remains a parody today, but any period suggestions of reaffirmation, the aforementioned "genre thriller," have long since gone.

Continuing this examination of *Brunette* as broad parody, a passing comedy aside by *Newsweek*'s review—"anything Sherlock Holmes can do, Sherlock Hope can do better"[34]—invites a connection between film noir and the antiheroic Hope. The noir private eye is just the opposite of Sherlock Holmes. Sherlock is all-knowing; he can look at a footprint and tell how much change the suspect had in his pants and whether he preferred peach cobbler to pumpkin pie. With his brilliant deductions, the last page of the Holmes story has all the loose ends tied together. Now, the film noir detective is tough, but he is often no further ahead in solving the mystery than a member of the audience, and some questions even go unanswered. In arguably the greatest film noir, the revisionist *Chinatown* (1974), Jack Nicholson's central character is never ahead of the viewer and ends up defeated by John Huston's figure of evil. But, though the "last page" of *Chinatown* is difficult to accept, one has enjoyed the equal-ground nature of the "trip" to the end. Bob Hope can only comically fill the film noir shoes of an Alan Ladd or Jack Nicholson, and thus film noir is parodied. Yet, it is appropriate that Hope should be spoofing a then-new, more vulnerable private eye. Indeed, *The New York Times* review of *Brunette* included an observation—"As for clarity, what would it want with such as that?"[35]—that could apply to many legitimate examples of film noir.

An additional point with regard to *Brunette* is the mistaken period connection drawn between it and Hope's earlier *My Favorite Blonde* (1942), where the comic is *not* in search of adventure.[36] While some parallels exist, such as a pretty girl and an antihero with "delusions of courage,"[37] *Blonde*'s parody has a different pre-noir target—Hitchcock's political thriller *The 39 Steps*. Hope's character in *Blonde* is hardly setting the entertainment world on fire—a secondary sidekick to a penguin in small-time variety theaters. But his lack of interest in getting involved (unlike Hope's wanna-be private eye in *Brunette*) is central to the parody success of *Blonde*, since *The 39 Steps* plays upon one of Hitchcock's favorite themes, a "wrong man" forced into involvement.

It is unfortunate that most people think only of Mel Brooks' spoof of the director—*High Anxiety* (1977)—when one mentions parody and Hitchcock. *Blonde* complements Brooks' work, since the Hope vehicle focuses on one Hitchcock movie, and *High Anxiety* takes a shotgun approach that attempts to refer to as many of the celebrated director's movies as possible. If truth be told, the Hope picture is the better spoof. Brooks's film, because of its broad comic attack, is often uneven in getting laughs. But comparison of these two affectionate but different spoofs of Hitchcock will have to be saved for some future study.

Brunette sometimes seems a model for Woody Allen. For instance, Hope's false bravado on death row (the framing device from which the flashback occurs) anticipates Allen's demeanor in *Love and Death* (1975) as he awaits execution; both characters anticipate a pardon. Consequently, these normally devout cowards act as calm wise guys. For instance, Hope's Ronnie Jackson, on the verge of his walk to San Quentin's gas chamber, sneers at a penitentiary that has not yet converted to electricity. Even this comment is topped with the closing reaction of the disappointed executioner (Bing Crosby) when Ronnie's last-second pardon arrives. Hope's character responds, "That guy will take any part." *Road* picture footnotes such as this, always at Crosby's expense, occur in many of Hope's solo films, including *Blonde*.

There is also an engrossing link between *Brunette* and Allen's dark comedy *Crimes and Misdemeanors* (1989), which shows Hope's continued influence on the comedian, even when parody is not the focus genre. In Hope's *Brunette* a confession that would clear the antihero of murder charges has been recorded. But a switch is made, and when Ronnie plays what he thinks will clear him, he hears a speeded-up version of Betty Hutton singing "Murder He Said," from the film *Happy Go Lucky* (1943), a comic surprise that seems to keep pointing the murder finger at Hope's Ronnie. In *Crimes* Allen has a dual-focus narrative, with a murder in one story and more comic frustration for his antihero in the other. And at precisely the moment when one character decides to murder, the film cuts to a theatrical screening of *Happy Go Lucky* and Hutton belting out "Murder He Said." It is an inspired surprise comic transition to the world of Allen's antihero character, a film fan at a revival house screening of the Hutton movie. Allen the director has set up the transition by an earlier scene with his character at the screening of another old film. Thus, one character plans a murder, while another merely toys with the idea in the safety of a darkened theater.

A good parody acts as a guide to a genre, and *Brunette* does just that. The film noir woman is sexually manipulative. When Dorothy Lamour's character, Carlotta Montay, mistakes Ronnie for a detective, he is reluctant to take her case. But she comes on to him, saying: "We Montays are generous. If you will just find my husband [actually, it is her uncle] I will be so grateful. You'll see." With that promise and the appropriate sexy body language, the word *no* drops out of Ronnie's vocabulary. Period reviews often treated Lamour as just another pretty face: "She is little more than a comely prop in a one-man [Hope] job of bumbling clowning."[38] Though being drop-dead gorgeous is certainly in the genre's femme fatale job description, Lamour goes beyond beauty as a plot catalyst. In part because of earlier *Road* pictures, as well as two other pre-*Brunette* screen teamings with the comedian, she and Hope have excellent film chemistry. And with no Bing Crosby in sight, save for the cameo, the viewer can safely assume the comedian will get the girl. Moreover, despite Carlotta's initial film noir–given manipulation, Lamour's many previous movie pairings with Hope convince the viewer they belong together.

Film noir oozes sexuality, and *Brunette* is saturated with it, starting with the comic given that Hope's screen persona both thinks of himself as God's gift to women, and is obsessed with sex in general. For instance, when his *Brunette* character finds out Carlotta is not married, he drools, "So he's not your husband. Well, did I quote you any rates? I may work cheaper, you know." When Hope's Ronnie is being chased and escapes through an apartment building, he buzzes nearly all the apartments to unlock the main door, repeating the line, "Hello honey, this is Joe." Countless women replying in a "come hither" nature lead him to observe in the midst of his flight, "I must remember this address." Even events not associated with sex are described in a sexual manner. For example, when Ronnie comes to after being knocked out, he says, "I was playing post office with the floor." (This comic patter after a concussion is also reminiscent of the 1944 noir classic *Murder, My Sweet*, in which Dick Powell as Philip Marlowe is forever responding with a quip after being knocked out by bad guys.)

Another noir characteristic is the suggestion that the femme fatale or a member of her immediate family is mentally unstable. For instance, the strange behavior of younger daughter (Martha Vickers) in *The Big Sleep*

(1946) includes Humphrey Bogart's Philip Marlowe complaint that she tried to sit on his lap—while he was standing up. The period noir films often imply ties to incest, but the era's censorship policy forbade anything that provocative. Only later, when restrictions were dropped, could a noir movie such as *Chinatown* (1974) or *The Grifters* (1990) deal directly with incest. In *Brunette*, Ronnie is told Carlotta has mental problems and asks, "Does she snap her cap very often?" Carlotta's waffling on just who is missing, her husband or her uncle, could also be construed as someone being a victim of, or having a propensity toward, incest. Ronnie has to rescue Carlotta from a mental sanitarium, and this requires Hope to act crazy, something he finds upsetting: "I think I do this too well."

Parody films frequently spoof specific films and/or genres in addition to the key genre under attack—rather a nothing-sacred policy. And *Brunette* includes many examples. For instance, when Ronnie is having difficulty climbing a tree in order to break into a second-story window, he mumbles, "It always looks so easy in those *Tarzan* pictures." Later, when he finds himself hanging from a chandelier during a chase, he discovers a bottle and immediately quips, "Ray Milland has been here." This is a reference to Milland's Oscar-winning performance as an alcoholic in *Lost Weekend* (1945), forever hiding bottles in odd places.

Film noir often also features a magnificent old mansion in which the decadent heavies reside, or at least appear to live. Ronnie says in voice-over, "It's the kind of house that looks like you can hunt quail in the hallway." But as in Hitchcock's later noir-ish *North By Northwest* (1959), the central character (in this case, Ronnie) brings in authorities only to find the house empty of boarders. Things are seldom as they seem in film noir, and even the sanity of the lead figure appears to be in question. Whether occupied or not, such a mansion represents old money obtained in shady deals. The decay of such families is sometimes symbolized by age, sickness, or incest. For example, in *The Big Sleep* a hothouse for plants is attached to the mansion, with the elderly patriarch in a wheelchair constantly there. Though not as blatant as this, *Brunette* manages to create that ambience, including a heavy pretending to use a wheelchair.

Even Ronnie's quips have a way of resurfacing in later noir films. For instance, when he finally manages to hold a gun on the diminutive, knife-obsessed Peter Lorre, he cracks, "One move and you're a dead midget." In *Chinatown*, Jack Nicholson's character makes the mistake of calling director Roman Polanski's knife-carrying cameo figure a midget and nearly loses his nose. And as *Chinatown*'s wounded private eye observes, "I like my nose and I like breathing through it."

In these and so many other ways, Hope's *Brunette* manages to take apart film noir, one genre component after another. In answer to a later revisionist critic's article titled "Bob Hope: More Than a Gagster?" the answer has to be a resounding—yes![39]

HOPE'S *THE PALEFACE*

Though Hope was frequently drawn to the Western parody, this segment focuses on *The Paleface* because it is the best of the series and arguably the greatest of his non-*Road* pictures. There is, however, a comparison made with the sequel, *Son of Paleface*, because of its more saturation comedy approach to parody.

Life magazine's "Movie of the Week (January 3, 1949) salute to *Paleface* paid high tribute to Hope's spoofing abilities when it linked them to America's premier genre: an "astute combination of two ingredients which have always served the movies well: a standard cowboy-and-Indian plot and the standard gags and gimmicks of a Bob Hope comedy."[40]

The comedian plays the most anitheroic of characters—a mail-order dentist named Painless Peter Potter. Business is not going well in the Old West (he has a tendency to pull the wrong teeth), so he plans to head East before any unhappy customers return for revenge. (When one tough character gives him just fifteen minutes to get out of town, Painless replies, "The last town gave me twenty minutes.")

Strangely enough, *Paleface* co-screenwriter Frank Tashlin (with Edmund Hartmann) would later claim the vehicle was conceived as a takeoff on the Western classic *The Virginian*.[41] Not surprisingly, since the film bears few obvious ties to the novel, this picture was the impetus for Tashlin to move on to an acclaimed directing career . . . as a way of protecting his scripts. Fortuitously for Hope, they would later collaborate on *Son of Paleface*, with Tashlin directing and scripting (along with Robert L. Welch, Joseph Quillan, and an army of Hope gag writers).

Tashlin's disappointment on *Paleface* notwithstanding, the movie is an imaginative spoof of Westerns. Early in the action, Hope's character meets a sexy Calamity Jane (Jane Russell), who is a secret agent for the government. Her assignment is to discover who is smuggling guns to the Indians. Calamity marries Potter as cover (a couple apparently going West to homestead) to succeed in her mission. This puts Painless in constant danger, but Calamity always manages to shoot their way out, while making it appear as if Potter is the real hero. Hope's character, not unlike Harry Langdon's silent screen persona and Peter Sellers' later Inspector Clouseau, is oblivious to this assistance. And therein lies much of the comedy, with Painless thinking he is a gunfighter and even searching out danger. Moreover, the comedy ante is heightened all the more when he decks himself out with a cowboy outfit more elaborate than that of a six-year-old with wealthy parents. It quite possibly influenced Dustin Hoffman's *Little Big Man* (1970) costume when his character was going through a gunslinger stage.

The year after *Paleface* came out, film critic James Agee gave Bob Hope and the picture left-handed praise by describing the actor as a "good radio comedian with a pleasing presence."[42] Agee felt the film was a standout for the period but could not rival the classic silent comedies; although a visual gag could be milked for several laughs, he noted, the verbal joke received just one, if that.

In 1952, *Saturday Review* critic Hollis Alpert took Agee to task for those comments when Alpert reviewed the sequel to *Paleface—Son of Paleface*.[43] This *Review* essay focused on the sequel but defended the propensity for sight gags in both pictures. Though Alpert does not provide *Paleface* examples, he might have described the inspired marriage sequence. The viewer sees the hands of the minister, Potter, and Russell's new bride in close-up for a single long take. When the reverend calls for the ring, Painless cannot find it and searches several pockets. After the ring has been found, the clergyman explains what it symbolizes. Hope's character then puts the ring back into his vest pocket. The minister's hand impatiently gestures to get the ring back. A confused Potter now retrieves his watch from another pocket and tries to hand that over. Further gesturing from the minister has Potter fishing out the ring again. But now he puts it on one of the reverend's fingers. The exasperated bride grabs the ring and tries to give it back to Painless. But Potter keeps mistakenly arranging his hand so that Jane twice accidentally puts the ring on one of her antiheroic husband's digits. Losing patience, Jane slaps Painless's hand and personally guides him in the placement of the ring on her finger. Potter then puts his hand over Jane's, as if to say, "I can't chance having the ring come off and go through this ordeal again." At last they are officially husband and wife, though it remains a mere cover for Jane.

Scenes such as these do not make Hope another Chaplin, but they should help correct the misconception that he is merely a radio (that is, verbal) comedian. In fact, the ring sequence is reminiscent of Frank Capra's use of visual comedy in sound films. An example is the long-take, close-up scene of title character Jimmy Stewart's hat in *Mr. Smith Goes to Washington* (1939). Smith is very nervous when he finds himself in conversation with the most beautiful woman he has ever seen. Capra showcases this uneasiness by following Smith's hat from hand to hand, held behind his back, dropped, and more hand-to-hand movement.

Bob Hope's comedy is often an effective combination of sight and sound. Shortly after the wedding scene, Potter comes into his bedroom thinking Jane is behind a dressing screen. However, it is an Indian (Joseph Vitale), periodically giggling from previously inhaling Potter's dental laughing gas. When Hope's character comes to the dressing screen, he affectionately reaches over and touches "her" shoulder saying, "My but you're a muscular little thing, aren't you? Those dresses are awful deceiving." Then Potter rubs "her" arm and the Indian giggles from the laughing gas. Hope's character says, "I'm sorry; I didn't mean to tickle you." He feels "her" hair, observing, "Isn't that sweet, you put your hair up in braids."

Painless says, "Come out Mrs. Potter. ["She" giggles.] I know you're modest. But it's all right. I'll keep my eyes closed." He pulls "her" toward him and as they kiss, the Indian whacks him on the back of the head, causing Potter to say, "Boy, can you kiss!" He then passes out on the bed.

In and of itself this is an effective comedy scene. *But* it goes beyond this. Agee had wanted as much as possible to be milked from a gag, and Hope's mistaken identity scene does just that. But in addition, it includes two other components. The laughing gas had comically been set up earlier in the movie, and part of the scene's charm is tied to that previous routine. The laugh is thus being stretched out. Later in the film all we need to hear is a high-pitched giggle to know the gas has been put to comic use again. Along similar lines, Vitale's Indian hitting Potter in the back of the head is funny. But it is all the more amusing given that this is precisely what Jane does every time Painless tries to kiss her. She whacks him, and he attributes it to great kissing; then he passes out. Inventive comedy has not only ingenious scenes but also shared material that connects and enrichs later routines.

With recognition of these visual skills, it is time to briefly examine Hope's brilliant verbal talent. His comic dialogue ranges from the comic throwaway description of a patient's mouth (a "happy little dungeon") to the elaborate word game he must play in preparing for a gunfight. One cowboy advises Painless that his opponent "draws from the left, so lean to the right." Another bystander tells him, "There's a wind from the east, so you better lean to the west." A third cowboy warns him that his adversary "crouches when he shoots, so stand on your toes." With each additional tip Potter comically repeats them all. But then, as if anticipating the criticism that verbal humor cannot be stretched, Painless attempts to run through the advice one more time and it comes out, "He draws from the left so stand on your toes. There's a wind from the east, better lean to the right. He crouches when he shoots, better aim to the west. He draws from his toes so lean towards the wind." Painless has comically topped the original elaborate directions. Hope's character tops it still one more time by observing, "Ha, ha, I've got it." The addition of a sight gag and a comic aside further stretches this comedy. That is, Potter decides he should take a practice shot before the gunfight, but he misses his target badly. He immediately alibis, however, by licking a finger, holding it up in the air and observing, "Wind shifted."

Hope's tongue-twisting dialogue is reminiscent of Danny Kaye's famous verbal virtuosity, best showcased in the ingenious *Court Jester* (1956), with lines such as "The pellet with the poison's in the vessel with the pestle." Kaye is a phony jester in this parody of court romance, intrigue, and general swashbuckling. Former Hope writers Melvin Frank and Norman Panama both scripted and directed the picture.

Of course, *The Court Jester* appeared much later than *Paleface*. A period parody with verbal gymnastics that opened almost simultaneously with

Red Skelton is one happy spy in *A Southern Yankee* (1948).

Hope's film was the Red Skelton Civil War spy spoof *A Southern Yankee* (1948). Skelton is at his best as a visual comedian, helped in this picture by gag suggestions from Buster Keaton, with *The General* representing a loose foundation for *A Southern Yankee*. But even physical comedians from the 1940s had to make with the tricky wordplay. Thus, Skelton's burlesque of a spy must remember, "The paper's in the pocket of the boot with the buckle. And the map is in the packet in the pocket of the jacket."

Fittingly, *A Southern Yankee* was based on a lengthly original story by the ever-present Frank and Panama, which features "the packet in the pocket" dialogue. Whereas, most story treatments run 10 to twenty pages, the surviving Frank and Panama tale (University of Southern California Archives of the Performing Arts) is seventy pages! The best parody component of their ambitious story did not even find its way into *A Southern Yankee*. In a special "alternate ending" they have Skelton's character losing track of his love interest, only to meet her years later. But she has married and is now Mrs. Butler. When the disppointed Red is introduced to the husband, Frank and Panama propose a spoofing bombshell—a Clark Gable cameo as *Gone with the Wind*'s (1939) Rhett Butler . . . a Civil War tit-for-tat.

While Skelton holds the edge for physical comedy in the sound era, and

Danny Kaye was a master of funny phonetics, Hope was the king of combining these skills in his parodies. Hope was also the most prolific creator
of quality spoof films. Consequently, Kaye and Skelton notwithstanding,
Hope parody is what so influenced Woody Allen. In a 1980s revisionist
review of *Paleface*, movie critic Marilyn Wilson says the "Hope film *persona* is much like the Allen one—the good-hearted but inept man whose
main weapon is the wisecrack. . . . Hope's speeches in this film would fit
perfectly into one of Allen's early films."[44] Wilson goes so far as to suggest
that an offscreen voice that convinces Potter to rescue Jane works much as
the Bogart adviser figure in Allen's *Play It Again, Sam.*[45]

Despite the old vaudeville joke about Hollywood being the place where
everything is created sequel, it took several years, in spite of *Paleface*'s huge
success, before *Son of Paleface* appeared. Regardless, movie sequels are
generally interesting both for what they tell the viewer about the original
and/or for any new directions they take. In *Son of*, Hope plays Junior, the
only child of Painless and Jane. He has recently graduated from Harvard
and comes West to retrieve a fortune in gold allegedly left to him by Potter.
It is now early in the twentieth century, and young Potter arrives via a
noisy horseless carriage. It makes for a great sight and sound gag. The
viewer has been led to believe that gun-shooting desperadoes are about to
descend on the town. When this offscreen automobile backfires several
times, one merely assumes the plot is proceeding on course. And then Junior
arrives in this bright red vehicle, complete with the full-length slicker, gog-
gles, gloves, and cap. The viewer is amused at the comic trickery, and
Hope's costume adds to the fun.

Though sequels are often panned for not capturing the unique qualities
of the original, *Son of* also found great critical and commercial success.
Broader in its parody than *Paleface*, *Son of* plays more along the "anything
goes" philosophy that later became synonymous with the parody world of
Mel Brooks. For the time period, as at least one critic observed, the movie
"comes so close to the style of those old 'Road To—' pictures . . . you
might almost shut your eyes (if you can manage) and think you are enjoying
one of the same."[46]

Before the movie opens, the viewer is reminded of the *Road to Utopia*'s
prologue with Robert Benchley. Bob Hope does voice-over narration of
what to expect from the film, and then on the screen is Bing Crosby driving
an automobile at night. Hope observes, "Ah, ah, what's this? This is an
old character actor on the Paramount [film studio] lot we try to keep working. He's supporting a large family, but I guarantee this fellow will not be
in the picture tonight." Hope's voice-over occasionally returns during the
film, such as his commentary about the statue of his father, which graces
the main street of Paleface Potter's Western hometown, Sawbuck Pass.
Chiseled onto the statue's base are the words "He won the West." Hope
says, "If he won it, he was using loaded dice."

Like the *Road* pictures, *Son of* is peppered with Hollywood film references. For instance, when an old tintype photographer suddenly appears for no discernible reason and Junior says, "Who do you think you are, Cecil B. DeMille?"—that is precisely who it is. Later, when Potter's son attempts a lengthy horseless-carriage trip across the desert, two buzzards alight on the back seat. Junior orders, "Hey, Martin and Lewis [Dean Martin and Jerry Lewis], no hitchhiking; it's a state law!" Speaking of law, when this picture was made (1952), Hollywood still had a censorship code. Consequently, during one flirtatious scene, young Potter's dialogue briefly cannot be heard. Immediately, Junior turns to the camera in direct address and says, "You should have heard that line." It is reminiscent of a fifth columnist moment in *Never Give a Sucker an Even Break* (1941), when W. C. Fields (playing himself) is in a soda fountain that resembles a bar. He turns to the camera and observes, "This scene's supposed to be a saloon, but the censor cut it out. It'll play just as well." Both gags are effective, but Hope's version has a surprise element (beyond the direct address), since the viewer's first assumption is that the soundtrack has gone dead.

As with *My Favorite Brunette*'s inclusion of film noir star Alan Ladd, *Son of* includes a Western star, Roy Rogers, playing himself. But there is a decided difference. Ladd's detective is revered by Bob Hope's wannabe private eye. Rogers' secret agent cowboy is seen as something of a joke by Potter Junior. This is largely based on Rogers's preference for horses, particularly his famous Trigger, to women. He even sings a ballad about the subject, titled "Four-Legged Friend." Obviously, this situation plays on the old Western stereotype of the special bond between a cowboy and his horse. But Rogers's macho quotient is further comically damaged when he turns down the sexual advances of Jane Russell, who is again co-starring with Hope. For the oversexed Junior (just like Dad), Rogers's disinterest is incomprehensible. In fact, at one point in the film Junior gives Rogers a look that goes well beyond comic pity, almost as if to suggest that Rogers *loves* his horse. (Of course, one should give Rogers credit for leaving himself open to such spoofing.) Ironically, Junior later spends time in bed with Trigger, as he and the horse have a lengthy fight over the covers; the horse ends up the winner. This is just another example of how much broader the parody is when contrasted with *Paleface* or especially with *My Favorite Brunette*.

Comic use of animals in *Son of*, be it Trigger, "Martin and Lewis" buzzards, or a stuffed moose that pours forth coins like a Las Vegas slot machine (after Junior shoots it), are also consistent with director/writer Tashlin's fascination with funny animals and animal-like heroes. A former newspaper cartoonist and animator, his early film resume included work for both Disney and Warner Brothers' Looney Tunes. And the year prior to *Son of*, he authored the cartoon book *The Possum That Didn't*.

Since comic creatures are a given in the parody world of Hope (such as the aforementioned talking bear and fish of the *Road to Utopia*), Tashlin's humor inclinations complemented a predisposition of the comedian's burlesque work. Of possible greater *Son of* Tashlin influence was his talent for maximizing Hope's visual comedy. For example, the sometimes cartoonist was responsible for the inventively surreal scene in which Junior's moving automobile loses a wheel but manages to continue when the onboard comedian easily holds up the axle with a rope. Appropriately, however, the sight gag is all the funnier with a standard Hope wisecrack addition, an admonishment to Roy Rogers to "Hurry up—this is unbelievable."

With Rogers's *Son of* preference for Trigger, Junior wins Jane Russell's Mike (she is a good bad girl in each picture) by comic default, which sets up the film's biggest laugh and inspired close. Mike has had to serve a long prison term. Thus, the ending is a fast-forward to parole day. Junior (once again in driving attire) and Mike seem to have been married before she was incarcerated. As Roy and Junior await her release, Rogers observes that it must have been difficult biding one's time all those years. Hope's character answers, "I saw Mike on visiting days but it wasn't any fun talking to the woman you love through a wire screen." Mike soon exits the prison and after a short delay, four little boys follow. An incredulous Rogers asks, "Yours?" But unlike the close to *Utopia*, in which Hope's character has obviously been cuckolded, these children are his, as evidenced by their wearing early motoring garb identical to Junior's. As Rogers and the viewer ponder the provocative making of babies and wire screen, Hope's character says, "Let's see 'em top this on television!" (By the early 1950s, when *Son of* was made, the new squeaky-clean medium of television had begun to cut into movie attendance.)

As the credits close on *Son of*, Roy Rogers rides off into the sunset (a classic Western conclusion), while Potter Junior drives his new family east in his horseless carriage. Junior, like his father, prefers the comforts of civilization. Indeed, in *Paleface*, Painless Potter sings the Academy Award–winning song of 1948—"Buttons and Bows"—whose East versus West lyrics decidedly embrace the former. Potter had planned to return to the East when Calamity Jane essentially kidnapped him West. Fittingly, Painless takes part of the wagon train off course when he pays more attention to singing "Buttons and Bows" than to following the correct fork in the road. (The popular song again resurfaces in *Son of*.) Dentist Potter does, however, represent one of the basic pioneer types going West—the young professional (maybe *semi*-professional in his case) looking for a ready market of less-demanding customers. It is precisely this kind of Western immigrant who needs the protection of the stereotypical good guy cowboy. Thus, when Potter, thanks to Jane's shooting, is mistaken for just that capable cowboy type, the parody success of *Paleface* is heightened. As a footnote, Hope brings off the dental humor most impressively. Numerous comedians have not fared as well when dealing with this subject, whether

W. C. Fields in *The Dentist* (1932) or Red Skelton in *A Southern Yankee* (1948). Laurel & Hardy are not much more successful in their dental comedy *Leave 'Em Laughing* (1928). But the saving grace for this team is the introduction of laughing gas. Possibly Hope took a page from this sketch, because the best part of his *Paleface* "dental work" also involves laughing gas. In fact, the use of laughing gas becomes a comic motif in Hope's picture.

The East-West dichotomy is expanded in *Son of*, because it is 1896 and the end of the standard period associated with the Western genre (post–Civil War to the turn of the century) is fast approaching. Junior accents this further by arriving in an early automobile and forever referring to his eastern alma mater Harvard (the letter *H* is plastered over everything he wears or owns). And there is never any doubt about Junior returning to "Boston, Mass." Moreover, at exit time Potter is just as comically incompetent as when he arrived from Harvard. In contrast, most Western spoofs involve comic characters who either prefer the West (such as Buster Keaton in *Go West*, 1925) and/or have grown from the experience (like Jerry Lewis in *Pardners*, 1956). It is not until Mel Brooks' *Blazing Saddles* (1974) that another spoof of the genre both left the West (literally breaking out into modern Los Angeles reality) and learned little from the experience.

Hope's spoof of the macho Western hero in both *Paleface* pictures is bolstered by his dominating, malelike co-star Jane Russell. (She is even called Mike in the sequel.) Indeed, her somewhat wooden acting skills are less bothersome here because one associates her with the genre's strong, silent type—the traditional male hero. But the parody of Hope's Western character by way of Russell's Mike can be taken a step further. *Son of* director/co-writer Tashlin's later often-acclaimed work, such as the period satire *Will Success Spoil Rock Hunter* (1957, starring Jayne Mansfield), is also known for its lampooning of sexuality by way of casting bosomy women. Tashlin's view of America's breast fetish is that it represents an additional comic way of showing "the immaturity of the American male." He amusingly expands on this by adding: "Imagine a statue with breasts like Mansfield's. Imagine *that* in marble. . . . We make an idol of a woman because she's deformed in the breasts. There's nothin' more hysterical to me than big-breasted women—like walking leaning towers."[47]

Tashlin's take on breasts and comic male immaturity, though associated with his post-Hope work, is applicable to the two *Paleface* pictures and the well-endowed Russell. Of course the ski-nosed comic has a head start on sexual immaturity every time he makes that high-pitched growling sound after perceiving how handsome he is. But the bosom factor immediately comes to mind after one Hope *Paleface* growling session when his misperception on personal looks is accompanied by the winningly egocentric line, "What are you doing to that glorious beast [Russell's character]?"

Although America's breast fetish is most associated with the 1950s and

Jane Russell and Bob Hope pose for *Son of Paleface* (1952), in which Russell is another bosomy leading lady for writer/director Frank Tashlin.

Marilyn Monroe (as well as Russell and Mansfield), Russell's much-ballyhooed film debut in the "sex Western" *The Outlaw* (1943) was a major catalyst for the country's increased interest in cleavage. *Outlaw* producer and credited director Howard Hughes (though largely megaphoned by Howard Hawks) had conducted a well-publicized nationwide chest hunt for the movie's leading female role, as well as designing a special brassiere to maximize her "gift."

With only one other film to her credit prior to *Paleface*, Russell undoubtedly owed her initial Hope teaming to Hughes' bosomy Western. (And by frequently giving her characters in *Paleface* and *Son of* a masculine twist, she manages to spoof her "sex Western" debut.) Russell also had a cameo in Hope and Crosby's *Road to Bali*, which appeared the same year as the *Paleface* sequel (1952). Hope might best have caught the tenor of the times when he introduced her once as "the two and only Miss Russell." Certainly the comedy lesson was not lost on parody master Mel Brooks, who later provided his *Blazing Saddles* (1974, see Chapter 4) governor with a distractingly large breasted secretary. And no one plays the immaturity level better than Brooks' "Gov," though it is a minor character devoid of the wit associated with Hope's two *Paleface* roles, or any of Brooks' other burlesque figures.

All in all, this portion of the chapter has been an examination of Hope at his antiheroic spoofing best, from the *Road* to film noir and way out West. No one was better at film parody, nor produced as many still laugh-out-loud examples of the genre. His longevity in this area has been matched by Brooks. But the latter burlesque artist has been neither as prolific, nor as consistently funny in his later work. Hope is a unique talent whose parody legacy continues to help define the genre, both as a body of work and in its influence on such major artists as Woody Allen.

WOODY ALLEN'S *PLAY IT AGAIN, SAM*

Fantasy has always been associated with the comedy world of Woody Allen. Coupled with that is the pervasiveness of his comic antihero stance, which has come to represent a view of the frustrations of modern society. Add to this an early propensity for Bob Hope–influenced parody and an ongoing interest in the nature of love, and one has all the ingredients for a rich spoof in *Play It Again, Sam.*

At its heart the movie is a parody of film noir cool, Bogart style, à la his classic *Casablanca* (1942). Allen's title is drawn from dialogue often attributed to the earlier film, which uses World War II as a backdrop for its love story. Though Bogart's nightclub-owning Rick never uses exactly those words, one of *Casablanca*'s many memorable scenes is when he asks Sam the piano player (Dooley Wilson) to again play the haunting "As Time Goes By," which conjures up tortured memories of a Parisian affair with Ingrid Bergman's Ilsa.

Her character has now come back into Rick's Casablanca (North Africa) life with a husband in tow. Paul Henreid's Victor Laszlo is a leader of Europe's underground movement against Nazi Germany. It seems that when Rick and Ilsa fell in love, she thought Victor was dead. But she suddenly and mysteriously left Paris when she realized her husband was alive. With the fall of France, Rick relocated to Casablanca and tried to forget Ilsa.

Casablanca became a key gathering place for refugees from Nazi-occupied Europe, with the next goal being hard-to-obtain exit visas to Lisbon, the departure point for America. Rick controls the letters of transit needed by the Laszlos. Understandably bitter, Bogart's character initially refuses Ilsa's plea for help. Desperate, she threatens him with a gun, but her lingering love for Rick negates any possibility of violence. When this love becomes apparent to Bogart's figure, as well as the reason for the enigmatic exit from Paris, he tells her they will use the letters of transit themselves.

At the airport, however, Rick puts the Laszlos on the plane, convincing Ilsa that love must be sacrificed for the importance of her husband's work. Ironically, by giving up the girl, the role of Rick made Bogart a romantic star, adding a new dimension to his defining film noir toughness in the genre's *Maltese Falcon* (1941) starting point. Since that time, critics and the public alike have often made Bogart a candidate for best Hollywood star of all time, with *Casablanca* frequently receiving a nod for the movie capital's greatest production, *Gone With The Wind* notwithstanding.

Play It Again, Sam uses *Casablanca*'s airport scene as a framing device. Allen begins the picture with his character in a film theatre watching the celebrated finale. As the movie cuts back and forth between Bogart on screen and its antihero audience member, it is clear that Allen, like a Bob Hope figure, has momentarily become Bogart. He underlines this after the close of *Casablanca* (and his first fantasy) by saying, "Who'm I kidding? I'm not like that. I never was, I never will be. Strictly movies." For the next several minutes the film avoids fantasy, allowing the viewer to become acquainted with the real-world situation of Allen's character. It is familiar ground: Allen is a film journalist who is feeling especially frustrated sexually because his wife has recently divorced him. But by *Sam*'s close, a comedy metamorphosis has taken place. Allen's character essentially replicates the *Casablanca* conclusion himself, sacrificing love in his own life, and despite the loss, finally finding romantic self-confidence. What falls between the framing device is a complex parody with Bogart as the fantasy mentor of Allen's film critic.

The optimum word in this parody is *fantasy*. It drives Sam's spoof of both film noir and romance, as well as periodically burlesquing itself—undercutting the genre's normal expectation that one can keep a positive spin to our daydreaming fantasies. But before exploring the ambitious enchantment labyrinth that is *Sam*, the general importance of fantasy to Allen's work merits attention. It has been nearly as integral to his films as frustration, be it the short sketches from *Everything You Always Wanted to Know About Sex (But Were Afraid to Ask)* (1972), in which antihero consistency is maintained even when he appears as a sperm, or the moment of supreme self-satisfaction in *Annie Hall* (1977), when Allen suddenly pulls Marshall McLuhan out of nowhere to put down a pompous intellectual. Director Allen even underlines the fantasy magic of this moment by then giving his comedy character the direct address line, "Boy, if life were only like this."

For the student of comedy, it is quite natural to link the frustrations and fantasies of Allen's world with an earlier author who helped bring the comic antihero to center stage in American humor—James Thurber. In fact, if one's sense of a comedy chronology were a bit shaky, it would seem logical to note the Woody Allen–like nature of James Thurber's classic fantasy, "The Secret Life of Walter Mitty" (which also spoofs the action adventure story):

Captain Mitty stood up and strapped on his huge Webley-Vickers automatic. "It's forty kilometers through hell, sir," said the sergeant. Mitty finished one last brandy,

"After all," he said softly, "What isn't?" The pounding of the cannon increased. There was the rat-tat-tatting of machine guns . . . Something struck his shoulder. "I've been looking all over this hotel for you." said Mrs. Mitty. "Why do you have to hide in this old chair?"[48]

That the Allen fantasy does not always represent the joyful escape associated with Mitty's secret life is, of course, nothing new. Charlie Chaplin is shot in the heaven scene from *The Kid* (1921) after he has succumbed to sin; and in the more modern variation on this in *The Seven Year Itch* (1955), Tom Ewell gets conflicting fantasy messages from heaven and hell about what to do when upstairs neighbor Marilyn Monroe comes visiting. Goodness wins—if you can call that a victory.

What is so unique about Allen's depiction of frustration in the fantasy world is that it occurs so often. In fact, *Sleeper* (1973), in which Allen is defrosted in a Big Brother–like world 200 years in the future, might be termed a science fiction fantasy of frustration—a comic nightmare. As John Brosnan has noted, Allen had completed science fiction trial runs for *Sleeper* the previous year (1972) with some of the episodes from *Everything You Wanted to Know About Sex (But Were Afraid to Ask)*, particularly one involving a giant, mobile, killer breast.[49]

But apart from underlining the deep-seated nature of his comedy persona's frustrations, this aspect of Allen's imaginary world does not offer the viewer much new insight, however comically diverting your standard giant killer breast might be, not to mention *Sleeper*'s giant lethal chicken, or weapon-sized strawberry. But when more realistic concerns, such as the nature of love and sacrifice, are examined in tandem with escapist fantasy elements in his movies, insights as well as laughter are provided.

This is best exemplified in *Sam*. By casting Bogart (played by Jerry Lacy) in a number of the fantasy scenes, Allen raised viewer identification to the nth degree. From this comes a broad-based parody story that still embraces such traditional Allen themes as his relationship with women, movie history, personal identity, and a general antiheroic world view. *Sam* has no fewer than eighteen often-lengthy fantasy scenes (his longest and most consistently integrated use of fantasy in a parody film). It is Allen's most effective balancing of the fantastic and the real for both comic effect and maximum viewer identification. The following pages address the majority of *Sam*'s fantasy scenes and their relationship to burlesque.

Early in the film, after the *Casablanca* screening and two flashbacks with his ex-wife (Susan Anspach) documenting the breakdown of the marriage (her boredom), Allen's Felix asks himself, "What's the secret to being cool?" Suddenly Bogart appears and essentially tells him to toughen up. The "naturalness" of this icon's appearance is helped by the fact that Felix's apartment is like a Bogart museum, with posters from *Casablanca* and *Across the Pacific* (another Bogart film, 1942) dominating, while smaller bits of Bogart memorabilia, stills, and books, lie scattered about. Allen, like an updated Bob Hope, tries Bogart's prescription of bourbon and soda while doing an imitation (voice and mannerisms) of the actor. Felix passes out.

The parody is funny because Allen's character falls so short of his tough guy idol. He even betters Hope's amusing *Brunette* inability to drink like a traditional film noir detective (Alan Ladd), because at least the ski-nosed comedian remains conscious. Moreover, Allen's scene is more spoofingly pointed, since alcohol is closely associated with Bogart's *Casablanca* role. Indeed, when a Nazi officer asks Rick his nationality, Rick replies, "Drunkard."

After Felix's failure with the hard stuff, he is joined by his supportive friends Dick and Linda (frequent Allen co-stars Tony Roberts and Diane Keaton), who make it a point to play matchmaker. But Felix is so depressed now, he has another fantasy. It is a short vision/nightmare of his ex-wife on a wild date with a biker type, during which she sneers about Allen, "He fell off a [push] scooter once and broke his collarbone." The scene is a generic spoof of the then-in-vogue motorcycle movie, which had taken off with the huge critical and commercial success of *Easy Rider* (1969). If forced to be more specific, the macho Allen biker reminds one of Joe Namath's feature debut as a sexy but simple biker in the innocuous *C. C. & Company* (1970).

Felix's friends manage to get him a date, and as he dresses, Lacy's Bogart again appears. What follows works on several parody levels. First, there is the fun of seeing Bogart as a dating consultant. The power broker who runs "Rick's" nightclub is now giving advice to an antihero. It is as if he has pulled aside *Casablanca*'s token underdog (Peter Lorre) for tips on picking up women. Second, although mentors for childlike heroes are standard fantasy fare, having Bogart in the role makes this basic component of the genre amusing; his tough talk film noir cool is incongruous to the fairy godmother/good witch stereotype. Fittingly, however, for an adviser from a minimalist genre, Bogart tells Felix to keep it simple; tone down the mouthwash, deodorant, aftershave, and baby powder, or "you're gonna smell like a French cathouse."

This Bogart-as-mentor works on a third parody level. Felix, encouraged by the cult hero, mimics Bogart's mannerisms and inflections, and with a reflection of a Bogart poster in the mirror before him, he fantasizes about seducing his blind date—curing her of frigidity. And he kindly offers to help any of her friends with similar problems. A fourth spoofing slant comes from the manner in which Felix mimicks Bogart—it is very much in the misguided "aren't I drop-dead handsome" pose of Bob Hope's parody persona. And ski-nose's character frequently admires himself in a mirror.

As might be expected, all this is comically undercut when the blind date is a failure, as are Felix's next several interactions with different women.

These refusal types range from a spoof of existential angst (a suicidal girl interested in the dark mind-set of painter Jackson Pollack), to another derailing of bikers when his blind date takes him to a Hell's Angel–like bar. But the biggest parody laugh in this parade of dating frustrations comes from Allen casting an actual porn star as a dinner companion. Appropriately, her dialogue suggests a sexually obsessed character. But when Felix makes his romantic move, she responds with shock as if he were a rapist. For the viewer it is a wonderful moment of burlesquing surprise, which Felix accents by observing, "How could I have misread those signs?"

This series of dating failures is the longest *Sam* passage without a fantasy break, but this merely seems to justify the fantasy escalation (if Felix is to become a lover) for the rest of the film. Moreover, by this point the viewer has started to realize, though it has not yet become apparent to Allen's character, that this frustrated outsider has a lovely rapport with Keaton's Linda. Since she is married to his best friend, Linda is the only woman he has not been trying to impress—a basic fantasy lesson that success is tied to being yourself. And since her nonstop businessman husband is a "phone man" (a continuing gag finds Dick constantly either calling in deals or calling his answering service to leave new numbers where he can be reached), Linda and Felix have lots of time together. This phone shtick is a spoofing way to showcase a normally melodramatic situation—Dick's neglect of Linda.

As Felix and Linda become closer, they make a dinner date for an evening Dick is out of town on business. And it is not long before Felix briefly imagines seducing Linda. Appropriately enough, Felix immediately feels guilty, which just as logically brings Jerry Lacy's Bogart to the rescue, trying to downplay the guilt. This soon becomes the most important fantasy since the *Casablanca* opening, because Felix's ex-wife appears and proceeds to argue with Bogart about what Allen's character should do. It is a pivotal fantasy because it brings together for the first time the two poles of Felix's fantasy world—the castrating ex-wife and the macho legend—who later battle for control of his real world. The scene takes place in a grocery store, giving it an added comic touch, which Felix accents at the fantasy's close by saying, "Fellas, we're in a supermarket!"

The parody quotient for the grocery fantasy is high. First, it is funny because once again Felix cannot control his daydreams. Second, it also amuses when tough guy Bogart is henpecked by Felix's ex-wife. Third, the image of Bogart as a grocery store consultant for dinner date shopping is straight out of spoof heaven—what could be less likely for *Casablanca*'s world-weary Rick? But Bogart is a no-nonsense noir male. A supermarket setting is not alien to the more typically vulnerable noir hero, such as Fred MacMurray's character in *Double Indemnity* (1944). In that film there is just such a scene, with his insurance salesman and a sexy client (Barbara Stanwyck) concocting a plan to kill her husband as they stand among the canned goods. Thus, a fourth way that *Sam*'s grocery setting embraces parody is to remind the viewer of the *Double Indemnity* scene, a classic with which cinema junkie Allen had to figure noir fans would connect.

On the way home from the market, Felix fantasizes how much easier it would be if his friends were getting a divorce and Dick asked him to take care of Linda. The spoofing fantasy that follows, though very brief, maintains beautiful consistency with the rest of the movie. Neglectful husband Dick leaves by plane (echoing the *Casablanca* opening airport scene and anticipating its return at the close), and tops all previous telephone numbers at which he can be reached: he is meeting an Eskimo lover at "Frozen Tundra six, nine two nine oh."

At home now, preparing for the dinner date, Felix imagines all his advances being misunderstood, with the cry of rape quickly dispatching this nightmare fantasy. Besides being a funny send-up of traditional love story expectations (one does not normally worry about accusations of rape in, say, *Romeo and Juliet*), this *Sam* scene is also a tribute to an earlier parody of romantic comedy—average married man Tom Ewell's guilty fantasies about upstairs neighbor Marilyn Monroe in *The Seven Year Itch* (1955). Indeed, some of Felix's dialogue before Linda arrives borrows from the guilty monologue of Ewell's antihero. Regardless, the understandably sobered Felix plays it very detached upon Linda's arrival.

Bogart soon appears as sort of an on-the-job date counselor. It will represent his longest scene thus far in the film, as well as his funniest. Allen, like Buster in *Sherlock Jr.* (1924), effectively uses this example of a "real" screen love to guide his film life. And once again the mise-en-scène of the apartment enhances the effectiveness and believability of Bogart stepping out of the shadows to coach Felix. Bogart posters seem to turn up in every shot, and bits of room decor push the parody envelope by aping the Moroccan set design of the original *Casablanca*, from the beaded curtain in the kitchen to the living room's rattan chair and shutters. But just as Felix is about to become Bogart's *A* student, following Mr. Film Noir's every tip while sitting on the couch with Linda (who is oblivious to this other presence), the ex-wife appears and guns down Teacher.

Needless to say, this is a bit disconcerting to pupil Felix, especially since the fantasy assassination takes place right over the living room sofa on which he is courting Linda. After the shooting, only the couple remain. But Bogart's pointers are not wasted, because everything romantic comes to pass; thus, a long take of a very passionate Felix/Linda smooch is intercut (once again courtesy of Felix's imagination) with a similar Bogart/Bergman kiss from *Casablanca*.

The next scene finds Felix and Linda in bed the morning after, and though we seem to have returned to total reality (that is, if you can accept his character in bed with anyone), the cue still seems to be taken from Bogart—a huge film poster of *Across the Pacific* appears over the bed, completely dominating the couple. This morning-after scene opens with a close-up of the poster, in which Bogart is "scoring" a one-two punch, as if suggesting a sexual pun on what has occurred the night before.

Felix and Linda decide that they have found something good and that Dick must be told. Since Linda insists she will tell him, Felix has time alone to imagine how his best friend will respond. Thus, his next three fantasies represent different possible reactions from the cuckolded husband. The first fantasy is a monocle-and-pipe spoof of a theatrical English drawing room drama with two gentlemen (Felix and Dick) discussing things ever so rationally. Allen's character refuses to let there be any hostility by giving Roberts' character a terminal disease and closes the scene with proper British civility—a toast and "cheers."

Cuckold-husband fantasies two and three are both movie parodies and do not run so pleasantly for interloper Felix. The first plays upon his guilt and finds Dick walking into the sea, and implied suicide, à la the watery death chosen by the alcoholic husband played by Fredric March in *A Star Is Born* (1937), which is repeated by James Mason in the 1954 remake of the same name. (Ironically, Allen will use a straight variation of the scene, to mixed critical response, in *Interiors*, 1978.) For *Sam*, however, any lingering melancholy is undercut by Dick's parting soliloquy on the beach: "Why didn't I see it coming? Me, who had the foresight to buy Polaroid at eight and a half."

In the final fantasy of this trilogy it is Felix, however, who bites the dust. Passing a theatre playing the Italian film *Le Coppie* (1970, a large display poster acting as a backdrop for the fantasy opening, not unlike the earlier use of Bogart memorabilia), Felix imagines Dick as a humiliated, hot-tempered Italian out for revenge. The knife-wielding husband corners Felix, a most unlikely baker, who tries to defend himself with some of the limpest dough ever to put in a movie appearance. The little baker never has a chance. And the comic perversity of the revenge is maximized by having Felix take a fatal wound to the privates. Yet, it somehow seems consistent with an impassioned Italian vendetta, especially as this culture is perceived through the movies. Strangely enough, the ambiance provided by the *Le Coppie* poster begins and ends with it being an Italian film. That is, said movie (a now-obscure anthology comedy with three stories) does not have a jealous male, though each episode humorously deals with couples.

Felix is jarred back to a welcome reality (after the imagined stabbing) when, outside his apartment, he runs into Dick. Though Allen's character fears the worst, Linda's husband senses marital trouble but does not suspect his friend. Dick pours out his love for Linda and the concern that she is involved with some "stud." Up to this point Allen's spoofing wannabe Bogart was dealing with more guilt. But the "stud" reference immediately sends him into an entertaining bit of Bob Hope "aren't I God's gift to women" parody posturing. Still, Felix decides he cannot break up the mar-

The only believable homework Bob Hope's persona might be caught doing, as Dorothy Lamour looks on in *The Road to Morocco* (1942).

riage. Thus, his primary anxiety becomes how to let Linda down easily. With a lingering of the Hope persona (the incongruity of ego and the antiheroic), Felix reasons the break will not be simple, since "I was incredible last night in bed. I never once had to sit up and consult the manual." (Bob Hope might have been an indirect source for the manual joke, since he can be seen reading the book *How To Make Love* in *The Road to Morocco*.)

The next two fantasy parodies occur as Felix rushes to the airport to tell Linda he has reconsidered, while she is rushing there to tell her husband *she* has reconsidered (he, of course, is just rushing off on more business). In the first burlesque, Linda takes Felix's decision poorly, with the scene borrowing directly from *Casablanca*. Linda asks for a mysterious letter and pulls a gun, à la Ilsa's (Bergman) threatening demands for the letters of transit. The fantasy closes just as Felix screams, "Don't pull the trigger; I'm a bleeder." So much for being Bogart.

This near-disaster then cuts directly to Felix's second fantasy on the ride to the airport, in which Bogart is his cab driver, ready to give him more pointers and settle him down. After a passing reference to actress Lizabeth Scott (who played another threatening film noir woman opposite Bogart in *Dead Reckoning*, 1947), the cool one stops the taxi. Lacy's Bogart then shows Felix how to break it off with a "dame," again played by a gun-toting Linda. This, along with Bogart's praise of Felix's sacrifice "for a pal," prepares the little guy for the big romantic finish with Linda.

The final spoofing fantasy brings one full circle to the film's opening. This time, however, instead of cutting back and forth between mesmerized audience member Felix and the projected image of *Casablanca*, both the situation (romantic triangle preparing for airport farewell) and the mise-en-scène (incoming fog and the separate starting of the plane's engines) of *Play It Again, Sam* actually recreate *Casablanca*. Then, when the plane is safely away, Bogart joins Felix in his walk into the enveloping mist, just as Claude Rains' character joins Bogart at the end of *Casablanca*.

Unlike earlier fantasies, however, in which Felix blindly tried to ape the complete Bogart persona, the closing scene uses the Bogart legend as a point of reference to aid Felix in the final liberation and acceptance of his own identity. That is, he essentially plays the part on his own; Bogart is not giving him cues from the wings, as he did earlier in the apartment. And though Felix does restate part of Bogart's farewell speech from *Casablanca*, it is the act of a mature person merely using past experience, rather than the alienated incompetent in search of a style who opened the movie. Still, a fun sense of Bob Hope bravado remains.

Allen's character summarizes it quite nicely when he says, "I guess the secret's not being you [Bogart]; it's being me." As if to illustrate this, Bogart and Felix break up their stroll at the close; after the former's, "Here's looking at you, kid," Felix walks off into the darkness of the night (and into his future?) alone, but not quite so lonely.

Like Thurber's antihero Walter Mitty, these parody fantasies have at times provided Allen's Felix with unique adventures (hobnobbing with Bogart) in what is otherwise a banal life. Unlike Mitty, however, the fantasy world itself has been spoofed when Allen's character is frustrated in what should be a controlled environment—one's daydreams. Yet the key difference between Felix's parody-directed fantasy and Mitty's lies not so much in the latter point (important as it may be) but rather in the fact that Allen's comedy persona (unlike Thurber's) is allowed to take his spoofing fantasy beyond mere distraction, using it to learn both to be and to accept himself.

In achieving this level of maturity, Felix no doubt needs both poles of burlesque fantasy, from the confidence Bogart provides to the occasional fantasy frustration that keeps his values in perspective—which eventually steer him away from being just a Bogart clone. Though one can never know the answers to life's eternal questions, by the close of *Play It Again, Sam* Allen's persona is in a healthier state of mind for coping with the darker side of existence.

The close also represents a basic fantasy component: choosing between two worlds, such as Dorothy picking Kansas over the Land of Oz, or Wendy making a similar decision in *Peter Pan*, opting for home over Never, Never Land. As with these two examples, Felix has made the mature, coming-of-age choice. But this is not to say Allen is locked into this position.

In his celebrated fantasy *Purple Rose of Cairo* (1985), which (like *Sam*) also spoofs the genre, Mia Farrow's Depression-era waitress Cecilia has romantic movie star Tom Baxter (Jeff Daniels) walk off the screen and into her life. But instead of fueling a reality-based maturation, like Bogart's impact upon Felix, Baxter's eventual abandonment of Cecilia leads to her forever hiding away from life's harshness by watching movies. The heart-breaking close comes about because Farrow's character cannot move beyond the mere fantasy escape level of film, just as Daniels' AWOL screen shadow does not know how to act in real life. The picture's last image of Cecilia has her alone again—at the movies.

Additional fundamental fantasy components in *Sam* are found in three character types unique to the genre: supernatural villain, child hero, and an immortal wise mentor for the human hero. The individuals Allen assigns to these types jump-start the film's parody slant. For instance, any male who has gone through a difficult divorce can comically relate to Felix's witchy villain being an ex-wife, especially the part about grieving even *after* a relationship is over.

For the film fan, Allen's casting of Bogart as the immortal mentor immediately makes this figure user-friendly, while affectionately spoofing one's mindset for the stereotypical fairy godmother. And fantasy's standard deployment of a child hero comically plays into Allen's frequent use of his boyish antihero. As with an ex-wife for a supernatural villain, these decisions are inherently funny, whether or not the fantasy derailment is recognized.

The realistic tone in the *Sam* fantasy scenes—no pink ball of light that heralds the arrival of *Oz*'s good witch Glinda here—is consistent with the majority of other such excursions in Allen's films prior to the 1990s. (*Alice*, 1990, includes a flying fantasy, and *Deconstructing Harry*, 1997, offers a colorful look at hell.) Allen's pre-1990 realistic spin also might help explain the tendency for his more exotic spoofing fantasies not to reach the final print stage. One example of such cut material is playing a spider caught in Louise Lasser's black widow web (shot for *Everything You Always Wanted to Know About Sex (But Were Afraid to Ask)*, 1972). Another is the giant chess game using real people as chess pieces (filmed for *Sleeper*), with Allen's character appropriately playing a white pawn about to be sacrificed but not without a winsome bargaining argument: "Hey, fellas, it's only a game. We'll all be together later in the box."[50]

The generally natural tone of Allen's pre-1990 fantasies, particularly *Sam*'s Bogart scenes, might best be classified as what film theorist Siegfried Kracauer labels "fantasy established in terms of physical reality."[51] That is, the plot of *Sam* takes "the existence of the supernatural [in this case Bogart] more or less for granted, its presence does not simply follow from these visuals. . . . [T]he spectator must from the outset conceive of them as tokens of the supernatural."[52] Plus, by not camping up Bogart's appearances, his film noir aura remains intact; this maximizes any parody factor involving the ultimate example of cinema cool.

To relate to the fact that a fantasy is in progress whenever Bogart appears, one must already be a practicing member of the modern world's biggest fantasy club—the filmgoing public. And by getting the joke (Felix's inadequacies and Bogart's giving home lessons in self-assertiveness), we go a long way toward becoming part of it. Who has not felt similar inadequacies, at least in comparison with our favorite cinema superhero, whether Bogart or 007? Contrasted with a screen legend, most everyday lives resemble parody.

Allen represents his own best example of daydreams peopled with cinema heroes even as a child: "I remember seeing *Tom, Dick and Harry* [1941] advertised and saying, 'I can't wait to see that.' It was one of those things that became a part of my consciousness because I lived in the movies and identified with that."[53]

His comedy persona in *Sam* restructures part of his life to use the "experience" of his film fantasy existence, slipping in and out of this other world as someone else might do with an old pair of shoes. All this activity tends to flirt with the tongue-in-cheek message of Oscar Wilde's essay, "The Decay of Lying": "Paradox though it may seem . . . life imitates art far more than art imitates life."[54] Of course, as already noted, Felix eventually emerges from the world of Bogart, with the implication that newfound maturity will now separate him from the affectionate spoofing of movie fantasy.

With each new Allen film of the fantastic, however, his comedy persona (or a designated antiheroic replacement) must face the same question: will he use fantasy as mere escape or as a step toward maturity? Much of this section has examined the struggle in the light of an opening reference to Thurber's most celebrated short story, the spoofing fantasy "The Secret Life of Walter Mitty." To come full circle, an apt closing observation on this duality might best chronicle Allen's own most honored short work, "The Kugelmass Episode," which won the O. Henry Award as number one story of 1977. (With *Annie Hall* winning the best picture Oscar for 1977, Allen had a banner year.)

"The Kugelmass Episode," reminiscent of both the Mitty story and a spoofing of H. G. Wells's *The Time Machine*, examines the life of an unhappily married professor (Kugelmass) out to put some excitement back into his life, preferably on a sexual level. His parody-related adventure, or escape, comes in the form of a fantasy-making invention that can transport a subject into the world of the written word. For Kugelmass, this means an opportunity to date "any of the women created by the world's best writers."[55] Walter Mitty could not have gone for it any faster. Plus, as in *Sleeper*, Allen has another scenario for burlesquing both romance and science fiction.

Kugelmass goes all out and has an affair with Emma Bovary. But there are complications when the invention breaks down, causing the frustrated professor mental and financial ruin. Therefore, when the crisis is over, he swears off these fantasy time trips, happy that at least his wife has not found out (more antiheroic shades of Mitty) and grateful that "I learned my lesson."[56]

Kugelmass' maturity is short-lived, and he tries another trip (into sexy *Portnoy's Complaint*), but the fantasy quickly becomes an eternal comic nightmare. The novel-hopping apparatus shorts out and is destroyed (science fiction's love/hate relationship with the machine), the operator/inventor dies of a heart attack on the spot, and poor Kugelmass, instead of finding himself projected into *Portnoy's Complaint*, turns up in "an old textbook, *Remedial Spanish* . . . running for his life over a barren, rocky terrain as the word tener ('to have')—a large hairy irregular verb—races after him on its spindly legs."[57] Parody-happy Allen is again gently warning us that total fantasy escape can be dangerous if not directed toward character growth, as in *Sam*. Otherwise, we might metaphorically end up like Kugelmass, forever running away.

CONCLUSIONS

No one embraced the parody antihero better than Bob Hope. Although other comedians occasionally essayed the burlesque part, Hope made spoofing the heart of his film work. Indeed, as a child of the '50s (television's first generation), my love of parody was a direct result of watching rebroadcasts of old Hope pictures. I bonded with my equally spoof-obsessed dad watching such early ski-nose parodies as *Ghost Breakers* (1940) and *My Favorite Blonde* (1942). In the late 1970s, Hope disciple Woody Allen observed, "If I wanted to have a weekend of pure pleasure, it would be to have a half-dozen Bob Hope films." Allen was merely echoing what an army of parody lovers might have said.[58]

It would be my hypothesis that the key reason Allen's early Hope-like screen persona was so popular is that the real Hope had committed the cardinal sins of getting both old and hawkishly political (the antithesis of parody). As comedy historian/critic Maurice Yacowar implies in his still-insightful look at Allen, *Loser Take All*, the comedian's early work constantly conjures up vintage Hope—such as the science fiction spoofing scene from *Sleeper* in which Miles (Allen) and Luna (Diane Keaton) attempt to clone the leader, working only with his surviving nose. Miles gets them by security with the patented Hope line, "We're here to see the nose. We hear it's running."[59]

As comedy theorist Frank Krutnik observes, such "verbal resilience is the ammunition which allows him [Hope, or in this case, Allen] to master whatever misfortune his character suffers."[60] That is, the smooth patter is part of the balance that allows Hope and his disciple Allen to fluctuate between the most incompetent of comic antiheroes and the cool parody—conscious, egotistical wise guy. The smart aleck crack also serves to protect a vulnerable ego.

Unlike the *Sleeper* scene, Allen's work is not simply a cloning exercise (à la Hope). Allen takes Burlesque Bob's art to a higher level. Hope's skewering of various genres makes us laugh. Allen started here, and by *Sam*, had us thinking beyond the parody. For instance, in *Sam* he could both have fun with film formulas (burlesque) and entertainingly challenge us to contemplate how the mythic Bogie affects our lives. In fact, as movie theorist and award-winning filmmaker William C. Siska notes, by the late 1970s, Allen's work could often be placed under the art-house-as-genre umbrella.[61] Like many great artists, Allen's gift is an amalgamation of old traditions and new interpretations. And film parody has been made all the richer for it.

NOTES

1. Jeffrey Couchman, "Bob Hope: More Than A Gagster?," *New York Times*, May 6, 1979, section 2, pp. 1, 15.

2. Raymond Durgnat, *The Crazy Mirror: Hollywood Comedy and the American Image* (1969; reprint, New York: Dell, 1972), p. 171.

3. William Robert Faith, *Bob Hope: A Life in Comedy* (New York: G. P. Putnam's Sons, 1982), p. 185.

4. Bob Hope and Bob Thomas, *The Road to Hollywood: My 40-Year Love Affair with the Movies* (Garden City, NY: Doubleday and Company, 1977), p. 127.

5. Ibid, p. 137.

6. Louella Parsons, "Paulette Goddard and Bob Hope Scheduled for Another Thriller, 'The Ghost Breakers,' " *Los Angeles Examiner*, November 22, 1939, section 1, p. 17.

7. Hope and Thomas, p. 137.

8. Arthur Marx, *The Secret Life of Bob Hope* (New York: Barricade Books, 1993), p. 137.

9. *Road to Singapore* review, *Hollywood Reporter*, February 21, 1940, p. 3.

10. *Road to Utopia* review, *The New Yorker*, March 2, 1946, p. 81.

11. Jack Moffitt, "Back to Utopia," *Esquire*, April 1946, p. 63.

12. Wes D. Gehring, *Mr. "B" or Comforting Thoughts About the Bison: A Critical Biography of Robert Benchley* (Westport, CT: Greenwood Press, 1992).

13. *Road to Utopia* review, *New York Herald Tribune*, February 28, 1946.

14. Moffitt, "Back to Utopia," p. 63.

15. Brooks Riley, "Words of Hope," *Film Comment*, May-June 1979, p. 24.

16. Bing Crosby (with Pete Martin), *Call Me Lucky* (New York: Simon and Schuster, 1953), p. 95.

17. Bob Hope (with Melville Shavelson), *Don't Shoot It's Only Me* (New York: G. P. Putnam's Sons, 1990), p. 34.

18. Ibid., p. 34.

19. Moffitt, "Back to Utopia," p. 63.

20. Frank Tashlin, "*Son of Paleface* Went Thataway," *New York Times*, October 5, 1952, section 2, p. 5.

21. Faith, *Bob Hope*, p. 183.

22. *Road to Utopia* review, *New York Herald Tribune*.

23. Raymond Durgnat, *The Crazy Mirror*, p. 170.

24. Ibid.

25. Henry Jenkins, *What Made Pistachio Nuts? Early Sound Comedy and the Vaudeville Aesthetic* (New York: Columbia University Press, 1992), p. 282.

26. Charles Thompson, *Bob Hope: Portrait of a Superstar* (New York: St. Martin's Press, 1981), pp. 78–79.

27. *My Favorite Brunette* review, *Time*, March 31, 1947, pp. 99–100.

28. Howard Barnes, *My Favorite Brunette* review, *New York Herald Tribune*, March 20, 1947.

29. Robert Benchley, "Carnival Week in Sunny Las Los," in *The Treasurer's Report and Other Aspects of Community Singing* (New York: Grosset and Dunlap, 1930), p. 41.

30. Jack Thompson, *My Favorite Brunette* review, *New York Daily Mirror*, March 30, 1947, p. 16.

31. Ibid.; "Laughing with and at," *Commonweal*, April 4, 1947, p. 614.

32. Robert Warshow, "The Gangster as Tragic Hero" (1948) and "Movie Chronicle: The Westerner" (1954), in *The Immediate Experience*, ed. Sherry Abel (New York: Atheneum, 1962), pp. 127–33 and 135–54; James Agee, "Comedy's Greatest Era" (1949), in *Agee on Film*, vol. 1 (New York: Grosset and Dunlap, 1969), pp. 2–19.

33. John G. Cawelti, "The Question of Popular Genres," *Journal of Popular Film and Television*, Summer 1985, pp. 55–56.

34. "Everybody's Favorite Hope," *Newsweek*, March 31, 1947, p. 92.

35. Bosley Crowther, *My Favorite Brunette* review, *New York Times*, March 20, 1947, p. 38.

36. Ibid.

37. *My Favorite Brunette* review, *Time*, March 31, 1947, p. 99.

38. Barnes, *My Favorite Brunette* review.

39. Jeffrey Couchman, "Bob Hope: More Than a Gagster?" *New York Times*, May 6, 1979, section 2, pp. 1, 15.

40. "Movie of the Week: *The Paleface*," *Life*, January 3, 1949, p. 61.

41. Claire Johnston and Paul Willemen, eds., *Frank Tashlin* (London: Vineyard Press, 1973), p. 56.

42. Agee, "Comedy's Greatest Era," p. 18.

43. Hollis Alpert, "The Wild Man Is Coming," *Saturday Review*, August 9, 1952, p. 36.

44. Marilyn Wilson, "*The Paleface*," in *Magill's Survey of Cinema*, 2d ser., vol. 4, ed. Frank Magill (Englewood Cliffs, NJ: Salem Press, 1981), p. 1852.

45. Ibid.

46. Bosley Crowther, review of *Son of Paleface, New York Times*, October 2, 1952, p. 32.

47. Johnston and Willemen, p. 57.

48. James Thurber, "The Secret Life of Walter Mitty," in *The Thurber Carnival* (New York: Harper and Brothers, 1945), p. 52.

49. John Brosnan, *Future Tense: The Cinema of Science Fiction* (New York: St. Martin's Press, 1978), p. 218.

50. Ralph Rosenblum and Robert Karen, *When the Shooting Stops . . . the Cutting Begins: A Film Editor's Story* (New York: Penguin, 1979), p. 261.

51. Siegfried Kracauer, *Theory of Film: The Redemption of Physical Reality* (New York: Oxford University Press, 1960), p. 90.

52. Ibid., p. 91.

53. Eric Lax, *On Being Funny: Woody Allen and Comedy* (New York: Manor Books, 1975), p. 69.

54. Oscar Wilde, "The Decay of Lying," in *Critical Theory Since Plato*, ed. Hazard Adams (Chicago: Harcourt Brace Jovanovich, 1971), p. 680.

55. Woody Allen, *Side Effects* (New York: Random House, 1980), p. 44.

56. Ibid., p. 54.

57. Ibid., p. 55.

58. Leonard Maltin, *The Great Movie Comedians* (New York: Crown Publishers, 1978), p. 185.

59. Maurice Yacowar, *Loser Take All* (New York: Frederick Uncar Publishing, 1979), p. 156.

60. Frank Krutnik, "Jerry Lewis: The Deformation of the Comic," *Film Quarterly*, Fall 1994, p. 17.

61. William C. Siska, "The Art Film," in *Handbook of American Film Genres*, ed. Wes D. Gehring (Westport, CT: Greenwood Press, 1988), p. 363.

4

Mel Brooks

Interviewer (1966): "What did you think you'd be when you grew up?"
Brooks: "Tall."[1]

Interviewer (1975): "Speaking of blue, you've been accused of vulgarity."
Brooks: "Bullshit!"[2]

BROOKS' BACKGROUND

Since the phenomenal commercial success of Mel Brooks' controversial parody *Blazing Saddles* (more than $100 million in its initial 1974 release), no name has been more associated with the genre than Brooks. In fact, one critic observed—in the spirit of Brooks and no doubt inspired by *Blazing Saddles'* bean-eating scene—that the director was "the Farter of his country [parody]."[3]

Born Melvin Kaminsky (1926), he later borrowed his mother's maiden name (Brookman) to avoid being confused with trumpet player Max Kaminsky. The name was a good fit; like many comedians, including Charlie Chaplin and W. C. Fields, Brooks attributed much of his comedy talent to his mother:

My mother had this exuberant joy of living, and she infected me with that. By the time my . . . [three elder] brothers were old enough to work, she could stay at home and she was my company. There was Kitty [Mom] and Mel and we got to know each other, and she really was responsible for the growth of my [comic] imagination.[4]

Brooks' early years had been a severe challenge, however, for Kate "Kitty" Brookman Kaminsky. Russian immigrant Kate had met and married Polish-born Maximilian in Brooklyn. They lived in the Jewish tenements of Brooklyn, where the comedian's father worked as a process server. But when the boy was two-and-one-half, his young thirty-four-year-old father died of tuberculosis of the kidney. Moreover, it was 1929, the year of the stock market crash, with America about to enter the Great Depression. Even with extended family assistance, Kitty found herself working ten-hour days in Brooklyn's sweatshop garment district, bringing home piecework to sew half the night away as well. Ironically, the most frequent take-home work for this woman without free time in a cold-water apartment was sewing bathing suits by lamplight.

In reference to his father's early death Brooks observed in 1971: "I think that unconsciously, there's an outrage there. I may be angry at God, or at the world, for that. And I'm sure a lot of my comedy is based on anger and hostility."[5] Thus, comedy was used both to cover this wrath and to get on with life. And like the New York childhoods of the Marx Brothers a generation before, Brooks learned comedy could be a form of self-defense if one found himself outside the neighborhood. Indeed, bullies are seldom lacking, comedy was sometimes helpful in the neighborhood, too. But unlike the Marxes, who would fight if their comedy passport around the city failed, Brooks was also a very good runner.

Just as comedy is all about resiliency, be it Wile E. Coyote resurfacing after every Road Runner–induced flattening or Laurel & Hardy surviving every kind of tit-for-tat comic violence, Brooks' family was resilient. Indeed, the comedian would soon be the spoiled one. "With the other sons forced into premature adulthood, it was almost as if Melvin had become an only child."[6] And unlike Groucho, who suffered because his mother preferred her oldest sons (Chico and Harpo), Brooks was his mother's favorite. But in interview after interview Brooks says he was the adorable favorite of the *whole* family. For instance, "I was always in the air, hurled up and kissed and thrown in the air again. Until I was six, my feet didn't touch the ground."[7] Brooks took it upon himself to be the family clown: "I always felt it was my job to amuse those around me."[8]

Despite any repressed anger over the premature death of his father, the comedian remembers his childhood as full of love. Contradicting the stereotype of people going into entertainment to find the love they missed as a child, Brooks suggests many comics enter "show business to recapture the love they had known as children when they were the center of the universe."[9] Interestingly enough, this was the track Billy Crystal took when he made the underrated comedy *Mr. Saturday Night* (1992). Playing the character Buddy Young, Jr., a composite of many famous comedians, Crystal (who directed, co-wrote, and starred in the picture) makes the figure's career very much an outgrowth of a beloved child who doubled as the family clown. (The very name "Buddy Young, Jr." accents a childlike stance.) Certainly critics have long "read" Brooks' need to be funny along these lines. For example, *New York Times* writer Herbert Gold observed, "*The 2,000-Year-Old Man* record [a Brooks character to be discussed shortly] made him a cult figure, although the cult wasn't large enough for a man who needed everybody's love, everybody's, and right now."[10] Gold went on to suggest Brooks was driven by a "heart which defies the loss of his father, the loss of childhood, by insisting on childhood everywhere. The extended family of show business helps to keep him well-stocked with relatives."[11] Fittingly, Brooks answers fan mail only from children—"They really care."[12]

During his youth, comedy was not limited to being the family clown, or to being used as the safety valve from the occasional bully. It also helped Brooks fit into the neighborhood as entertainer. "They [local kids] wanted no part of me. I was little. I was funny-looking. I couldn't smoke. But I could talk [be funny] better than any of them. I wormed my way in with my jokes."[13] The power that came with comedy was, however, dependent upon knowing his audience. The material he did in the streets, sometimes expletive laden and forever earthy (no doubt anticipating the *Blazing Saddles* bean-eating scene) was verboten at home. Regardless of setting, however, young Brooks always pursued the laugh with the energy of a "1,000-watt kid."[14] Fittingly, this is consistent with his mother's aforementioned "exuberant joy of living," a philosophy of life Brooks also made the cornerstone of his comedy.

For a future off-the-wall comedy auteur, it seems appropriate that his family would move in 1939 to Brighton Beach, which elbows Brooklyn's Coney Island. One is reminded of Woody Allen's comedy character in the Oscar-winning *Annie Hall* (1977), who claims to have been born and raised in a house under Coney Island's roller coaster. This famous, anything-goes amusement park might have been a partial catalyst for Brooks's future saturation comedy tendencies. However, credit for that approach would have to be shared with the machine-gun patter of period movie comedians such as Groucho Marx or the Ritz Brothers, of whom Brooks was a big fan.

A more immediate entertainment connection that came out of the Kaminsky move was living near the Buddy Rich family. A young Rich was just then starting a career that would soon establish him as arguably the greatest drummer of all time. And, surprise of surprises, teenage Brooks suddenly thought he might enter show business as a drummer.

For a young Jewish wanna-be performer, show business meant just one thing—the Catskill Mountains summer resorts known as the Borscht Belt. Brooks first worked there in 1940 as a jack-of-all-trades, which could cover everything from busboy, to the assistant to the assistant social director. Being close to show business made it seem more and more possible. And one-time thoughts about being a pilot or chemist (like an older brother) faded. Eventually he did do some Catskill drumming. Of course, there were distractions, such as finishing high school and trying higher education (a year at Brooklyn College). But the big entertainment derailment was something called World War II.

Brooks was trained to be a combat engineer. The job description, at least as it pertained to a future comedy filmmaker, was *rather* unusual—deactivate land mines before the army goes into action! But then again, considering all the zaniness he brought to his work, such as cowboy tollgates in the middle of the prairie, maybe his army assignment was not that strange.

After the war he returned to the Catskills and drumming. This was an entertainment circuit where old jokes went to die. But they were tolerated and sometimes even celebrated with the help of a drummer doing a "rim shot" (hitting the snare drum) right after some ancient punch line. Brooks studied this and as a drummer occasionally provided the rim shot himself. In fact, the first time he appeared as a comic (a last-minute substitute) he fell back on the same Methuselah material. But on this occasion these museum gags proved a revelation. Brooks decided not to go that route in the future. Without being obscene he would return to his street corner style— from improvising zany observations and noises to "found humor"—comic comments about the equally zany world in which we live. This did not mean rim shot gags were forever banished from his set. For instance, one can easily imagine him making a crack about fear of "bombing" on his army job. Still, it would be comedy from his own warped perspective.

If Brooks had a mentor besides his mother, it was celebrated television comedian Sid Caesar, for whom he wrote throughout the 1950s. Caesar was another Catskills musician (saxophone) more attuned to being a comic. The two became friends in the post-war Catskills, where Caesar had arrived as a comic and Brooks was still struggling. Caesar had been in the service, too. But unlike Brooks's *invaluable* entertainment training of deactivating land mines, Caesar had an opportunity to hone his comedy skills. He was able to showcase his talent in a Coast Guard review called *Tars and Spars*, which toured the country. It was so successful it found its way to Hollywood and was made into a film (1946). Caesar stole the show with two routines, one of which was a conversation between Hitler and Donald Duck, something he originally had worked on in the Catskills.

Caesar played both parts, using the German double-talk he had experimented with since he was a child. Besides Donald's quack-quack German gibberish, an occasional bit of English would sneak in, such as, "Aw, why don't you sit down, you crazy bastard."[15] I refer to this German double-talk routine as a possible influence on Brooks's future Nazi dark comedy interests. In a note written for Caesar's 1982 autobiography Brooks observed, "I went into the army and when I came out, I saw *Tars and Spars*. I studied what Sid did in the picture and I said, 'This guy is really funny, uniquely funny.' "[16] (Of course, in the 1940s no one had a copyright on a comic Hitler shtick; the closest would be Chaplin's inspired German gibberish takedown of Hitler in *The Great Dictator*, 1940.) Regardless, years later Brooks planned to cast Caesar as the Nazi playwright (author of *Springtime for Hitler*) in *The Producers* (1967). But because Caesar had a substance abuse problem at the time, the producing studio refused to let Brooks use him.

Beyond any German comedy shtick connections between the two, Brooks began his serious show business career as a comedy disciple of Caesar. The latter observed, "He [Brooks] didn't hang around Milton Berle or Jimmy Durante. He was funny and ingenious and he liked my type of humor, so he hung around me."[17]

Besides his comedy, "hanging around" was what Brooks had always done best. His persistence in hanging around the neighborhood eventually made him the area clown. His persistence in hanging around the Catskills eventually gave him work as a comic. His persistence in hanging around Sid Caesar eventually landed him a job as writer on the 1950s watershed comedy (often parody) NBC television program *Your Show of Shows* (1950–54; see Chapter 1).

Working for the show, and then for *Caesar's Hour* (1954–57), Brooks became part of a creative group that rivaled the celebrated story conference people of Mack Sennett's heyday. Fittingly, Caesar's writing team themselves would later inspire comedy projects. For instance, Caesar regular Carl Reiner would create television's classic *Dick Van Dyke Show* (1961–66), about three writers toiling for the fictional TV program *The Alan Brady Show*, a New York–based comedy-variety series with a Caesar-like over-the-top but seldom seen star (Reiner). And the model for Caesar writer Neil Simon's critical and commercial smash Broadway play *Laughter on the 23rd Floor* (1993–1994) was the inspired comedy chaos that went into the making of *Your Show of Shows* (written on the twenty-third floor of Rockefeller Center). A veteran of *Your Show*'s program staff described the situation as such. Caesar would read an outline of a previously prepared sketch, then: "everybody jumped up like a bunch of madmen [though Brooks was easily the maddest of the mad]. They screamed at each other, and hurled jokes at each other, improvising bits of dialogue, until they were tired out from laughing and sat down again."[18]

This television program was also the catalyst for a classic film comedy—*My Favorite Year* (1982). The Richard Benjamin–directed film takes place in 1954, a year in which Benjamin was an NBC page and Caesar was, well, the "Caesar" of NBC comedy. The movie is funny, poignant, and like its television model, parody was at the heart of its inspiration—spoofing the adventure films of the Errol Flynnish guest star (Peter O'Toole). The fictional in-film program, *The King Kaiser* [German for Caesar] *Show*, also starred Joseph Bologna in an inspired performance as the arrogant yet eccentrically brilliant Kaiser, easily believable as a Sid Caesar–like comedy force that could both inspire and lead a most eccentric writing team.

The youngest member of the troupe is the boy/man Benjy Stone (Mark Linn-Baker), an energized writer/gofer for the group who might be seen as the young Mel Brooks. Like Brooks, Benjy is Jewish, Brooklyn born, mesmerized by the movies, imbued with a spirit directly traceable to his mother, and willing to do anything to be in show business. This passion to belong is directly related to Brooks's persistent trait of "hanging around," and prompted Caesar to affectionately describe him as a "groupie."

To borrow from the Yiddish, Brooks had an unbelievable amount of *chutzpah* (gall), what an old Jewish story likens to the man who murders his mother and father, then asks the judge to forgive a poor orphan. Although Brooks's effrontery initially alienated the *Your Show of Shows'* producer, Caesar was an instant fan and actually paid Brooks' salary out of his own pocket the first two seasons.

Caesar's writing crew and the young Brooks bring to mind the legendary Sennett story conference people for another reason, too. The earlier group had what was called a "wild man," someone who might sit quietly on the sidelines offering little assistance for most of a session, only to provide some zany finishing bit of business to a routine that had otherwise become blocked. If a footnote example of this phenomenon is needed, one might turn to the cast of the early 1980s hit television situation comedy *Taxi*, about the lives and funny times of its drivers. The show offers two variations on the "wild man" type—the peripheral players Latka (Andy Kaufman) and Reverend Jim (Christopher Lloyd). Latka is a mechanic of indeterminate nationality and a fractured English peppered with his own gibberish-sounding language. Taxi-driving Jim's distracted ways are seemingly the result of a drug-induced meltdown from the hippie 1960s. Both characters are capable of providing the suddenly-out-of-left-field topper to some comic *Taxi* dilemma—Latka in the sometimes fast-paced indecipherable patter of a mechanic from Mars, and Jim with the slowly drawn out commentary of a cracker-barrel philosopher on acid.

On *Your Show of Shows*, Brooks represented that same type of comedy closer, a talent he first demonstrated on Caesar's 1949 television program *The Admiral Broadway Revue*, the prototype for *Your Show of Shows*. Indeed, the Sennett phrase of "wild man" could not have been more appropriate, since Brooks's first comedy save was a weird sound. Caesar and company were working on a routine about a jungle boy ordering breakfast, and they were stuck. They finally turned to Brooks, whose crazy rendition of a hungry crow *made* the skit.

Like fellow Caesar comedy writer Woody Allen, Brooks's focus turned to performing his own material in the 1960s. Teamed with another Caesar colleague, Carl Reiner, they came up with a character—a 2,000-year-old man. (Befitting Brooks's "wild man" background and his gift for improvisation, the birth of this character was an outgrowth of his clowning around with Reiner at private parties.) Once again, parody was at the heart of the material. Straight man Reiner, brilliant as the quasi-reporter/interviewer, would lob provocative questions at Brooks' very Jewish, very ancient wise man/wise guy. What followed was the spoofing of a crackerbarrel figure, Hebrew style.

With a 2,000-year range, Brooks' character could comment on everything from Jesus' bookcase-making skills to the sexy side of First Lady Dolley Madison. And as is often the case with parody, a little satire occasionally slipped in. For instance, the first god worshiped on earth was a guy named Phil. But when he was struck by lightning, everyone knew there was something bigger than Phil. Even though this was a spoof of the oldest crackerbarrel figure on record, Yiddish or otherwise, Brooks managed (as in all real parody), to show affection for his target character. Consequently, his 2,000-year-old man could, on occasion, provide legitimate insight. For example, when discussing his legion of children (none of whom ever wrote or called), he observed, "We mock [as young people] what we are to become."

The 2,000-year-old man was at the heart of his first film project, a mix of satire and parody titled *The Critic* (1962, see Chapter 1). This short subject consisted entirely of a series of abstract images projected on a screen while an elderly Jewish member of the audience provided voice-over comic commentary. Although no mention is made of the 2,000-year-old man, the narration is clearly that of the character who once described Jesus as "thin, nervous, wore sandals. Came into the store a lot. Never bought anything."

As noted in Chapter 1, the 1960s also saw Brooks create (with Buck Henry) the television parody *Get Smart* (1965–70), a spoof of the phenomenally successful James Bond films. (Ten years later Brooks would create the critically acclaimed television spoof of Robin Hood *When Things Were Rotten*, 1975. Unfortunately, audiences were not as smitten and the program was canceled.) Despite his many successes in television, which would also include dozens of variety show appearances as the 2,000-year-old man (with Reiner), by the mid-1960s Brooks was determined to succeed in film.

Before making his watershed parody *Blazing Saddles* (1974), Brooks made two feature films. Neither *The Producers* (1967) nor *Twelve Chairs* (1970) was a critical or commercial success, though the former would eventually be hailed as a cult comedy classic. Indeed, *The Producers*, like the Marx Brothers' *Duck Soup* (1933, also a critical and commercial failure upon its initial release) now often turns up on "Top 10" polls of film comedy's greatest movies. For example, in *Entertainment Weekly*'s October

16, 1992, "Special Collector's Issue" of the "100 Funniest Movies," *The Producers* came in at number six, followed by *Duck Soup* at seven.[19]

Besides the aforementioned parody elements that anticipate *Blazing Saddles* (see Chapter 1), *The Producers* foreshadows Brooks' left-handed homage to the Western in another way. Both films embrace characteristics that qualify them for inclusion in film theorist William Paul's 1994 approach to the "gross-out" film as genre. In his provocative *Laughing Screaming: Modern Hollywood Horror and Comedy* he includes *Blazing Saddles* as a pivotal part of the type.[20] He appropriately examines the sexual ramifications of Madeline Kahn's delightful Lili Von Shtupp, an obvious spoof of Marlene Dietrich's character type in *The Blue Angel* (1930) and *Destry Rides Again* (1939, see Chapter 2). But surprisingly, Paul makes no mention of the infamous campfire farting scene, which not even the more recent flatulence turn in Eddie Murphy's 1996 remake of *The Nutty Professor* has managed to top. Moreover, given Paul's attention to sexual gross-out material, and the power associated with the dominant partner, it is doubly surprising he makes no reference to *The Producers*, because Zero Mostel's lead character bankrolls his Broadway work by playing comically carnal games with innumerable kinky but wealthy little old ladies.

Despite Brooks' obvious anticipation of the popular gross-out film as genre (which says nothing of *The Producers*' showcasing a musical comedy play called *Springtime for Hitler*), and his earlier ongoingly successful ties with parody, *Blazing Saddles*' astounding critical and commercial success came as an industry surprise. As film critic Peter Schjeldahl observed in *The New York Times* upon its release, "Brooks has brought to the screen a brand of convulsive comedy so completely original that it seems to have dropped out of the sky. . . . Brooks is unique and irreplaceable; let us cherish him for that."[21] *Blazing Saddles* even moved Richard Schickel, arguably America's greatest film critic/scholar, to praise the movie in Western parody prose: "But goldarned if it doesn't work [despite gross-out comedy]. Goldarned if the whole fool enterprise is not worth the attention of any moviegoer with a penchant for what one actor, commenting on another's Gabby Hayes imitation [the famous Western character actor known for his comic toothless speech], calls 'authentic Western gibberish.' "[22] And the critic for Britain's scholarly periodical *Film and Filming* confessed, "I started chortling from the outset when the Warner Brothers trademark was demolished in flames."[23]

BLAZING SADDLES

John G. Cawelti's pioneering genre study *The Six-Gun Mystique* notes seven fundamental Western plots:

1. The Union Pacific Story centering around the construction of a railroad, telegraph or stagecoach line or around the adventures of a wagon train;

2. The Ranch Story with its focus on conflicts between ranchers and rustlers or cattlemen and sheepmen;

3. The Empire Story, which is an epic version of the Ranch Story;

4. The Revenge Story;

5. Custer's Last Stand, or the Cavalry and Indian Story;

6. The Outlaw Story; and

7. The Marshal Story.[24]

Blazing Saddles combines elements of the Union Pacific and Marshal stories, with a footnote to the Indian plot when Brooks turns up briefly as a Yiddish-speaking Sioux chief. (The Marx Brothers' *Go West* might have influenced Brooks' railroad slant—see Chapter 2.)

Though set in 1874, *Blazing Saddles* opens with what might very well be the laying of tracks for the transcontinental railroad (circa 1865–69). It is an operation of epic proportion, with the work largely being performed (as is historically accurate) with Chinese and black laborers. But a large area of quicksand necessitates the rerouting of the track through the town of Rock Ridge, which will soon be in need of a new marshal (to be addressed shortly). The crooked state attorney general Hedley Lamarr (Harvey Korman), whose name becomes an ongoing comic anachronism when it is constantly confused with that of later film actress Hedy Lamarr, is determined to obtain control of Rock Ridge for the huge monetary gain tied to the rerouting of the railroad. The comic irony here is that the Union Pacific Story is about (ideally) bringing *civilization*—via communication, be it tracks or telegraph—to the wilderness. But it is society's corruption instead of civilization that is being brought West.

Hedley controls Governor William J. LePetomane ("the Farter" in French, played by Brooks), who is most interested in sex with his secretary, as was the case with Mostel's character in *The Producers*. Brooks' two roles, as the Jewish Indian and the crooked WASP governor (with GOV on the back of his coat) represent the character extremes of the film. LePetomane is a racist who appoints a black sheriff not out of liberalness but rather for possible political gain. In contrast, Brooks' Indian chief appreciates the minority status of blacks and is shown, by way of a flashback, to have rescued the future marshal from harm when the boy and his family were caught in the midst of a battle between Native Americans and intruding white settlers. But as is the case throughout *Blazing Saddles*, Brooks' characters always seem funny first; seriousness does not derail the humor, especially in reference to a Jewish Indian chief possibly inspired by W. C. Fields (see Chapter 2). Of course, as with any good spoof film, the material comes like a "gag-firing machine gun."[25] It is saturation comedy at its best.

Since Hedley controls this corrupt Western political machine, one might best examine *Blazing Saddles'* parody by the ways in which he attempts to take over the town and how he is constantly comically rebuffed. But this necessitates a word about his right-hand man, Taggart (Slim Pickens). It is difficult to overestimate the casting of Pickens, whose many Western appearances had already made him an icon of the genre. Indeed, no less a film great than director Stanley Kubrick used Pickens' cowboy image to inspire black humor effect in *Dr. Strangelove or How I Learned to Stop Worrying and Love the Bomb* (1964). In possibly the film's most memorable scene, Pickens' character Major "King" Kong joyfully rides a nuclear bomb like a bucking bronco as it falls toward a dark comedy apocalypse.

This dimwitted Western jingoism is precisely what makes his Taggart an entertainingly appropriate lieutenant to Hedley. He is comically loyal to an establishment that is decidedly not out for the good of the citizens, whether it is people of color laying railroad track, or the white bread population of Rock Ridge, where everyone's last name is Johnson. (This includes the original Howard Johnson, whose ice cream parlor has only one flavor—vanilla.) Brooks even seems to indirectly underline this misguided loyalty trait in Taggart late in the film. Brooks' picture quite literally pushes the Western parody *physical* envelope by having his near-movie-ending brawl break through a Warner Brothers soundstage wall and onto the set of a musical comedy in production. (Brooks' comedy is not just off the wall; it blows walls away.) When the in-film director of this musical, Dom DeLuise in a very funny cameo as Buddy Bizarre, protests this genre-crashing intrusion, Picken's Taggart replies, "Piss on you; I'm working for Mel Brooks." And consistent with his character, he proceeds to smack Buddy with a comic roundhouse punch.

Taggart's first meeting with Hedley in the latter's office is also of great significance, both in demonstrating Taggart's importance as a comic catalyst for action, and in providing viewer insights about the unfolding story by way of the physical objects in the room. For example, the first thing one sees in the room is a painting of a wedding couple from the backside. This works comically on several levels.

First, and most obviously (never underappreciate the obvious), it is funny and unexpected, just as the movie is going to be. Second, *Blazing Saddles'* spoofing *derailment* of a Western train saga is providing a rearview image of the genre. Third, the painting's two posteriors anticipates the film's fixation with breaking wind, whether it is the conspicuous bean-eating scene, or the more subtle implication of the title *Blazing Saddles*. As Brooks observed, "Shakespeare said hold the mirror up to life; I held it a little behind and below."[26] Fourth, the painting's less-than-positive take on marriage anticipates the film's suggestion that the primary interaction between the sexes in the Old West was a cash transaction between a cowboy and the saloon girl/prostitute, à la Madeline Kahn's Lili von Shtupp. Indeed, that is what she is implying by singing the song "I'm Tired." Lili has been in the "shtupping" business for too long. Again there is a Marlene Dietrich connection for Kahn's character. In *Blue Angel* Dietrich's Lola-Lola introduces "Falling In Love Again" in the most tired of tempos. She has apathetically "had" every man this side of Berlin . . . indifferently ruining each life as a given.

Two other objects in Hedley's office also merit attention. There is a statute of the famous Lady Justice, blindfolded and holding her scales of justice. When the attorney general becomes excited about the possibility of stealing the Rock Ridge land, he closes his eyes and starts to massage the figure in a sexual manner. Obviously, this represents a metaphorical reference to what is about to happen—a rape of justice. That such action is possible has already been established earlier in the scene, after Taggart accidentally knocks an object off Hedley's desk—a law book. This sets the crooked attorney general to thinking about legal precedent for "land snatching." Looking first under *land*, the volume directs him to see *snatch*, again suggesting sexual overtones to the whole proceeding. And sure enough, the law book okays such action, making the precedent-setting case sound like a sporting event—"Haley 7, United States 0." (One is reminded of Taggart's first line in the film: "What in the wide, wide world of sports is going on here?"—both a punning reference to a onetime television program and a possible foreshadowing that this will be another, though comic, exercise in justice according to the sexist, good old boy school of thought.)

Regardless, Taggart visits Hedley's office and offers two suggestions on how to steal the Rock Ridge land. Hedley turns down the first idea as too Jewish—scaring off the townspeople by killing the first-born male child in each household. One might pause here briefly out of comic defense for Brooks. Though this "male child" reference is not specifically earmarked by the always-provocative critic Pauline Kael, it is the type of comedy, or noncomedy, material that she saw as a *Blazing Saddles* flaw, claiming Brooks' Jewish jokes "aren't even jokes anymore but just an assertion of Jewishness—as if that were always good for a laugh."[27] But Kael entirely misses the comic *surprise* inherent in such a remark coming from a Western icon figure such as Pickens's Taggart. It is unexpected dialogue equivalent to the later comment by moron character Mongo (Alex Karras; to be examined shortly): "Mongo just pawn in game of life." Moreover, one might use Kael's own wording against her complaint. That is, Brooks has so effectively saturated *Blazing Saddles* with Jewishness, such as his Yiddish-speaking chief going on about saving the "Schwartzes" [the blacks]—"Abee gezint. Take off!"—that probably a mere "assertion of Jewishness" would be "good for a laugh."

Taggart's second proposal to Hedley, about how best to drive the people out of town, is more to the attorney general's liking: "We go a-riding into town a-whomping and whomping everything that moves within an inch of their lives." Even more important in demonstrating the significance of Taggart to Hedley is how Pickens' character leads into this suggestion: "We'll work up a number six on them [the townspeople]." Korman's Hedley has no idea what a "number six" is, but he is both eager to find out and seemingly impressed that Taggart (like any good genre icon) should be such an excellent resource. The student of the Western should be impressed, too; Taggart's scenario would fall under *number six* of Cawelti's plot lines— the Outlaw Story. Though this is undoubtedly a fascinating coincidence, it should be stated that the original story author for the film, and one of the co-scriptors, was Andrew Bergman, now a writer/director. A sometime parody auteur in his own right, such as his brilliant spoofing of Marlon Brando's *Godfather* (1972) figure in *The Freshman* (1990), Bergman received a Ph.D. in film studies when Cawelti was blazing new trails in genre studies. And Bergman is not averse to academic footnotes in his movies, such as the university film department setting of *The Freshman*.

Nonetheless, although Taggart's value to Hedley should be clear by now, this office scene also finds the former figure representing a catalyst to later *Blazing Saddles* business. Pickens' character first brings Cleavon Little's future sheriff to Hedley's attention near the scene's close, when Taggart requests that "that uppity nigger" be hanged (he had earlier smacked Taggart over the head with a shovel). Little's character is not seen in this segment. He is being held under lock and key in another room in the building. But a disturbance from outside, a series of official hangings taking place, encourages Taggart to make his request.

Though there is nothing new about lynchings in the Old West, the cutaways to the executioner and his victims (no hangings are actually shown) provide several variations of winning dark parody (quite literally a "gallows humor" touch). First and most pointed is the fact that Brooks' hangman is decked out in medieval garb, complete with a mail shirt. It is something that would have made even the West's infamous "Hanging" Judge Parker and Judge Roy Bean pause. And therein lies a deeper meaning. Western violence, either by or against the law, quickly removes man's thin veneer of civilization and returns him to a primitive past. But then Brooks comically clouds the issue further by making this refugee from the Middle Ages the most affable of fellows, to the point of having him smooch a soon-to-be victim on the noggin. Second, the spoofing send-offs of these alleged villains can embrace the bizarre. For example, one victim and his horse are being hanged simultaneously. Another felon makes his exit in a wheelchair.

With a hanging date booked for Taggart's black antagonist and a land "snatch" solution planned, Hedley's helper is moved to observe, with comic earthiness and the film's ongoing employment of anachronism, "We'll make Rock Ridge think it's a chicken that got caught in a tractor's nuts." Just then, however, the noise of the dual hanging of a horse and rider spooks Taggart, and he jumps into Hedley's arms. Now playing father figure to

his lieutenant, the attorney general calms Taggart by singing him a lullaby
as the office scene closes. Again parody turns things upside down. The
tough guy has been reduced to acting like a baby, and the self-serving
politician shows comic compassion.

The next stop is Rock Ridge shortly before the outlaw attack. The setting
looks like any number of Hollywood Western towns, though the intermin-
gling of cows and cowboys in the local saloon does give one comic pause.
Then the badmen blitzkrieg is on, and they stop at nothing. For instance,
one witnesses the beating of a little old lady, with the action stopping
momentarily for her to face the camera in direct address: "Have you ever
seen such cruelty?"

Things look bad, and a town meeting is held at the church. The people
appear to be finishing a hymn, but it is actually "The Ballad of Rock
Ridge," which has been heard before and during the attack. The people's
position is summed up in the ballad's final line, "Our town is turning into
shit." Again it is parody of comic surprise. When a student of the Western
thinks of archetypal church music for the genre, he/she thinks of something
populist, such as celebrated Western director John Ford's use of "Shall We
Gather at the River" in *My Darling Clementine* (1946), as Wyatt Earp
(Henry Fonda) and Clementine Carter (Cathy Downs) walk toward the
tolling bell of the church-to-be. Moreover, beyond being less than hopeful,
Brooks' ballad is obscene, à la the word "shit."

The use of such words, and the film's ever-present refrain of "nigger,"
is consistent with Brooks' parody overview for *Blazing Saddles*. As noted
in Chapter 1, this movie is unique in Brooks' spoofing career for its satirical
underpinnings, such as references to Western racism and violence. The use
of verbal obscenities, however, brings up a popular buzz phrase later applied to the blue language of stand-up comic Richard Pryor and a co-
scriptor of *Blazing Saddles*—"the theatre of real life."[28] That is, the comic
brilliance of the movie is that we laugh at its effronteries to an *image* of
the American West that is essentially mythic (read: false) in nature—racism,
violence, and obscenity were, ironically, the reality.

Brooks comically mines what Italian director Sergio Leone had stumbled
into with his now-classic "spaghetti Western" trilogy—*A Fistful of Dollars*
(1964; U.S., 1967), *For a Few Dollars More* (1965; U.S., 1967), and *The
Good, The Bad, and The Ugly* (1966; U.S., 1967; all starring Clint Eastwood). The movies are not without their own parody elements. Leone
would later observe, "The man of the West bore no resemblance to the
man described by Hollywood directors, screenwriters, cineasts . . . all these
molds are mixed together, before the happy ending, in a kind of cruel,
puritan fairy-story."[29] One cannot read about this mythic West without
thinking of John Ford, whose work did so much to shape the pre-Leone
concept of the genre. Indeed, probably the most famous line from a Ford
film, and certainly the most significant, directly addresses this subject.

Though first anticipated at the close of his *Fort Apache* (1948), it occurs in Ford's *The Man Who Shot Liberty Valance* (1962): "When the legend becomes fact, print the legend."

Why do the people need a legend, or a lie (depending on your perspective)? Ford's answer was, "Because I think it's good for the country. We've had a lot of people who were supposed to be great heroes, and you know damn well they weren't. But it's good for the country to have heroes to look up to."[30] It is a provocative slant, and hardly surprising, coming from a very patriotic son of an immigrant. But even Ford would come to second-guess it by the end of his career. The same year (1964) Leone did *A Fistful of Dollars*, Ford made the revisionist *Cheyenne Autumn*, with Native Americans (rather than the cavalry) as heroes.

To put this in historical perspective, Leone's statement reminds me of a highly pertinent John F. Kennedy quote my junior high class was asked to memorize during his short presidency (1961–63). "The great enemy of truth is very often not the lie—deliberate, contrived and dishonest—but the myth—persistent, persuasive and unrealistic." Leone, long a student of American history and popular culture, was no doubt aware of this insightful observation, too. Change was in the air.

Be that as it may, American critics were still not prepared for the "spaghetti Westerns." Though they immediately found a large commercial audience, reviewers initially attacked them for their gratuitous violence. Although little acknowledged at the time, there also seems to have been some jingoistic critical backlash for a foreign director to tamper with the most inherently American of genres, the Western. Richard Schickel later entertainingly labeled it "the invasion of the genre snatchers."[31]

All these things worked to Brooks' 1974 advantage with *Blazing Saddles*. He was an American artist toiling under the still-affectionate umbrella of parody. And any of Brooks's satirical thrusts had a more immediate and understandably positive meaning than the still largely misunderstood Leone. For example, when *Blazing Saddles* makes fun of racism, such as people who use the word *nigger*, the viewer is obviously encouraged to rise above prejudice. Moreover, like the title of a later Jackie Mason one-man show on Broadway, *Politically* In*correct*, comedy always has the propensity to be subversive, whether in politics or in genre expectations. Consequently, *Blazing Saddles'* parody bushwhacking of the Western also made some social points and, in the long run, possibly joined Leone in contributing to the eventual revitalization of the sagebrush genre. In time, of course, Leone and Eastwood became parody targets, too. For instance, in *Back to the Future III*, (1990), which is essentially a Western spoof set in 1885, series star Michael J. Fox calls himself Clint Eastwood and wears the signature "spaghetti Western" poncho and hat of Eastwood's "man with no name" character.

After "The Ballad of Rock Ridge's" closing "shit" reference set a certain tone, the *Blazing Saddles* minister further articulates the town's dilemma: "Sheriff murdered, crops burned, stores looted, people stampeded, and cattle raped [maybe there was something to those cattle in the saloon]. Now the time has come to act and to act fast. . . . [pause] I'm leaving." What started as an apparent pep talk has turned into an exit line of comic surprise. Yet one is reminded of the church speech by Thomas Mitchell's character in the classic 1952 *High Noon*, sometimes referred to as the first adult Western. Gary Cooper's sheriff, Will Kane, desperately needs assistance (the badmen are coming at twelve o'clock). Kane's best friend and the leading spokesperson for the town, Mitchell's figure, seems to be rallying the people to the marshal's aid. But then with a sudden verbal twist, he encourages Kane to run. It would not be in the best interest of the town to be involved.

This hypocritical perspective, an angry use of the Western form as a Joseph McCarthy metaphor, was a veiled attack (as was Arthur Miller's play *The Crucible*, 1953) against communist witch-hunting, when people were afraid to get involved, even if it meant helping a friend. *High Noon* was (and remains) a high-profile Western Brooks would have been very familiar with, especially since *Your Show of Shows* spoofed parts of the movie, titling it *Dark Noon*. Indeed, the exterior of the *Blazing Saddles* church bears a striking resemblance to the *High Noon* building.

Although the people do come around in Brooks' movie, both films embrace a perspective Western purists find blasphemous. For instance, pioneering popular culture/genre critic Robert Warshow was disgusted that the *High Noon* sheriff would go to the people. To incorporate the "social drama" (McCarthyism) "is to raise a question which does not exist in the proper frame of the Western movie, where the hero is 'naturally' alone."[32] Notable director Howard Hawks, who excelled in so many genres (including the Western, such as *Red River*, 1948), even did a classic rebuttal to *High Noon*—the quintessential Hawks Western *Rio Bravo*, 1959. In this film John Wayne's marshal would never think of asking the town for help, though he is assisted by several flawed deputies, including Dean Martin's alcoholic gunslinger and Walter Brennan's lame old man. (Martin's character seems to be the model for *Blazing Saddles*' hard-drinking Waco Kid, played by Gene Wilder.)

Warshow was also bothered by the "antipopulism" of *High Noon*'s townspeople.[33] While his concept of the Western myth isolated them from the capable sheriff, they were still worth protecting. Seemingly to maximize the comic effect, Brooks' spoof toys with the legend of the populist people and has it both ways. For example, by linking the townspeople with the soon-to-be-appointed black sheriff, Brooks has more potential Western types to spoof, from the Gabby Hayes old-timer to the pioneering businessman Howard Johnson. But though the people reluctantly do the right—populist—thing, their bigoted background has been comically showcased.

The Waco Kid reminds the viewer of both as he observes, "These people are simple farmers, people of the land, the common clay of the new West. You know, morons."

This notwithstanding, Taggart's suggestions to do a "number six" (attack) on the town fails, and the people petition the governor to appoint a new marshal. Now Hedley must come up with a sheriff who will make the people leave Rock Ridge. The attorney general is so perplexed he even asks the viewer for advice, via direct address. But being the most entertaining of crooks, he comically insults the audience by implying that an answer is beyond them. Providentially, it is at this moment that Taggart's nemesis Black Bart is about to be hanged. And Hedley suddenly sees the perfect way to acquire the Rock Ridge land—appoint Cleavon Little's character sheriff and watch the population exit town.

This is not, however, the response he receives. It looks more like Bart will be leaving . . . in a box. But with every available Rock Ridge gun pointing in his direction, he *takes himself hostage*. Holding a six-shooter to his own throat and playing both victim and villain, Bart convinces the crowd to drop their weapons or "the nigger gets it." And with this spoof of the standard Western hostage scene, Bart makes his escape to the safety of the jail office.

Once again the townspeople meet at the church, this time to hear the schoolmarm read her letter to the governor complaining about his appointment of a black sheriff. Though it is a brief scene, Brooks manages another inspired spoof of a key Western figure. Since Owen Wister's classic novel *The Virginian* (1902), as pivotal to the genre as Mary Shelley's *Frankenstein* (1818) is to the horror film, the schoolteacher has symbolized Eastern education come West to civilize the wilderness. I am forever reminded of Cathy Downs' title character in *My Darling Clementine*. She initially goes West to find her lost love, the legendary Doc Holliday. But although this relationship is not meant to be (he is an Eastern refugee fleeing civilization and dying of tuberculosis), the film closes with her deciding to stay in Tombstone and start a school.

With this cornerstone of the mythic Western in mind, Brooks delivers a double-whammy parody attack. The schoolmarm, one Harriett Johnson (Carol Arthur—another Johnson!) is not only the spokesperson for Rock Ridge's lowbrow racism, she talks like the proverbial sailor. For example, she closes her letter to the governor with, "The fact that you have sent him [Black Bart] here just goes to prove that you're the leading asshole in the state." If time had permitted, it would have been comically fascinating to see how Brooks would have spoofed her classroom lesson plans. (See Chapter 2 for Mae West's take on the time-honored schoolmarm.) Thereafter, despite the letter, the town reluctantly accepts the new sheriff.

In the lull until the next disruption to Rock Ridge, time is allowed for background material on both Bart and a prisoner who turns up in the jail, the Waco Kid. The marshal's brief biography has already been alluded to—Brooks' Yiddish-speaking Sioux chief having allowed the then-boy and his Westward-bound wagon train family to escape death during an Indian/pioneer running gun battle.

The Waco Kid had been the fastest gun in the world. Indeed, according to Gene Wilder's Kid (speaking in the third person), "he had killed more men than [film director] Cecil B. DeMille." But he had fallen victim to the familiar Western tale of everyone out to make a name for themselves by gunning for Wilder's character. Indeed, this represents a flashback to my own childhood fascination with this Western phenomenon. One of my most prized possessions as a youngster was a ten-cent Dell comic book (echoes of the nineteenth-century dime novel) rendition of the popular 1956 film *The Fastest Gun Alive*. Here, too, was a name gun trying to escape his reputation. But I am no different than most American children, regardless of the era, enamored of the "shootist" (the original Western term for the famous gunslinger), who has become a prisoner of his six-gun prowess. I am reminded, for example, of James Thurber's comic reminiscences in *The Beast In Me and Other Animals* (1948) about the childhood allure of Western legend Wild Bill Hickok.[34]

Brooks' spoof of this fastest gun dilemma does, however, find comedy in a revisionist slant on the subject. That is, for one last time Waco had heard someone say, "Reach for it, Mister." But when he spun around to confront his stalker, he found a six-year-old kid. In disgust, Wilder's character threw down his guns and walked away, only to have the "little bastard shoot me in the ass. So I limped to the nearest saloon and crawled inside a whiskey bottle and I've been there ever since."

The wannabe gunman out to make a name for himself by dueling a famous shootist is invariably young. But to make him a mean-spirited six-year-old is both inspired parody and an insightful reflection of a then-new development in the Western genre—the less-than-innocent child. This is particularly true in the late 1960s work of Sam Peckinpah, who successfully pushed the Leone revisionist Western envelope further in *The Wild Bunch* (1969). As celebrated genre critic Jim Kitses observed, "Like birds on a string, children are a part of a violent [Peckinpah] world."[35] Indeed, one could argue they set the tone. At the very beginning of *The Wild Bunch*, a group of youngsters happily watch a scorpion fall victim to an army of killer ants. As one boy pokes at the insects with a stick, there is the sense that they are not mere observers but rather cheerful participants in this cruelty. Later events in the film seem to reinforce this position. For instance, children playfully ride on the body of the romantically idealistic character named Angel as he is dragged behind an early automobile. And at story's end a small boy is one of the figures who shoot the central character to death. Consequently, as funny as the Waco Kid's rendition of being shot in the tush is, as with all good parody, it also functions as entertainfully perceptive criticism. (For an earlier look at the Western child as innocent figure see, for example, the boy, Brandon de Wilde, who worships director George Steven's mythically mysterious stranger, Alan Ladd, in *Shane*, 1953. In the post–Leone/Peckinpah era even the good youngster, such as Ron Howard's character in *The Shootist*, 1976, can no longer blindly idolize the gunslinger.)

As the Kid and Bart begin to establish a friendship, it is time for another attempt by the comic heavies to gain control of the town. In this case, Taggart, acting independently of his boss Hedley, unleashes the most literal of *heavies* upon Rock Ridge—former Iowa All-American football player Alex Karras' slow-witted giant, Mongo. Taggart is sure that "Mongo will just mash him [Bart] up into little sheriff meatballs."

As in a cartoon, Mongo's bull-riding entry into town causes earthquake-like tremors and hysteria by a populace who seem all too familiar with the bullying chaos for which Mongo stands. Building upon the cartoon motif, complete with Warner Brothers' Looney Tunes music on the soundtrack, a Bugs Bunny–like Bart manages to tame the giant with an exploding candy-gram. (The marshal had been forewarned that "if you shoot him you'll just make him mad.") Moreover, the now-subdued Mongo, like a verbal puppy dog, pledges unending loyalty to Bart.

Again, the Hedley/Taggart goal of Rock Ridge control has been comically thwarted. Indeed, Cleavon Little's sheriff has even received a thank-you pie, though under cover of darkness, for domesticating Mongo. As Hedley attempts to brainstorm what to do while enjoying a bubble bath (though he will be temporarily traumatized by misplacing his rubber froggy), Taggert is once again the catalyst for a new plan. As if emulating the comic flowery language of a *word*smith such as W. C. Fields, Harvey Korman's character provokes the amusingly earthy Taggart response, "You use your tongue prettier than a $20 whore."

Immediately, Hedley draws a Beauty and the Beast analogy, deciding if Mongo cannot change things, maybe Hedley can control Bart with the importation of the sexy Lili von Shtupp (Madeline Kahn in her devastating German lisping takeoff on Marlene Dietrich). In film critic Maurice Yacowar's otherwise insightful examination of *Blazing Saddles*, he unexplainably observes that Hedley "is impervious to the charms of Lili von Shtupp."[36] But Korman's character is more than a little taken by the German bombshell. When he goes to propose his plan, he acts and sounds more like a prospective suitor than a political sneak. Even after she nonchalantly tosses the flowers he brought, Hedley is reduced to babbling, "Oh Lili, Lili, Lili, legs [Dietrich was known for her beautiful legs, and Kahn's are bared], Lili, Lili."

Hedley is all hands around her and seems to have forgotten his purpose in coming. Consequently, von Shtupp must ask him about the assignment. And even later when she has invited the sheriff back to her room, Hedley interrupts the seduction, supposedly to monitor her progress—but the real reason is best equated with his request, "Oh, just let me have a little feel."

I draw attention to this lustful Hedley for four reasons. First, even in this broad parody story line, it is necessary to establish that Lili is capable of turning men into Silly Putty. Second, it is important to set the record straight: Hedley is taken with Lili. Third, Korman's scenes with Kahn are among the film's funniest, and merit the deference. Fourth, as with all good jokes, there must be a topper. And when Lili meets her sexual match with Bart, as the viewer knows she must, her lust for the marshal is all the more comic as it apes Hedley's obsession with her.

Blazing Saddles takes aim at most Western clichés, but the sexual sparks between Bart and Lili provide fresh comedy ground for the genre. Normally, the romantic image of the cowboy is caught between the chaste WASP schoolmarm and the sexy saloon girl/prostitute. And, of course, there is the comically perverse innuendo about a cowboy and his horse (see the *Son of Paleface*, 1952, section of Chapter 3 as it applies to Roy Rogers and Trigger). But with Black Bart, Brooks suddenly has a new sexual component to work with—the stereotype of the African American male as superstud. Indeed, it is so ripe for comedy that as soon as Lili gets the marshal alone in the dark, she asks if it is true what they say about his people. There is the sound of a zipper and then Kahn's lisping cartoon-sounding voice, "Oh yes, it's twue! It is twue!"

The film cuts to the next day and the breakfast serving of industrial-strength-sized sausages, with Little's sheriff claiming fifteen is his limit. Although subtlety is hardly a word in Brooks' vocabulary, it effectively further milks the situation. But from a revisionist historical perspective, the director was no doubt actually exercising subtlety with the lights-out scene, given early 1970s restraints on the sexual screen interaction of a biracial couple.

Ironically, in 1994 author William Paul questioned whether the scene ends up "reinvoking older American attitudes towards blacks that they initially seem to be [comically] sending up."[37] Brooks would seem to have spoken to this concern by his everything-is-a-target policy. That is, he goes on to dismantle the black stud image by having Bart return to the jail a physically wasted lover. Paul's concern would be more applicable to Norman Lear's groundbreaking situation comedy of the same period, *All in the Family*, which was television's top-rated show from the 1971–72 season through the 1975–76 period (*Blazing Saddles* was released in 1974).[38]

Attacking racism was the number one issue on Lear's many-sided political agenda. The series' chief character and target is Archie Bunker (brilliantly realized by Carroll O'Connor), an uneducated, prejudiced, outspoken blue collar worker who believes in every ethnic stereotype. O'Connor brings such a mesmerizing flair to the characterization that many viewers, unfortunately, missed the message. "Liberals and intellectuals could cite it as an example of the absurdity of prejudice, while another large segment of the viewing audience could agree with Archie's attitudes and enjoy him as their kind of guy."[39] While such varied interpretations contributed to the show's huge popular success, it also somewhat diffused its war on racism. In contrast, *Blazing Saddles* does *not* have any comparable figure to distract from an issue.

Regardless of *All in the Family*, the upshot of the Lili and Bart dalliance is that Hedley has failed once again. Critic Yacowar's misreading of the attorney general's relationship to the saloon girl no doubt stems from this point in the movie, when a jealous, betrayed-feeling Hedley calls her a "Teutonic Twat." Besides an opportunity to use an amusing phrase, via its mildly taboo slang (and its double *t* comic consonant sound), the insult moves the plot along when Lili tells Hedley he will need an "army" to stop the marshal.

This inspires Korman's character to advertise for the worst "shit-kickers" in the West (including "Methodists"). Brooks responds with the movie's funniest visual scene—the camera slowly tracks the length of the bad man applicant line. Of course, this allows the director an opportunity for his pet comic indulgence—including some Nazi storm troopers, a hilarious anachronism. Other parody heavies include bikers, Ku Klux Klanners, and Mexican bandits. If selected for inclusion in this army, one receives a badge (Hedley is the law), which sets up *Blazing Saddle*'s most amusing footnote to an earlier film. That is, when the Mexican outlaws qualify for the army, their leader accepts, but with the wonderfully predictable crack from *The Treasure of the Sierra Madre* (1948), "We don't need no stinking badges!"

Just the sight of the fliers advertising for this comically evil horde is enough to send Rock Ridge's citizens packing. But Bart delays their flight with the promise of a plan. Being a cowardly racist group, however, they do not initially respond. No, he has to jump-start their attention by telling them they would do it for Randolph Scott. There is silence. The people respect the name as if referring to deity, which fittingly reflects the significance of this actor as icon to the genre. Men stand. Hats are taken off, and an angelic chorus from somewhere on high beautifully sings his name. Bart gets his chance. But before exploring his plan, Brooks' use of Scott merits further attention. Why use Scott? To play devil's advocate, a 1974 reference to John Wayne would probably have generated more name recognition laughter, something that is even more true today. When *Blazing Saddles* appeared, Scott had already been retired thirteen years, having last appeared in Sam Peckinpah's *Ride the High Country* (1962). But in pure parody terms, Scott is the better choice. He is *the* Western hero personified. No less a film theorist than the great André Bazin praised Scott's genre lineage by comparing him to silent film's definitive Western figure, William S. Hart. Though Scott starred in an assortment of film genres since the

1930s, (including a good number of Westerns), he had concentrated on horse operas from the 1940s on.

In the 1950s Scott's career peaked in a series of movies under the Western director auteur Budd Boetticher. The Scott persona was finely honed. Like the literary Virginian, this sharply featured, handsome screen cowboy had a dry sense of humor that complemented a sometimes spare use of words. The signature line of Wister's novel, "When you say that, smile," might very well have been written for Scott. The Boetticher films had been well received by both critics and public, with academics heaping further praise on them in the 1960s, such as in Jim Kitses *Horizons West* (1969).[40]

With all this attention, the movies still often seemed deceptively simple. For instance, in *The Tall T* (1957), Brennan (Scott) hitches a ride on a stage driven by an old friend, which is held up with an accompanying kidnapping. As a child growing up in the 1950s I happily accompanied my Western aficionado dad to all the Boetticher/Scott collaborations, exploring them more deeply only in later graduate school years. That Scott's name should surface in *Blazing Saddles* seemed all the more fitting since such analysis revealed the movies to exist as sophisticated "*parodies* of the morality play . . . to recognize that violence and injustice are less the property of a malignant individual than of the world itself."[41] As critic Andrew Sarris so elegantly put it, Boetticher's Scott work is "elemental but not elementary."[42] Consequently, the apparent spoofing broadness Brooks brings to his work in cases such as this (the seemingly heaven-sent use of Scott's name on the citizens of Rock Ridge), sometimes has a subtlety befitting a genre connoisseur. I am only surprised that Brooks did not find a way to incorporate the Statler Brothers' 1973 song "Whatever Happened to Randolph Scott?" into *Blazing Saddles*.

Marshal Bart's use of Scott gets the town's attention, but they still must execute a plan to defeat Hedley's army of the comically damned. From the layered levels of meaning attached to Scott's name, the scheme itself returns us to cartoonland: a replica of the town is going to be constructed overnight by the citizens and the railroad workers. Besides the comic impossibility upon which this builds laughter, it also reinforces a basic Brooksian satirical point: the American West was made up of morons. Who else would be gullible enough to mistake a false-front town for the real thing!

The modern artist often plays games with his or her audience—suckering the too-accepting "reader" into truths they might not otherwise have recognized, had it not been for some conning storytelling. Thus, when one laughs at this "moron" insight, there is also a sudden realization that if the viewer ever bought into the mythic WASP view of the West, he or she probably qualifies for moron status, too. Such huckster artists also have the "nasty habit of revealing the worm in the American Eden apple; he's mostly got a worm, or a snake, eating away at his own conflicting heart."[43]

That is, it is payback time for these artists. And the worm eating at Brooks, as alluded to earlier, is the unacknowledged racism and violence inherent in the traditional approach to the West. So, despite parody's general avoidance of passing judgment on the follies of mankind, it is something Brooks cannot avoid in *Blazing Saddles*.

Before leaving this element of message in Brooks' film, I am reminded of a passage from the second volume of black novelist Chester Himes' autobiography. One might set it up by saying Brooks' career could be described as a study in comic absurdity of a largely nonpolitical nature. But Himes reminds us, by way of writer Albert Camus, "that racism is absurd, Racism introduces absurdity into the human condition. . . . If one lives in a country where racism is held valid and practical in all ways of life, eventually, no matter whether one is racist or a victim, one comes to feel the absurdity of life."[44] In *Blazing Saddles*, therefore, absurdity comes in many shapes.

Another provocative perspective (though in a return to our spoofing focus) is that in building a replica of Rock Ridge, the townspeople are essentially playing at being parodists themselves. In fact, one assumes some of the sets allegedly put up overnight are merely Rock Ridge sets now revealed by different camera placements to be fake. This all becomes academic when the fight following the outlaws' attack on the fake town breaks through a soundstage wall into a musical comedy production. Aptly, in terms of in-film parodists, Taggart makes the aforementioned statement that he (and by implication, all cast members) are working for Mel Brooks.

With Hedley being thwarted for the last time, the action eventually spills off the Warner Brothers lot. Bart follows the crooked character to Grauman's Chinese Theatre, a location made famous by its cement foot-and handprints of the stars. For a parody film, which by its very nature spoofs a broad assortment of movies (besides its target genre), Grauman's is the perfect setting for a finale. For instance, as milling tourists peruse these tributes to Hollywood royalty, someone mentions film star Hedy Lamarr, whose first name has been mistakenly applied for comic effect to Korman's Hed*ley* Lamarr throughout the picture.

His character, a con artist to the very end, tries to get into the theater at a student rate. (With more than a touch of the comically surreal, *Blazing Saddles* is the main attraction.) As Hedley settles into his seat with some candy, he watches the approach of Sheriff Bart on the screen. Hedley attempts to escape, there is an impromptu shoot-out, and the Western politician buys the farm at the cement square honoring Douglas Fairbanks, Sr. Hedley's comic closing remarks are amazement that anyone with such small feet (Fairbanks) could have done the swashbuckling stunts for which he was famous. (Fittingly, Fairbanks also often brought a touch of parody to his early action adventures, spoofing the Western in *Wild and Woolly*, 1917.)

The film ends with Bart and his sidekick, the Waco Kid, riding off into the sunset . . . almost. They stop, dismount, and hand their horses over to a trainer, only to make their final exit in a stretch limousine. One is reminded of Max Bialystock's (Zero Mostel) line in Brooks' *The Producers* when another pricey automobile appears: "When you've got it, flaunt it!" *Blazing Saddles'* black marshal has not only sideswiped the traditional Western at every turn, he has also outclassed it. And like Brooks, he now leaves Rock Ridge behind not merely because his job is done, but because a true Western town could be b-o-r-i-n-g.

YOUNG FRANKENSTEIN

Before Gene Wilder signed on to be the Waco Kid in *Blazing Saddles*, he was working on a script called *Young Frankenstein*. Brooks and Wilder had been a mutual admiration society since the early 1960s (Wilder appeared on Broadway in *Mother Courage and Her Children* with Anne Bancroft, who would eventually marry Brooks). Wilder played the parody cowboy with the understanding that the refugee from *Your Show of Shows* would direct the monster spoof. But Wilder soon found he had a *Frankenstein* soul mate, and the two were reworking the horror script even before *Blazing Saddles* made it to the big screen. Brooks would explain:

Some things are sacred, and to me horror movies of the 1930s are. When I was a kid in New York, I used to go see them at 9 o'clock in the morning. I stayed through the day, existing on O'Henry [candy] bars until suddenly there was light shining in my face. It was the theatre usher with a woman [Brooks' mother] behind him screaming, "Come home. Come home."[45]

In another interview Brooks comically related how he had Frankenstein nightmares while sleeping on the fire escape during hot, pre-air-conditioning summer nights, invariably scaring everyone this side of Brooklyn when he woke up screaming, "Frankensteiiiiiiiiin!"[46] (In 1975 Wilder, after working with Brooks on *The Producers*, *Blazing Saddles*, and *Young Frankenstein*, called the older man a comedy "teacher."[47])

In completely rewriting the initial *Blazing Saddles* script with Brooks, Wilder observed, "My job was to make him more subtle. His job was to make me more broad. I would say, 'I don't want this to be *Blazing Frankenstein*,' and he'd answer, 'I don't want an art film that only fourteen people see.' "[48] And as any student of the film is aware, it was a comedy marriage made in parody heaven. More restrained than anything Brooks had done before or since, it still has the ability to be inspiringly outrageous, such as when the good doctor and his monster don top hat and tails to perform "Puttin' On The Ritz." *Time* critic Jay Cocks so nicely described it as "some sort of deranged high point in contemporary film comedy."[49] Indeed, another reviewer suggested it was "the funniest conception to appear in a comic film since Chaplin's deadpan dinner of one roasted shoe in *The Gold Rush* [1925]."[50] A future criticism of Wilder's solo work seems applicable to this routine: he "lacks Brooks' bludgeoning energy, which can transform a comic set piece into a tour de force."[51]

The plot catalyst for the "Ritz" number is a medical convention in Bucharest where the young doctor can demonstrate his accomplishment. This high camp vaudeville turn brings to mind the equally zany "Springtime for Hitler" number in *The Producers*. Brooks has a special gift for spoofing the musical routine, regardless of his film's target genre. Thus, it is fitting that *Blazing Saddles'* over-the-top finale finds itself invading a musical comedy soundstage. And as the signature statement goes, so goes the movie. Neither "Springtime for Hitler" nor *The Producers* was fully appreciated on its original release, and the film did little box office. However, "Puttin' on the Ritz" found high praise, and *Young Frankenstein* was a "monster" commercial hit.

Interestingly, Brooks himself has a penchant for often comically expressing himself (to the media and/or whoever happens to be around) in a musical comedy manner. Years later on the talk show circuit, he labelled the tendency his "Frank Sinatra syndrome," and he also aped the celebrated singer in a *High Anxiety* (1977) number. During the production of *Young Frankenstein* it was widely reported that between takes a very "on" Brooks would imitate the "Singing in the Rain" steps of Gene Kelly as well, belting out, "Fellini and Dick Lester are great directors, but are they tops in taps?" I am also forever reminded of that energy level in a wonderful moment from Brooks' uneven spoof, *Robin Hood: Men in Tights* (1993), when the title character (Cary Elwes) suddenly asks an off-camera orchestra for a B-flat and then bursts into song, as if Count Basie and his band were just standing by in the bushes of Sherwood Forest, as they were in the desert of *Blazing Saddles*.

The entertainer gene of a Brooks central character is not, of course, limited to music. One sees basic vaudeville traits in Wilder's *Young Frankenstein* character from the film's beginning. The viewer first sees the grandson of the infamous doctor in an American university classroom before an attentive student audience somewhere in Baltimore (not New York City, as is sometimes stated). He performs a demonstration of man's voluntary and reflexive impulses, which comically involves a knee to the groin of a Mr. Hilltop (the underrated character actor Liam Dunn, the cowardly judge of *Blazing Saddles*). Before this educational low blow, the young doctor introduces him with the slick nightclub-act-like disclaimer, "Mr. Hilltop here, with whom I have never worked or given any prior instruction . . ."

When it was apparent long before its release that Brooks, the consummate showman, had something special with *Young Frankenstein*, he had critics in to see the unique set, as well as to watch him toy with the editing process. Moreover, it never hurts to be a funny lobbyist for your movie. Thus, with tongue firmly in cheek, he bragged to critic Roger Ebert, "We can turn out a monster an hour during peak production."[52]

The movie opened to rave reviews, with possibly the most enthusiastic praise coming from *Time*'s Jay Cocks, who placed Brooks even ahead of comedy contemporary Woody Allen: "His best scenes are madder, funnier, more inspired than anything being done in movies today, including the rather coddled comedy of Woody Allen."[53] Brooks' own take on such a comparison, for *New York Daily News* critic Kathleen Carroll, was succinctly comic:"Woody, he's more cerebral; I'm more visceral, dirtier probably."[54] Carroll also noted Brooks' tendency to express himself in a music-related manner: "After looking at *Young Frankenstein* [she had been invited to an editing session], he was so exuberant that he nearly danced down the stairs and out to the street."[55] (One is reminded of the old Steve Martin routine about extremely pleased people having "happy feet.")

Kudos could take, however, rather roundabout paths. *The New Yorker*'s always provocative and often elitist Pauline Kael, never a Mel Brooks fan, said nice things by way of praising Wilder's performance, as well as using her description of his persona, "a magnetic blur," as the title of her review.[56] And though his comic turn merits high praise, when Kael makes statements such as, "he [Wilder] delivers what Harpo promised," one feels she has jumped the critiquing tracks a bit in trying to honor the film without honoring Brooks.[57] If any further evidence of bias is necessary, there is the post-Wilder portion of the review in which she calls this "crazy comedy" a movie "to go to when your rhythm is slowed down and you're too tired to think."[58] It is as if to say, "Okay, I laughed, but it's a no-brainer."

A much more honest celebration of the film came from *The New York Times*. Again, here was a source where Brooks' batting average had never been too high. The review also starts by singling out Wilder's performance, but with more palatable (and entertaining) praise: "This Dr. Frankenstein is a marvelous addled mixture of young Tom Edison, Winnie-the-Pooh and your average *Playboy* reader with a keen appreciation of beautiful bosoms."[59] Moreover, once past Wilder's character, reviewer Vincent Canby insightfully credits the film with being better because it is "more disciplined": "Mr. Brooks sticks to the subject, recalling the clichés of horror films of the nineteen-thirties as lovingly as someone remembering the small sins of youth."[60]

Since past critics had sometimes taken Brooks to task for being a loose cannon with his shtick, it is ironic that some reviews bemoaned the loss of this trait. For instance, *Newsweek* liked the movie but felt Brooks' "search for such [horror film] authenticity sometimes overly smooths out his normally anarchic, scatter-shot humor."[61] Brooks' relationship with critics might remind one of the catchphrase of Gilda Radner's Roseanne Roseannadanna—"It's always something."

Regardless, *Newsweek* was right about *Young Frankenstein*'s sense of "authenticity." As noted in Chapter 1, Brooks attempted to emulate the mood of the early 1930s horror classics by shooting in black and white and using dated optical devices such as wipes and iris-outs. He even brought back the once-standard 1:33 nearly square frame proportion. He was lucky enough to have access to the original *Frankenstein* (1931) laboratory sets, and when *Young Frankenstein*'s principals first discover that area of the castle, Brooks includes a sound montage of life being created from the earlier movie.

Black and white was an especially controversial call for two reasons. First, the money men behind the scenes wanted color because they felt black and white would hurt the potential sale to television. Second, Brooks' version faced competition from *Andy Warhol's Frankenstein* (1974), a campy in-color blood and gore fest. But Brooks held to his convictions, and the parody is all the more effective for it.

The movie opens, fittingly, at midnight on a dark and stormy night at the Frankenstein castle in Transylvania. The coffin of Victor's (creator of the monster) father (Beafort) is opened, and his boxed will is comically pried from rubbery, bony fingers. Convinced that the family name has been disgraced by the experiments of his son, Beafort leaves the estate to his American great-grandson, Wilder's Frederick. The hope is that the family name's dignity will be restored.

Frederick seems a great choice to return the name of Frankenstein to prominence. Already a noted brain surgeon and academic in America, he has also attempted to distance himself from the acts of his grandfather. This dissociation is comically showcased almost immediately in the film when Wilder's character informs a student that Frankenstein is really pronounced Franken*steen*. But later, Marty Feldman's Igor, Transylvanian servant to the young doctor, puts just the right amount of self-aware ("I am a character in a classic story") sarcasm on this new pronunciation when he observes, "You're putting me on!"

After baiting Frankenstein by asking why Frederick is not pronounced "Freaderick," Feldman's servant is inspired to change from "ee-gar" to "eye-gore" (so comically apt a description of Feldman's bulging eyes). And when Frankenstein attempts to reassert himself by stating this is not what he had been told, Igor continues to comically rule the day by saying, "Well, they were wrong, weren't they?" Brooks' fun with comic names is part of a long tradition of comic monikers in American humor, such as the 90-proof W. C. Fields calling his *Bank Dick* (1940) character Egbert Sousé but with straight-face sobriety, pronouncing it "Su-zay."

As with any Brooks action, however, including his funny use, or misuse, of names, he can push the envelope to extremes. For example, Cloris Leachman's caretaker of the Frankenstein castle (Victor having been her "boyfriend") is Frau Blücher, a name that makes the horses neigh whenever it is mentioned—and it is mentioned a lot. Saying "Blücher" is no doubt

Young Frankentstein (1974) principals Marty Feldman, Cloris Leachman, Gene Wilder, and Teri Garr do some brainstorming.

upsetting to horses everywhere, because the name means glue in German. Yet rare is the audience member who is aware of this. In fact, even Brooks' most insightful critic, Maurice Yacowar, seems oblivious to the fact, as he goes to punning extremes to make sense of it: "her name arouses the eternal neigh-sayers."[62] In classroom screenings, most students laugh simply because it is both a funny-sounding name and because Brooks effectively bludgeons us with so many repetitions (the best of which is Igor's—the only one specifically aimed at bugging the horses).

Funny names notwithstanding, Wilder's character naturally succumbs to the temptation of playing God, just like Grandpa, especially after he discovers Victor's lab book with the laugh-out-loud title, *How I Did It.* Fittingly, later in the film, after having questioned at times what he was doing, young Frankenstein symbolically demonstrates his peace at creating life by comically returning to the traditional pronunciation of the family name. He has come a long way from his opening classroom description of Victor as a "famous cuckoo."

While still wrestling with the ethical dilemma of his heritage, however, the early film finds Frederick spending his first night at the Transylvania family castle in Grandpa's bedroom. He has a nightmare, awakening to his repeated refrain of, "Destiny, destiny, there's no escaping destiny." The plus side to this situation is that he finds his sexy assistant Inga (Teri Garr) next to him, having come to his room when she overheard his ramblings. Inga represents Brooks' homage to all those voluptuous yet vacuous B-horror movie heroines. She is also a counterpoint to Dr. Frankenstein's frigid American fiancée Elizabeth (Madeline Kahn). (Though *Young Frankenstein* is supposed to be contemporary in setting, Elizabeth is a throwback to the repressed sexuality of a Victorian age that replicated the characteristic so well in its frequent genre of choice—horror.)

The awakened doctor and Inga are suddenly aware of strange but enchanting music coming from "behind zee bookcase" in the bedroom. After a delightful bit of slapstick, as they try to figure out the triggering device to get behind the bookcase (the comic high point being Wilder's character trying to use his body as a wedge between the wall and a spinning case), the two find a hidden passageway.

Their adventure leads them to Victor's secret laboratory. They are joined on the way by Igor, whose appearance at this point is one of the movie's comic high points. Frankenstein and Inga are slowly filing past a cabinet row of decomposed heads/skulls labeled "3 years dead," "2 years dead," "6 months dead," and "freshly dead"—the last being that of Igor. This wonderful sight gag surprise is immediately topped by Igor breaking into the punning lyrics: "I ain't got no body [we've just seen his seemingly bodyless head], and nobody cares for me."

Besides the humor, the scene is significant for two reasons. First, it again demonstrates the entertaining self-awareness of Marty Feldman's character. Though other figures occasionally demonstrate the trait, such as Frederick knowing enough about the horror film he is in to look for a bookcase triggering device, it is Igor who constantly toys with the genre's conventions. As with direct address, which Igor also uses more than any other character in the movie, story awareness makes the viewer feel he/she has special insider status with Feldman's figure. For that reason one often identifies strongly with him, his "eye-gore" notwithstanding.

Second, Igor's musical turn is significant because it underlines again the importance of singing and/or dancing in Mel Brooks' best parodies. As a footnote to the phenomenon, this is a key reason why one might argue that classic Brooks characters are superior to the more one-dimensional figures of, say, the Zucker Brothers and Jim Abrahams' *Airplane!* Although the latter film has imaginative spoofing antics, its characters merely deliver lines, whereas Brooks' figures seem more a part of the parody premise itself. Moreover, these characters could be called a throwback to an earlier comedy tradition predicated on a marriage of music to merriment, be it the harp and piano solos of Harpo and Chico Marx, or the song and dance routines of the Hope and Crosby *Road* pictures. This music connection was a personality comedy expectation that lasted from the early sound era, such as Groucho's "Hooray for Captain Spaulding" number in *Animal Crackers* (1930), to the Martin and Lewis duets of the 1950s. It was a time when comedians often had their own theme songs (i.e., Bob Hope's "Thanks for the Memories," or Laurel & Hardy's "Cuckoo Song." "Hooray for Captain Spaulding" later became the signature song of Groucho's solo career.) Brooks' early parody figures seem all the richer for having tapped into that tradition.

After Igor's "I Ain't Got No Body" bit, Frederick discovers Victor's "how to" monster book and spends the rest of the night mesmerized by it, reading aloud from the text while Inga and Igor fight off sleep. The following morning at breakfast the book remains the focus, with Dr. Frankenstein sharing the information that Victor used large body parts to simplify the life-producing procedure.

As the breakfast party ponders this, sexy Inga fittingly observes, "He [the monster] would have an enormous schvantzstucker [sticking tail-penis]." And the thought gives her so much pleasure she makes a "woof" sound. The scene brings to mind Philip Stevick's essay "*Frankenstein* and Comedy," in which he examines unintended humor in Mary Shelley's original novel, as well as its ripeness for parody. Stevick observes that the doctor "has assembled anatomical parts so as to make a creature *eight feet tall*. No thought of the social problems of an eight-foot creature crosses his mind."[63] Although Stevick may be missing out on the possibilities of popularity via a large "schvantzstucker," his article gets to the heart of why the story made such a rich parody target for Brooks. The creature's size increases the comedy quotient of most scenes, be it the "Puttin' on the Ritz" number, or the obligatory off-camera sex scene.

That night Frederick and Igor go to the graveyard to dig up a recently buried criminal. The doctor complains, "What a filthy job." When his assistant tells him it could be worse and Frankenstein asks how, Igor replies, "It could be raining." Naturally, in the world of Brooks, it immediately begins to rain. Though it is a funny set-up by Feldman's character, it is more important as another example of Igor as a casual comedy counterpoint to Frederick's more childish, easily frazzled figure. For instance, earlier in the film Frederick describes a once-hidden area of the castle as "filthy." Igor's wonderful comeback is, "I don't know, a little paint, a few flowers, a couple of throw pillows."

The ultimate example of this contrast occurs later in the film when Frankenstein thinks his attempt to create life has failed. As Inga and Igor attempt to comfort him, he initially seems to be able to handle it: "If science teaches us anything, it teaches us to accept our failures as well as our successes with quiet dignity and grace." But then he totally flips out in the most entertainingly over-the-top manner by inexplicably trying to strangle an organism he thinks to be dead anyway while pitching a verbal temper tantrum of kindergarten proportions. When Igor and Inga finally calm him, Feldman's character turns to the camera and observes (after an ironic eye-rolling reference to the doctor), "Quiet dignity and grace." (Besides being a masterful spoof, *Young Frankenstein* is about the eventual maturation of its title character.)

After the graveyard, Frederick and Igor must get the exhumed body back to the castle. But they lose control of their cart and the coffin slides off, exposing an unusually large arm. Just then a policeman approaches, and though they manage to get their boxed body back onto the cart, the doctor is forced to pretend the arm is his, picking at the cuticles of the dead hand. (Frederick's cape covers his corresponding arm and presumably Igor, who is in charge of maneuvering the dead arm when Frankenstein has to shake hands with the officer and later salute him.)

The verbal interaction between the doctor and the constable is comically contingent upon several punning references to the word *hand*, such as, "If you have everything in hand" (spoken while Frederick is actually holding on to the stiff's hand as if it were his). The scene exemplifies the parody trait (see Chapter 1) that the genre should be amusing even without viewer expertise on the subject under comic attack, but it is most humorous when one is familiar with the spoof source. Thus, even without having seen the original *Frankenstein* (1931) Brooks' send-up of body snatching is funny. But the student of that work knows the doctor has a tendency to use that word frequently, such as when he tells his assistant, "The brain of a dead man, waiting to live again in a body I made! With my own hands . . . my own hands."

Safely back at the lab with the body, it is time for step two—procuring a brain. It is Igor's assignment to steal the noodle of one Dr. H. Delbruck, a gifted philosopher and medical man. And the wording on the brain depository door comically reminds the viewer that for all of the film's Transylvania period look, it is still supposed to be a contemporary setting: "After Five P.M. Slip Brains Through Slot In Door." Now, consistent with the 1931 movie but out of character for Feldman's Igor, he takes an "abnormal" brain (labeled Do Not Use This Brain!) after accidentally scrambling Delbruck's organ when he drops it.

Igor has much in common with actor Dwight Frye's hunchback assistant Fritz in the original film. And "no doubt, Fritz is descended from the imps and demons who accompanied medieval sorcerers, as well as the stock comic assistant of melodrama."[64] Both Fritz and Igor are grotesque variations on a basic popular culture figure, the sidekick. Both are afraid of the monster and electrical storms (so important to the doctor's creation process). Still, there is a key difference between the two. Although Fritz can be endearingly comic at times, he has a dark side, such as taunting the creature with fire, which eventually leads to Fritz's death at the hands of the monster. One Mary Shelley scholar has gone so far as to suggest Fritz "is the part of [Dr.] Frankenstein who must constantly be kept in check but always threatens to break out."[65]

In contrast, as has already been demonstrated, Feldman's Igor mixes such a marvelous self-aware mastery of the genre's conventions with an any-thing-goes musical comedy pastiche that viewers tend to identify with him ... versus the distancing tendency related to Fritz's negative behavior. Moreover, far from being a symbol for the doctor's dark side, Igor (his "ain't got no body" number notwithstanding) is a key figure in the evo-lution of Brooks' young Frankenstein into a mature human being, and even a loving parent.

The difference between Igor and Fritz also speaks to the great irony of *Young Frankenstein*. Though it is Brooks' most affectionately detailed hom-age to a film and/or series of films, the nature of the original material (the tragic fate of both master and monster) makes *Young Frankenstein* ulti-mately his greatest departure from an original source. (One is talking com-edy, after all.) With *Blazing Saddles* or such later works as *Spaceballs* (1987) and *Robin Hood: Men in Tights* (1993), Brooks is dealing with genres (the Western, science fiction/fantasy, and action adventure) in which an upbeat ending is generally a given. Hand in hand with this are central characters who generally triumph. Thus, the happy conclusion that parody strives for is not inconsistent with one's expectations for these genres.

Regardless, Igor does return to the castle with a brain, and while Brooks does not showcase its addition to the body, the picture soon moves to the re-creation of the famous platform in the sky scene, where an electrical storm is used to trigger new life. As comedy critics Bill Adler and Jeffrey Feinman so nicely describe it, "the laboratory becomes an electrical cir-cus."[66] This culminates with Igor throwing a final switch marked The Works. But as noted earlier, the experiment seems to have failed, and a comically distraught Frederick (crying for his "mama") is led away by Igor and Inga.

The film then cuts to a meeting of the local villagers. In the 1931 *Frank-enstein* this group of characters is most often associated with mindless mob mentality. They allow their fear of the unknown and/or the different to cloud their thinking; thus they call for the death of the monster at the film's close. They trap the creature in a mill tower and set fire to the structure, leaving him to a grizzly fate as a giant falling beam pins him to the floor. The fact that the fiery blades of the windmill resemble a burning cross has sometimes even been considered a commentary on the escalating activities of the KKK during this period.

Obviously, in giving the story a parody twist Brooks is going to cut the villagers some comedy slack. Still, to be consistent, as well as building upon the fact that the area has already experienced one member of the Frank-enstein family playing God, the villagers express serious concerns about Frederick's activities. More to the comedy point, however, Brooks uses the scene to introduce Inspector Kemp (Kenneth Mars), the wooden-armed, one-eyed official who wears a monocle over his eye patch.

Once again, the viewer doesn't need prior knowledge of the Frankenstein saga to enjoy the broad humor. But it is all the more entertaining when one recognizes the character as Brooks' take on Police Inspector Krogh, the monocled, wooden-armed official first introduced in *Son of Frankenstein* (1939, played by Lionel Atwill). He lost his arm to the monster as a child, when it was "torn out by the roots." And at the close of the 1939 vehicle the creature rips off the wooden limb—a brief triumph against authority.

The prior knowledge factor is especially pertinent as it applies to Inspector Kemp comedy, because the original model (Krogh) had much about him that was unintentionally funny to begin with, from a uniform that looked like a spoof of German militarism, to a swiveling wooden arm which produced shrill sounds when adjusted. With this as a foundation, Brooks has a field day with Kemp, including a whole routine on the mechanics of lighting a cigar, which involves placing one wooden digit (more hand humor) in the fire to use as a lighter.

Kemp counsels the villagers, when they can understand him through his thick German accent, not to act rashly toward Frankenstein. Comically, at one point, after a collective "What?" from his audience, the inspector is forced momentarily to drop his accent so the villagers can comprehend him. Kemp eventually informs the assembled mob, after an especially forceful bit of guttural Germanic pronunciation throws saliva on them and knocks the monocle from his blind eye, that he will himself visit the castle and see what the young doctor is doing. Character actor Mars again creates a superbly comic German figure, reminiscent of his Nazi playwright in *The Producers* or his German professor in Peter Bogdanovich's screwball comedy *What's Up, Doc?* (1972).

As the meeting of the villagers breaks up, the scene switches to dinner at the castle. But as Igor and Inga eat, the doctor continues to pout over his apparent failed experiment. When Inga observes that he has not touched his food, Wilder's character comically mashes everything on his plate with his hands. He has now touched everything on his plate. The doctor is still very much the child figure.

This is followed by a fantastic verbal shtick by Igor. As previously stated, this figure has come to represent a calming, mature influence on the doctor. Consistent with this mindset, Feldman's figure responds to Frederick's latest childish outburst with a soft-spoken, apparently affectionate memory of how his own dear old dad insightfully handled similar problems. Thus, one is momentarily lulled into a crackerbarrel philosopher-like expectation. (Here comes some collective wisdom born of experience.) Then POW! Igor blindsides the viewer with his rendition of an angry yelling father. "What the hell you doing in the bathroom day and night?! Why don't you get out of there and give someone else a chance?!"

The outburst is drop-dead funny for five reasons. First, and most basic, there is the comic surprise of not getting a helpful hint from Igor's dad. Second is the absurdity factor; this is not remotely connected to anything going on in the story. Third, the absurdity quotient is compounded when one scrambles to rethink just what he/she expected. That is, who has old tried-and-true wisdom to impart on how to handle childish behavior following failure to create life in the Transylvania castle of your choice? Fourth, on further reflection, Igor's comic eruption has a loosely left-field connection to his physical appearance. There is an old wives' tale that masturbation (which is implied in Igor's father's comments) can cause a hump to appear on your back. Fifth, the comedy builds upon the ever-increasing uniqueness of Igor. The viewer is already taken with his insider genre awareness. By also providing him with a broader popular culture cognizance of such peripheral funniness as folktale slants on masturbation, one comically relates to his character all the more. (Feldman's contributions to *Young Frankenstein* have never been fully acknowledged, given the tour de silly performance of Wilder, and the ongoing craziness, both on-screen and behind the screen, of a Brooks production. But he was a major comic talent on British television before his Brooks connection.)

As the post-experiment dinner continues, after Igor's impression of his father, noises from the lab reveal upon investigation that their work was successful; the creature lives. The exuberance is short-lived, however, when Igor spooks the monster by lighting up a cigarette (the original assistant consciously tormented him with fire), and the creature begins to strangle Frederick. Eventually this new life force is subdued with a needle-applied sedative—a solution comically arrived at via a game of charades, since the doctor cannot verbally communicate with Igor and Inga while being choked.

Given the monster's antisocial behavior, Frederick quizzes Igor about the brain his assistant brought him. It is then revealed to Frankenstein that instead of the requested Dr. Delbruck noodle, Igor has brought the brain of one Abby Normal. As alluded to earlier, character consistency has been sacrificed (Igor is too bright to have made this mistake) to both replicate Fritz's earlier error and go for the broad joke of a name drawn from the term *abnormal*. Moreover, the original Brooks/Wilder script would seem to have lessened Igor's mistake by revealing that Delbruck had died of venereal disease (such victims first going crazy), hardly a promising development when considering brain donors.

Regardless, the doctor goes a little crazy himself when this information sinks in, attacking Igor while comically admonishing his assistant that they have put an abnormal brain in what is essentially the body of a giant gorilla. Frankenstein's attempted revenge upon Igor is exactly the response the monster tried earlier—to strangle the focus of his anger. Besides being funny, this is a brilliant development, because it comically suggests the Doppelgänger (literally "mirror image" or "alter ego") theme of the original novel.

This technique, also known as "the Double," finds a character either self-duplicated or divided into two distinct personalities. For our purposes here (focusing on the horror genre), the classic example is Robert Louis Stevenson's 1886 *The Strange Case of Dr. Jekyll and Mr. Hyde*. (Fittingly, modern master of the genre Stephen King feels the foundation for all horror literature is a trilogy that includes this work, Shelley's *Frankenstein*, and Bram Stoker's *Dracula*, 1897.[67]) The Doppelgänger device came into widespread literary use during the nineteenth century, paralleling the golden age of the horror genre. Appropriately, this Zeitgeist (spirit of the times) of "divided self" generated further interest via Freud's period writings and the psychoanalytical criticism that followed.

Obviously, "the Double" can be used to address an author's conscious message and/or explore the many other angles of vision the artist might have unconsciously tapped into. For instance, Shelley's front and center communication is, "Don't play God." And although this message has not gone away, feminist critics in later years have pitched a myriad of provocative slants on Dr. Frankenstein's tragically flawed act of creation. The range encompasses everything from the monster symbolizing the lowly state of women in nineteenth-century society, to the ghastly *horrors* that were childbirth "creation" during the same time period.

The whole analytical "Double" process is given a fascinating further spin when it embraces a parody work such as *Young Frankenstein*. As a spoof artist, Brooks naturally uses elements of the defining work, such as the Doppelgänger effect, as a foundation for his takeoff. And to this he must add a comic slant. Moreover, one now has another author's (Brooks) angle of vision (beyond making people laugh) to explore.

Brooks is on record as having two deeper meanings to impart. The first is merely a comic variation upon what he sees as Mary Shelley's central message that men suffer from "womb envy." That is, "This [male] scientist . . . says, 'All right, so can I [sic] make a baby. I'll put a few rods in his neck and plug him in somewhere and we'll make a life.' That's really it: to create life, like a woman."[68] His second communication deals with the mob versus intelligent people. Brooks feels "the story of Dr. Frankenstein addresses itself to the fear quotient. The monster is just symbolic of his mind, and the mob hates his mind, they hate his imagination."[69] Interestingly enough, just as the 1931 *Frankenstein* played upon period mob mentality (see earlier comments in the chapter), Brooks also saw a mob mind-set affecting society during the period in which *Young Frankenstein* was made. "I think Watergate proves how serious gullibility is. Always mistrusting the intellectual. Any loud-mouth shithead they'll [the mob] buy."[70]

"The Double" device will be explored further later in the chapter as narrative examples in *Young Frankenstein* surface. Returning to the doctor's attempted strangling of Igor, Feldman's character is inadvertently rescued by Inspector Kemp's arrival at the Frankenstein castle. As an envoy of the villagers/mob, he is checking on the doctor's activities.

During a comic game of darts (for instance, Kemp keeps his spare darts stuck in his wooden arm) Frankenstein attempts to assure the inspector he is not following in the tradition of his infamous grandfather. Kemp, who cheats constantly during the dart match (comically underlining the less-than-trustworthy nature of authority figures in this gothic tale), leaves less than convinced. But his exit is the source of an inspired sight gag. During the dart game he constantly ruined the doctor's throws by suddenly raising his voice just as Frankenstein released each projectile. The darts flew every which way, including one that found a cat off camera (with the animal's squawk courtesy of Brooks). But most of the darts broke through windows in the castle. Fittingly, when Kemp returns to his car, two of his tires are flat and resemble pin cushions, punctured with countless darts.

With Kemp's departure, Frankenstein, Igor, and Inga rush back to the laboratory, only to witness the release of the monster by Frau Blücher. Leachman's character treats him like the son she and Frankenstein's grandfather never had. Thus, despite the doctor's warnings about the monster's "rotten brain" and the obligatory noting of Blücher's name (in order to get one more chorus of neighing from the horses), the creature escapes into the night. The doctor is sick over the danger now unleashed upon the countryside.

Fittingly, given Frankenstein's fear, the next scene finds Brooks' take upon what is arguably both the most memorable and controversial scene in the original 1931 film. In the earlier movie Boris Karloff's monster encounters a little girl tossing flowers into a lake to watch them float. At that time, children still represented innocence in the horror genre, and the girl movingly takes his hand and invites him to join in her game, unaffected by his scary appearance. (The scene is also ironic in that the child's father has been too busy to play with her.) The monster follows suit with his own flowers, only to move innocently toward the girl when they are gone. What follows was cut, at Karloff's insistence, upon the original American release of the movie: the creature throws the child into the water and she drowns. Karloff said:

My conception of the scene was that he [the monster] would look up at the little girl in bewilderment, and, in his mind, she would become a flower. Without moving, he would pick her up gently and put her in the water exactly as he had done to the flower—and, to his horror, she would sink. Well, Jimmy [director James Whale] made me pick her up and do THAT [motioning violently] over my head which became a brutal and deliberate act.[71]

For Karloff the "pathos" of the scene was then lost. Ironically, however, what follows this excising suggests something all the more sinister. When the girl is next seen she is a disheveled, inexplicably bloodied corpse being carried by a distraught father. Rape is now easily "read" into the scenario

. . . all from a bit of well-intentioned self-censoring (though now often restored to video copies).

So how does Brooks handle this provocative scene? He uses the same
basic ingredients but relocates the innocent little girl to a well with a single
flower, throwing in individual petals. Again the monster is invited to play.
But when the flower is gone, Brooks begs the question by having the child
say, "Oh dear, what should we throw in now?" With an inspired stroke,
the monster gives the viewer a genre-aware moment of direct address, as
if to say, "Don't tempt me." Though one just does not top such a wonderful in-joke, Brooks squeezes another laugh out of the scene by having
the girl play against type. Instead of her being genre-aware thankful that
the monster did not drop kick her down the well, she rudely orders him
to play on the teeter-totter, yelling, "Sit down!" When he does, his weight
catapults her through the open upstairs window of her room, and she lands
safely in bed moments before her concerned parents check on her.

The next stop for Peter Boyle's monster draws a chapter from a blind
hermit interlude in *The Bride of Frankenstein* (1935). The *Young Frankenstein* variation on this scene involves a brief friendship with another blind
hermit (a surprisingly comic cameo by Gene Hackman). Again, one need
not be a student of the earlier work to enjoy the parody update. On a
broad slapstick level Boyle's encounter with the hermit is laugh-out-loud
funny because this supposedly killer creature is turned into a comic antihero
by a *blind* man. The creature literally runs for his life from the hermit's
cabin after a series of accidents: hot soup is ladled into his lap . . . twice, a
hearty toast (accent on hearty) destroys his beer mug (followed by an entertainingly knowing rolling of the monster's eyes), and an attempt to light
a cigar results in a flaming thumb. (The delayed reaction of Boyle's character to the fire brings to mind Oliver Hardy's similar reaction to a toasted
thumb in *Way Out West*, 1937, Laurel & Hardy being a comedy team
Brooks is especially fond of. See Chapter 2.)

Enjoyment of the scene is further embellished when one knows this is the
setting in which Frankenstein's movie creature first learned how to talk. But
whereas the earlier film found the hermit teaching the monster simple sen-
tences (such as "Wine . . . good") through loving patience, Boyle's character speaks his first word here under radically different circumstances. Again,
it is a product of a comic accident. When the recognition and pain of a
flaming thumb finally sink in, the creature lets out a hilarious "W-O-W!"
and bolts through the cabin door like a cartoon character. Hackman's blind
hermit manages to put a topper to even this when he cries out, "Wait!
Come back! I was going to make expresso!"

By giving the hermit homosexual overtones—"Let me touch you. Let me
feel you. Let me hold you. Let me smell you. . . . You *are* a big one, aren't
you?"—Brooks lends the scene an additional comedy slant that reinforces
a basic horror genre motif, that of suppressed sexuality. Indeed, this subject

and "the Double" connection between Frankenstein and the creature will be expanded upon shortly. Besides the hermit's entertaining innuendo, like a lot of humor, a reality factor is at play, too. Society's perception of isolated individuals often paints them as sexually starved, regardless of their sexual orientation. Moreover, this was given an added timeliness in the late 1990s when director James Whale's homosexuality, and its impact on such works as *Frankenstein* and *Bride of Frankenstein*, became the subject of several books and the poignant darkly comic feature film *Gods and Monsters* (1998), a fictionalized account of the weeks prior to Whale's 1957 suicide. (Mary Shelley's *Frankenstein* refers to "gods and monsters" and the line appears in Whale's *Bride of Frankenstein*.)

It seems only natural that Whale's isolating homosexuality in 1930s Hollywood would have contributed to his sympathetic portrayal of cinema monsters (outsiders). It is hard to deny the winking gay overtones in his work, be it the scene with the hermit, or those involving Dr. Frankenstein's older colleague Dr. Pretorious (both from his *Bride of Frankenstein*). Thus, the suggestions of comic gayness in *Young Frankenstein* have definite Whale roots, representing once again the thoroughness of a Brooks parody. (The year after *Young Frankenstein*, the gay factor became even more provocative in the cult parody classic *The Rocky Horror Picture Show* [1975]—with a tour de force performance by Tim Curry as the bisexual Dr. Frank-N-Furter.)

The sexual suggestion of Brooks' hermit scene can be enjoyed on another level. *The Bride of Frankenstein*, makes the hermit out to be almost a religious figure, from his monkish garb to his loving kindness. Brooks' more realistic twist on the character thus acts as a satire of the original scene. The beauty of this "reading" is that Whale would no doubt have enjoyed it, since he frequently satirizes the church himself in his Frankenstein movies. For instance, more than one critic has found the grave-robbing scene in his first Shelley adaptation, shot under the shadow of a cross, as Whale's own perverse satirization of the crucifixion. More pointedly, in *Bride of Frankenstein* the monster is tied, for a time, in a crosslike configuration.

Horror is a genre in which the frequent suggestion of absolute evil predisposes, of course, the inclusion of good as personified by the church. And although that religious presence is more likely to be of a positive nature (such as the hoary example of a vampire's aversion to a cross held by a believer), the genre also includes its fair share of church negation. This is probably best personified by H. G. Wells' devastatingly effective satirization of the Ten Commandments in *The Island of Dr. Moreau* (1896).

Regardless, Brooks' hermit interlude shares one thing with Whale's scene, as well as the passage in Shelley's book: all end negatively for the monster. But a toasted thumb is a minor setback compared with the frightened reaction to the monster by the hermit's relatives in the novel, or the attack by the hunters in the 1935 film sequal that ends with the accidental burning of the hermit's cabin. As addressed earlier, despite Brooks' mirror (the genre tribute nature of *Young Frankenstein*), the comedy expectations of parody demand a happy progression of events (and conclusion), whereas the straight renditions of *Frankenstein* can offer only melodrama and tragedy.

Though the Brooks/Hackman portrayal of the hermit plays with satire, there is still a sense of the affection that Whale imparted to the monster-hermit *Bride of Frankenstein* scene, before the burning of the cabin. One is reminded of this when a feel good *Bride* moment (a clip of the hermit and the monster) movingly appears at the close of *Gods and Monsters*, commemorating another unusual friendship in the latter film. How does this connect to Brooks' *Young Frankenstein*? Even when the parody master lets elements of satire slip into his work, there is an underlying affection for his spoof target that creates a special bond with the Brooks characters. Thus, that *Bride* close to *Gods and Monsters* had me thinking of Whale *and* Brooks.

After leaving the hermit's cabin in the Brooks film, the monster is soon recaptured by the doctor and his assistants, lured back by the soothing music of a violin. Interestingly enough, the *Young Frankenstein* viewer is first made aware of the instrument's calming influence earlier in the movie but in Frankenstein lore it originally surfaced at the beginning of the hermit segment in *The Bride of Frankenstein*.

Brooks' film next addresses what the original doctor was incapable of doing—showing love and compassion for the creature. This naturally involves some comic bravery, since we are still dealing with a giant "gorilla" who has a "rotten brain." But Frankenstein has himself locked inside a room with the creature, giving explicit orders not to be released regardless of what follows. It is a risk Igor immediately puts in perspective! "Nice knowing you." As expected, the doctor initially begs with comic ardor to be freed when the monster first begins to growl. However, by quickly turning to fatherly praise, his words begin to work wonders both on the creature and himself.

The next scene finds Frankenstein preparing to show off the creature at a medical conference with the aforementioned "Puttin' on the Ritz" number. (Famous for bizarre turns, this Brooks routine is really around the bend.) The segment also obviously borrows from the original *King Kong* (1933), in which that creature, too, is unveiled before a stage audience. And both scenes end with the creatures terrorizing said audiences.

Brooks critic Yacowar sees the segment as an example of Frankenstein still not being sensitive to the monster.[72] The claim is not without justification. For instance, at one point the doctor slips his "son" a cookie reward, as if he were a trained animal. The position is also consistent with the exploitation slant of the model scene from *King Kong*. Still, this perspective seems unduly harsh on Wilder's character.

To better understand this, the "Puttin' on the Ritz" number also owes a left-handed tribute to George Bernard Shaw's *Pygmalion*, where what starts as a bet to transform a Cockney servant into a lady turns into love. Consistent with that, love is also present in Frankenstein's transformation of "zipper neck" to top hat and tails. This position is soon reinforced when Wilder's doctor risks his life by transferring part of his brain to the monster to counterbalance the sometimes violent behavior of his creation. This plot development is no doubt loosely inspired by *The Ghost of Frankenstein* (1942), in which an attempt is made to give the creature a healthy brain. (The production involved neither Whale nor Karloff.)

Prior to this serious *Young Frankenstein* development, however, there are several winsome comedy episodes largely dependent on the reappearance of Frankenstein's fiancée, Elizabeth (Madeline Kahn). The first showcases Feldman's Igor in another wonderful flight of bigger picture comic awareness. Kahn's sexy-looking but frigid tease has just arrived at the castle, and the doctor asks Igor to help with the "bags." Interpreting bags along slang lines, meaning women, Igor replies with a perfect impression of Groucho Marx's sex-driven voice, "Certainly, you take the blonde [Garr's Inga] and I'll take the one in the turban [Elizabeth]." He then starts lustily barking and biting at the animal fur around the latter's neck. Besides the comic surprise his popular culture awareness again gives the viewer, his turn as the dirty old man persona of Groucho is a barometer for several sex-driven scenes that follow.

The pivotal segments (actually one, periodically interrupted by footage of the village mob's hunt for the monster) involve the creature's dalliance with Elizabeth, whom he has kidnapped. He has his way with her . . . seven or eight times. But she is ever so willing. Indeed, once he starts to unzip his fly she begins making woofing sounds. Fittingly, her hair, after the turban is removed, resembles that of Elsa Lanchester's title character in *Bride of Frankenstein*—a thick mass streaked with lightning-like silver.

Of course, in the earlier work Lanchester's figure rejects the monster for whom she was made. So once again Brooks' parody rewrites the saga along comedy's demands for happiness. (In *Bride of Frankenstein* the doctor's new wife is kidnapped but merely to guarantee that he makes a bride for the creature.) The consistency between *Bride* and Brooks' work comes, however, in the suppressed sexuality of Dr. Frankenstein. Brooks has periodically had fun with this whenever the doctor and Elizabeth shared time together. In fact, her last assertion of a "don't touch" policy occurs, ironically, just prior to being abducted by the monster.

Inga is the wild card (the added player) in the *Young Frankenstein* sexual equation. Her eventual pairing off with the doctor allows the monster and Elizabeth to remain a couple. Frankenstein and Inga's comic consummation takes place just prior to Elizabeth's arrival. But throughout the movie, despite her sexy kookiness, she helps move the doctor toward a more natural spontaneous sexuality that matures into love. Undoubtedly, *spontaneous* is the optimum word here, because the monster brings that same natural and/ or animal-like quality (of Inga's) to his relationship with the formerly sexually distant Elizabeth. Thus, Kahn's character grows, too, from a comically frigid, motherlike figure for Frankenstein, to being a partner with the monster. And even the latter fellow finds some added maturity—he has no fear of fire when he lights up the obligatory two cigarettes following their sexual tryst (not to mention his sudden romance genre awareness that lovers always come down with a smoke).

Still, the phenomenon of "the Double" between Frankenstein and his "son" has to be played out one further step. A portion of the doctor's brain is transferred to the monster. But a mob, using Inspector Kemp and his wooden arm as a battering ram, breaks in on the procedure just as it is concluding. The angry villagers start to carry off the still-unconscious doctor. But surprise of surprises, a now verbally articulate creature rescues Frankenstein with a moving speech, concluding with, "I live now because this poor, half-crazed genius held an image of me in his mind as something beautiful."

It is an extraordinary scene for several reasons. First, it is touchingly well written, with its theme of love making a difference and transforming the tragedy of the original story into a legitimate (however expected) happy ending. Second, the comic surprise of a suddenly eloquent monster is, notwithstanding, consistent with the well-spoken manner of Shelley's original creature (though his closing comments hardly spoke of love—"Farewell, Frankenstein! . . . thou didst seek my extinction."[73]). Third, when shaking hands with Kemp, the monster accidentally pulls off the inspector's wooden arm. Thus, the scene technically repeats an incident from *Son of Frankenstein*. But instead of replicating the earlier work's violent hatred (the inspector was trying to kill the creature at the time), Brooks footnotes the event while turning it on its ear: Kemp and the monster are making up.

Consequently, like all art, Brooks' segment works on several levels. And it even closes with a touch of mystery. The doctor is still unconscious, and since the mob interrupted the experiment before it ran its full course, there is a question as to Frankenstein's mental condition. Since this is the land of broad parody, however, one is hardly sweating bullets about the outcome. And not surprisingly, the film next cuts to Frederick and Inga entering their post-wedding castle bedroom. As the doctor waits for her to slip into something sexy, the action briefly moves to our other couple—the monster and Elizabeth. In an ingenious sight gag, both funny and informative, the creature's increased brainpower is showcased by having him reading the *Wall Street Journal* in bed.

Kahn's character can be heard off-camera making with very domestic chatter, which is both comic (such as referring to a special clothes hamper just for his "socks [and] poo-poo undies") and distracts the viewer for the comic surprise of her entrance, where her hair is made up even more to resemble Elsa Lanchester's bride. Elizabeth accents the connection further with the sounds she makes, from that of electricity to Lanchester's throaty hiss. With wonderful genre awareness, the monster gives the viewer a look of resignation and begins a low growl.

The growl is an excellent touch since it represents, from past experience, sex . . . , which Elizabeth obviously is expecting. Yet given the creature's direct address apathy, the sound can also be equated with a moan of indifference. Fittingly, in a last example of "the Double" effect, the growl is used as a sound-cut transition back to Frederick and Inga. But here the doctor's growl is very much sexual in nature as he goes into an animal-like trance. And in a comic topper (pun optional), Inga and the viewer find that the transference process that gave part of the doctor's brain to the monster has also resulted in Frankenstein receiving some of the creature's substantial sex organ. Continuing with 1930s cinema technique, Inga's pleasing discovery (she breaks into a chorus of "Ah, Sweet Mystery of Life," just as Elizabeth did on her first night with the monster) occurs over a metaphorical flaming fireplace visual. (As gifted comic George Carlin once said of a similar scene in another film, "You don't have to be Fellini to know what that means.") And Brooks accomplishes the most difficult of tasks, a horror spoof that somehow manages to remain amazingly close to the original material, yet delivers an outrageously happy ending—hardly a norm for the genre.

NOTES

1. Larry Siegel, "*Playboy* Interview: Mel Brooks," *Playboy*, October 1966, p. 80.

2. Brad Darrach, "*Playboy* Interview: Mel Brooks," *Playboy*, February 1975, p. 48.

3. Ibid., p. 47.

4. Joanne Stang, "And Then He Got Smart," *New York Times*, January 30, 1966, sect. 2, p. 17.

5. Joseph Gelmis, "But Seriously, Folks, *Mel Brooks* Is One of the Brightest People You're Gonna Run Into In Your Life," *Newsday*, January 21, 1971, p. 3A.

6. William Holtzman, *SEESAW: A Dual Biography of Anne Bancroft and Mel Brooks* (Garden City, New York: Doubleday and Company, 1979), p. 3.

7. Darrach, "*Playboy* Interview," p. 49.

8. Philip Fleishman, "Interview with Mel Brooks," *Macleans*, April 17, 1978, p. 8.

9. Darrach, "*Playboy* Interview," p. 61.

10. Herbert Gold, "Funny is Money," *New York Times Magazine*, March 30, 1975, p. 16.

11. Ibid, p. 21.

12. Paul Zimmerman, "The Mad Mad Mel Brooks," *Newsweek*, February 17, 1975, p. 55.

13. Ibid., p. 56.

14. Gold, "Funny is Money," p. 28.

15. Sid Caesar (with Bill Davidson), *Where Have I Been? An Autobiography* (New York: Crown Publishers, 1982), p. 51.

16. Ibid., p. 94.

17. Ibid., p. 92.

18. Graham McCann, *Woody Allen: New Yorker* (1990; reprint, New York: Polity Press, 1992), p. 45.

19. "Mirth of a Nation," *Entertainment Weekly*, October 16, 1992, p. 17.

20. William Paul, *Laughing Screaming: Modern Hollywood Horror and Comedy* (New York: Columbia University Press, 1994, pp. 135–37.

21. Peter Schjeldahl, "How the West Was Won by Mel," *New York Times*, March 17, 1974, section 2, p. 15.

22. Richard Schickel, "Hi-Ho, Mel," *Time*, March 4, 1974, p. 63.

23. Gordon Gow, *Blazing Saddles* review, *Film and Filming*, August 1974, p. 43.

24. John G. Cawelti, *The Six-Gun Mystique* (Bowling Green, OH: Bowling Green University Press, 1971), pp. 34–35.

25. Schjeldahl, "How the West Was Won by Mel," p. 15.

26. Fleishman, "Interview with Mel Brooks," p. 8.

27. Pauline Kael, *Reeling* (New York: Warner Books, 1976), p. 380.

28. Jim Haskins, *Richard Pryor: A Man and His Movies* (New York: Beaufort Books, 1984), p. 64.

29. Richard Schickel, *Clint Eastwood: A Biography* (New York: Alfred A. Knopf, 1996), p. 138.

30. Peter Bogdanovich, *John Ford* (Los Angeles: University of California Press, 1970), p. 86.

31. Schickel, *Clint Eastwood*, p. 180.

32. Robert Warshow, *The Immediate Experience* (1954; repr. New York: Atheneum, 1972), p. 149.

33. Ibid.

34. James Thurber, *The Beast in Me and Other Animals* (1948; reprint, New York: Harcourt Brace Jovanovich, 1973), p. 48.

35. Jim Kitses, *Horizons West* (Bloomington: Indiana University Press, 1970), p. 161.

36. Maurice Yacowar, *Method in Madness: The Comic Art of Mel Brooks* (New York: St. Martin's Press, 1981), p. 104.

37. Paul, *Laughing Screaming*, p. 136.

38. Tim Brooks and Earle Marsh, *The Complete Directory to Prime Time Network TV Shows 1946–Present* (New York: Ballantine Books, 1979), pp. 808–10.

39. Ibid., p. 21.

40. Kitses, *Horizons West*, pp. 88–137.

41. Ibid, p. 96.

42. Andrew Sarris, *The American Cinema: Directors and Directions, 1929–1968* (New York: E. P. Dutton 1968), p. 125.

43. Kathleen Murphy, "Sam Peckinpah: No Bleeding Heart," *Film Comment*, April 1985, p. 75.

44. Chester Himes, *My Life of Absurdity: The Later Years* (New York: Thunder Mouth Press, 1976), p. 1.

45. Bob Thomas, "Mel Brooks 'Salutes' *Young Frankenstein*," *New York Post*, May 28, 1974, p. 22.

46. Darrach, "*Playboy* Interview," p. 52.

47. David Sterritt, "It's a Whole New Career for Gene Wilder," *The Christian Science Monitor*, January 29, 1975, p. 9.

48. Bill Adler and Jeffrey Feinman, *Mel Brooks: The Irreverent Funnyman* (New York: Playboy Press, 1976), p. 124.

49. Jay Cocks, "Monster Mash," *Time*, p. 104.

50. Adler and Feinman, *Mel Brooks*, p. 143.

51. Charles Moritz, ed., "Gene Wilder" entry in *Current Bibliography 1978* (New York: H. W. Wilson Company, 1979), p. 457.

52. Roger Ebert, *Young Frankenstein* review, *Chicago Sun-Times*, June 9, 1974, section 3, p. 2.

53. Cocks, "Monster Mash," p. 104.

54. Kathleen Carroll, "A Funny Thing Happened to Frankenstein," *New York Daily News*, December 8, 1974, Leisure section, p. 9.

55. Ibid.

56. Pauline Kael, "A Magnetic Blur," *The New Yorker*, December 30, 1974, pp. 58–59.

57. Ibid., p. 58.

58. Ibid.

59. Vincent Canby, *Young Frankenstein* review, *New York Times*, December 16, 1974, p. 48.

60. Ibid.

61. "Babbling Brooks," *Newsweek*, December 23, 1974, p. 79.

62. Yacowar, *Method in Madness*, p. 123.

63. Philip Stevick, "*Frankenstein* and Comedy," in *The Endurance of Frankenstein: Essays on Mary Shelley's Novel*, George Levine and U. C. Knoepflmacher, eds., (1979; reprint, Los Angeles: University of California Press, 1982), p. 224.

64. Martin Trapp, *Mary Shelley's Monster* (Boston: Houghton Mifflin, 1976), p. 90.

65. Ibid., p. 91.

66. Adler and Feinman, *Mel Brooks*, p. 135.

67. Stephen King, *Danse Macabre* (1979; reprint, New York: Berkley Publishing, 1982), p. 60.

68. Jacoba Atlas, "New Hollywood: Mel Brooks Interview," *Film Comment*, March–April 1975, p. 57.

69. Ibid.

70. Ibid.

71. Donald F. Glut, *The Frankenstein Legend: A Tribute to Mary Shelley and Boris Karloff* (Metuchen, NJ: Scarecrow Press, 1973), pp. 112–13.

72. Yacowar, *Method in Madness*, p. 127.

73. Mary Shelley, *Frankenstein; Or, The Modern Prometheus* (1818; reprint, New York: New American Library, 1965), p. 211.

5

Two for the Road

In *Hot Shots! Part Deux* (1993) Topper Harley (Charlie Sheen) temporarily leaves a violent world for a life of contemplation with Buddhist monks. As he explains to some visitors, "These men have taken a vow of celibacy, just like their fathers and their fathers before them."

Scream's (1996) Billy Loomis (Skeet Ulrich), sounding a bit like a horror film Forrest Gump, observes, "Life is like a movie. You just can't pick your genre." But as this chapter demonstrates, Billy seems to be one *Scream* character who has done just that.

BACKGROUND

Conjecture about murder motives is a hot topic in *Scream*. The wittiest response suggests that no explanation is necessary, what with an approaching millennium. If a comparable litmus test were applied to the topic at hand (why parody?), even a reference to the calendar would be superfluous. As long as there are popular movies, spoof artists will be out to affectionately deflate them. In this way the 1990s are no different from any other film decade. The only time one becomes parody specific is when addressing what are a particular period's top targets (popular films and/or genres).

This chapter's take on 1990s burlesque centers on two critical and commercial successes, *Hot Shots! Part Deux* and *Scream*. The former spoofs commando movies (among others), especially the Sylvester Stallone vehicles *Rambo: First Blood II* (1985) and *Rambo III* (1988). The Wes Craven–

directed *Scream* takes aim at teenage slasher films of the 1970s and 1980s, including his own *The Last House on the Left* (1972) and *A Nightmare on Elm Street* (1984). *Hot Shots! Part Deux* and *Scream* were also selected because they represent the two poles of parody—the broadside slant à la Mel Brooks (see Chapter 4), and the reaffirmation approach as personified by *Destry Rides Again* (1939) and *Butch Cassidy and the Sundance Kid* (1969; for more on both films see Chapter 2).

Although the Brooks stance is obvious, a quick review of reaffirmation parody is provided by British movie critic Damian Cannon's "reading" of *Scream*: "On one hand it is a spoof of the many terrible horror films that came before. . . . On the other hand he [Craven] seems to be making a serious [horror] movie. . . . [Generally] these two desires mesh success-fully."[1] In examining the parody dichotomy of *Hot Shots! Part Deux* and *Scream*, this chapter follows the basic burlesque characteristics delineated in the opening chapter. This something old is mixed with something new, for this book—critiquing spoofs of commando pictures and slasher films. But while the main lesson to be gleaned from the chapter is that basic parody (in all its diversity) continues to be alive and well in contemporary film, there is a fresh wrinkle or two. For instance, recent burlesques are much more likely to be self-referential, deconstructing the genre even before the critics. As Roger Ebert notes in his review of *Scream*:

Instead of leaving it to the audience to anticipate the horror cliches, the characters talk about them openly. [For example, the film's central figure observes:] "They're all the same [horror movies], some stupid killer stalking some big-breasted girl who can't act who's always running up the stairs when she should be going out the front door. It's insulting."[2]

Granted, self-referential parody did not start in the 1990s. For instance, Brooks's *Blazing Saddles* (1974) has several such moments, such as the scene in which Cleavon Little's black sheriff politics for more time by re-minding his town they would do it for Western legend Randolph Scott (see Chapter 4). And the 1970s dominant stand-up comedian, Steve Martin, had a self-referential act that spoofed the traditional comic routine. Or, as he has explained, "The joke was, 'Look, I'm doing stand-up!' The joke was not what I was doing but that I was doing it . . . a thing to be manipu-lated."[3] What is new about recent parody characters going the deconstruc-tion route is both the greater frequency with which it occurs, and the ambitious nature of these interludes. As this chapter will demonstrate, the genre's self-referential tendencies have moved leagues beyond throwaway references to a pivotal star such as Scott. Parody as "creative criticism," providing insights to the target genre and/or auteur, has never been more true.

One might best close this section by adding that the popularity of self-referential thought in the 1990s has it surfacing outside of parody, too. For example, as I write this (summer 1998) the most popular comedy ticket on Broadway is Yasmina Reza's Tony-winning *ART*. An international critical and commercial success in twenty-five countries (including Paris and London), the story chronicles the impact of a painting upon the friendship of three men. Serge (Victor Garber) has spent a fortune on a minimalist (white on white) work of art; his buddies Marc (Alan Alda) and Yvan (Alfred Molina) do not share his enthusiasm. Alda's character is the most entertainingly offended by what he sees as a waste of money. The amusing arguments that follow explore both deconstructive criticism and the nature of art. *Newsweek* playfully praised the language cross fire as sounding "like Don Rickles with a degree from the Sorbonne."[4] Appropriately, in looking at the 1990s as consciously self-referential, *The New Yorker* based the success of *ART* on the fact that audiences "have been in these [analytical] situations themselves."[5]

Of course, on a broader self-referential "canvas," in terms of audience size, *the* television comedy of 1990s, *Seinfeld*, was nothing if not a study in deconstruction. Thus, the chapter that follows merely documents this increased artistic self-consciousness, among other things, in the world of film parody.

HOT SHOTS! PART DEUX

The film begins with a commando-style secret mission statement being typed out on the screen. Just as this familar action adventure device is nearing completion, our unseen typist twice has difficulty spelling *assassination* and opts for the word *kill*. This represents an introduction to an entirely different "mission" statement, called parody.

The action starts with a commando raid upon the palace of Saddam Hussein (Jerry Haleva). Although this is played straight, the periodic cutaways to the dictator's bedtime routine are done with broad comic strokes. Saddam is a lisping cross-dresser whose fastidiousness has inadvertently put him on erotic terms with a Dustbuster. With this political footnote the movie technically embraces satire. But the dictator is "sketched" in such affectionately cartoon character hues (eventually sounding and looking like Sylvester the cat), satire almost seems too strong a word. It is more fitting to focus on the film's generally nonpolitical parody nature (derailing genre conventions instead of the follies of mankind).

Before exiting the subject of satire, however, one must also note Lloyd Bridge's Tug Benson, president of the United States. Again, it is the most gentle of satirized characters. And unlike Haleva's Saddam, Benson is not a caricature of one particular president, though he combines the forgetfulness of Ronald Reagan with the clumsiness of Gerald Ford. Fittingly, for a film that strongly accents parody over satire, the only Benson scene that replicates presidential reality is decidedly nonpolitical. Like George Bush, Lloyd Bridges' character finds himself upchucking at an Asian state dinner. Thus, as *The Washington Post* critic suggests, it is more instructive to see the Benson figure as "*Hot Shots* films' answer to the [straight parody character played by] Leslie Nielsen in *The Naked Gun* series."[6]

After the botched Middle East mission that opens *Hot Shots! Part Deux*, Benson decides retired commando Topper Harley must lead a rescue mission. His former superior, Colonel Denton Walters (Richard Crenna), and sexy CIA operative Michelle Huddleston (Brenda Bakke) track Topper to a Southeast Asian monastery. Crenna is the film's best early joke, since his character spoofs the straight similar role he had in the *Rambo* pictures.

They find Topper, however, in a nearby village, where he is earning pocket money in a martial arts fight against an opponent who resembles a Bruce Lee villain. The rough, rabid crowd is also reminiscent of the betting mob that follows the Russian roulette competition in the Vietnam War epic *The Deer Hunter* (1978).

The location of Harley's remote hideaway feeds the comic geography of *Part Deux*. That is, the parody is about the Middle East, showcasing everything from a comic Saddam to a POW map location as somewhere "between Iraq and A Hard Place." But the most commercially successful *Rambo* movie was *Part II*, in which Stallone's Vietnam veteran character is a one-man commando army who goes to Cambodia in search of American military men missing in action. *Hot Shots! Part Deux* constantly blurs the Middle East/Southeast Asia distinction, from Harley's remote Buddhist monastery, to the riverboat sequence later in the movie.

The opening of the latter segment is also the film's most inspired segment. Harley is in a boat going upriver, with the viewer hearing his thoughts on the mission in voice-over narration. It reminds one of Sheen's father (Martin) in Francis Ford Coppola's Vietnam War classic *Apocalypse Now* (1979). As the government assassin Captain Willard, Martin takes a patrol boat up another river in search of an enigmatic military man (Marlon Brando), a much-decorated officer whom the army claims has gone mad. This mesmerizing film frequently has Willard commenting on his assignment in voice-over narration.

No sooner has the astute *Part Deux* viewer made the *Apocalypse Now* connection than Willard's actual voice-over starts to compete with Harley's on the sound track. Quickly topping this is the bigger parody payoff appearance of Martin Sheen himself, à la Willard. Going downriver, his patrol boat ultimately meets his son's, with both Sheens shouting in unison as they pass, "Loved you in *Wall Street*!" This final in-joke, a reference to the 1987 movie in which the two co-starred, returns one to parody's scattergun effect, having fun with the most tangential material. Be that as it may, this *Apocalypse Now* footnote to Southeast Asia and the Vietnam War is another example of *Part Deux*'s comic skewering of Middle East geography.

There is one final *Apocalypse Now* link. Shortly before *Part Deux* was released, HBO broadcast a "making of" special titled *Hearts of "Hot Shots! Part Deux": A Filmmaker's Apology*. This is a knowing spoof of the acclaimed 1991 documentary *Hearts of Darkness: A Filmmaker's Apocalypse*. The latter film chronicles the difficult, tumultuous *Apocalypse Now* production through the eyes of the director's wife, Eleanor Coppola. So much went wrong during the making of Francis Ford Coppola's picture, from bad weather and Martin Sheen's heart attack, to an unprepared Brando and substance abuse by cast and crew, that *Hearts of Darkness* plays like a dark comedy. And it is precisely that edge that *Hearts of Hot Shots! Part Deux* manages to project in its parody. Thus, it details the ostensibly troubled production of *Part Deux* through the eyes of director Jim Abraham's daughter. Once again, what is essentially a Middle East spoof has a Vietnam connection.

Harley doesn't immediately commit to a rescue mission. Earlier, when Colonel Walters and Michelle visited the reluctant warrior at the monastery, after his pocket money fight, he turned down their patriotic pitch. And as befits a spoof film, both figures were excellent at derailing action adventure clichés. For instance, Crenna's Walters attempts to bring Sheen's Topper Harley aboard by playing the stereotypical paternalistic military commander. Thus, his recruiting line begins with, "Topper, let me tell you a little story." The fun starts when the tale being told is "Goldilocks and the Three Bears."

Sexy Michelle might be called the comic summary girl. Explaining to Topper that two missions to rescue American servicemen have failed, she manages the following overview with poker-faced aplomb: "Now we have to go in to get the men who went in to get the men who went in to get the men." After this tongue-twisting chronicle of failure, her response to Harley's question of "why me" is all the more comic: "Because you're the best of what's left."

Michelle is also used in a sequence of decentralized monastery comedy. The camera placement early in the colonel's dialogue with Topper has Crenna's character in the right foreground, while Michelle occupies the left background. As if preparing a treatise on parody and deep-focus cinematography, this compound scene is also a working definition of saturation comedy. That is, Crenna does a send-up of his *Rambo* character in the foreground, while Michelle has a series of horny monks showing off for her in the background. The comically incongruous monastery material includes two monks going through their bodybuilding programs, one directing a tutu-attired dancing dog, and another displaying his tops-in-tap routine. In a fitting close to this Buddhist talent show (especially for a group sworn to silence), several signs appear when the colonel and Michelle leave, with the largest proclaiming, Come Back Anytime, Michelle.

Crenna's character has not convinced Harley to join the mission, but he has made Sheen's figure think about why he is hiding in a monastery. Immediately after the colonel and Michelle exit, Topper sends the movie into a flashback—the romantic last dinner with the lover who then mysteriously left him, Ramada Hayman (Valeria Golino). This plays upon a similar sense of loss by Humphrey Bogart's Rick in *Casablanca* (1942), after Ingrid Bergman's character has suddenly left him. The *Part Deux/Casablanca* romantic link is fleshed out further as the parody continues.

Topper and Ramada are dining in an Italian restaurant, with the men at a neighboring table aping the cafe configuration where Michael Corleone assassinates a crooked cop and a rival mobster in *The Godfather* (1972). The gooey romanticism of Topper and Ramada is spoofed by having them recreate two scenes from the Disney animated feature about dogs in love, *Lady and the Tramp* (1955). First, the human couple find themselves nibbling on opposite ends of the same piece of spaghetti . . . with the telegraphed kiss. Then Harley, à la the mongrel stray Tramp, uses his nose to roll a meatball across their shared plate to Ramada.

As comedy theorist Henri Bergson suggested years ago, one's perception of comic animals is linked to their apparent replication of human activity. But *Part Deux*'s reversal does two things. It literally embraces the humorous stereotype of lovers acting less like thinking humans and more like gratification-seeking animals. Secondly, by having Sheen's character use a dog as a role model, it further burlesques the already less-than-bright image of the action adventure hero, especially as personified by Stallone's Rambo.

This leading man *stupid factor* goes perfectly with a character who, shortly after the meatball-rolling segment, tells his lover, "Don't worry, in a couple days we'll be on the train to Hawaii." The flashback then closes with a tour de silly; Ramada requests that Topper "kiss me like you've never kissed me before." His response is to bite her nose before giving it a smooch.

Part Deux's next scene opens two weeks later, at an Iraqi prison camp. Colonel Walters is being tortured with electric shock so strong the lights in Time Square are flickering. Like most American prisoners in earlier war films, Crenna's character can take it. But parody digs deeper to provide a reason for this toughness—Walters has been married . . . twice. Ultimately, he is forced to make a pro-Iraqi tape, but even here comic resistance surfaces. While he mouths his captor's words, his hands are busy negating this party line, such as when he mimics masturbating. These actions work on two levels. They continue the tough guy American hero stereotype, but in a breezy, obscene manner not available to earlier censorship-susceptible movies. The latter point strikes at the heart of parody: give the viewer a well-worn genre scene, and then do something surprising.

Luckily, Topper sees the tape and immediately shows up at the aforementioned state dinner, where President Benson has his sushi-puking incident. Sheen's character feels responsible for Walters' capture and wants to volunteer for the rescue mision. After a short session with Benson, Topper is *debriefed*, in a strictly sexual manner, by the leader of the forthcoming rescue operation, sexy Michelle Huddleston.

What follows are two comic sex scenes that spoof carnal segments from three films: *9½ Weeks* (1986), *No Way Out* (1987), and *Basic Instinct* (1992). The catalyst for this humorous study in eroticism is Michelle's reprise of Sharon Stone's infamous leg-crossing (sans underwear) scene in *Basic Instinct*. Protecting its PG-13 rating, *Part Deux*'s camera placement does not reveal all, but Brenda Bakke's sensualness makes the segment both funny and sexy. Plus, there are amusing lines, such as: "Now I know what to get you [underwear] for Christmas," not to mention the cartoon zaniness of having steam come out Topper's collar. And all this transpires before the two have even left the state dinner.

The limousine ride to her apartment is the perfect opportunity for a burlesque of Kevin Costner's libidinous limo outing with Sean Young in *No Way Out* (Costner and Young are also coming from a la-de-da state function). Though *Part Deux*'s mobile make-out is funny (driven by the sound track beat of the Pointer Sisters' orgasmic "I'm So Excited"), comedy kudos go to the inquisitive driver (Tony Edwards). His fascination with this backseat mating ritual begins simply with a desire to get a better view and culminates in his videotaping the event . . . as the limousine rolls merrily along.

This comedy riff by the driver also has roots in *No Way Out*. The man at the wheel (Gordon Needham) while Costner and Young get it on is equally taken with their activity. But whereas Costner's request for the privacy panel separating the front and back of the limo ends the voyeurism fun of the *No Way Out* chauffeur, raising the divider in *Part Deux* is merely an invitation for more comedy. For instance, the Sheen/Bakke driver is next seen taking pictures of the couple as he runs alongside the car.

As the athletic exuberance of the sex escalates at Michelle's, the parody model becomes the oh-so-steamy workout between Mickey Rourke and Kim Basinger in *9 ½ Weeks*. Michelle is riding Topper so hard the bed's headboard is squeaking. Consequently, she suddenly reaches under the sheet and pulls out a knife-like object, which she brings down in a half arc, as if to stab Sheen's character. But it turns out she is wielding a screwdriver, which she uses to "kill"/"screw" the headboard squeak. Obviously, Michelle's actions are meant to mirror Stone's ice pick dispatch of lovers in *Basic Instinct*. But it is a witty take on acknowledging an example of disturbingly sexy screen violence. This portion of the carnal spoof comes to an inventive full-circle conclusion when the limo driver turns up at Michelle's bedroom window for more erotic peeking.

The morning after these provocative escapades, a troubled Topper has another flashback—being stood up by Ramada at the train depot. It is a timely development, since Michelle has just expressed her devotion to him and he is doing an inventory of his romantic emotions. The movie cues for these two women are decidedly different. Ramada is the virginal girl on a pedestal whose memory is filtered through a Disney children's picture—*Lady and the Tramp*. Michelle is an R-rating, with designs on NC-17.

Besides a contrast that is a boon for burlesquing different types of romantic film, the Michelle target models, particularly *No Way Out* and *Basic Instinct*, hint at a dark side to her character. In the former movie Sean Young is torn between love and a sugar daddy who takes care of life's monetary problems. *Basic Instinct*'s Sharon Stone is to die for . . . literally. Her figure is a sexual predator, eventually killing her lovers. Until this point in *Part Deux*, Michelle has done nothing to arouse suspicion, besides be sexually easy, which goes against America's Goody-Two-Shoes stereotype for a heroine. But when it later turns out that Michelle is a double agent working for the enemy, one must credit this broad parody with an unlikely characteristic—subtle foreshadowing.

Topper is soon on a plane heading for the rescue mission. The best airborne spoof material comes courtesy of fellow commando Rabinowitz (Ryan Stiles), the demolition expert. He launches into a takeoff on a monologue one expects early in a war movie:

You know what I'm going to do if we make it? I'm going to go back to Eagle River and marry my gal, Edith Mae. I'm going to get us a nice little place with a white picket fence. You know the kind—two-car garage, maybe a fishing boat. And in fifteen years when they're all paid for, I'll set my charges and blow the shit out of them.

In a straight action picture, this sort of spiel helps establish what the good guys are fighting for, as well as frequently targeting its speaker as someone who will pay the ultimate price. Although Rabinowitz avoids the latter, his flawless delivery and inflections are an effective takedown of all such patriotic drivel. Moreover, the latter unhinged part of his comments knowingly targets a basic flaw in many traditional war films—the apparent ease with which good guys can compartmentalize violent activity and suffer no long-term psychological damage.

Besides this comically ambitious insight, the airborne portion of *Part Deux* offers several quick throwaway parody moments, from an intimidating commando knife having a soda-pop straw component, to a bailing out scene, which (after several paratroopers have yelled, "Geronimo"), includes the real thing in full Native American regalia singing out, "Me" as he jumps.

The unit's contact/guide on the ground turns out to be Topper's former lover, Ramada. His reflections on their last meeting (what she wore, the weather . . .) parallel Bogart's first *Casablanca* comments to Bergman after her mysterious disappearance. Of course, for the sake of spoofing, Topper sillies it up with the addition, "I wore chiffon."

Soon the commando group is heading upriver. When a radio transmission alerts them to a nearby enemy patrol boat, the film burlesques the elaborate coded messages that surface in war movies. One such cipher statement warns, "The vultures are circling the carcass." But the rescue unit's radio man Williams (Michael Colyar) is clueless: "I see a couple gulls?"

Sheen's character has his own distractions. Like a little kid, he accidentally causes a leak in the boat while playing with his giant, all-purpose knife. He comically but effectively covers the hole with his boot when Ramada comes on deck. Her attempt at conversation triggers another *Casablanca* connection. Topper's complaint about her resurfacing is a paraphrase of Bogart's famous grievance, "Of all the gin joints in the world." Consequently, Topper dissents, "Of all the missions, in all the jungles, in all the world, you had to come walking into this one."

Director and co-scripter Abrahams comically livens up the proceedings by having the love interest present. In *Casablanca*, Bogart's Rick complains about the reappearance of Bergman's figure in a soliloquy. *Part Deux* has a peeved Topper telling Ramada face-to-face. This allows her to get amusingly self-referential: "But it's a sequel; I had to come." And the movie is off and running on a deconstructive tit for tat. For example, Topper as film reviewer observes, "Do you have any idea what the critics will say [about your reappearance]? Same warmed over character." Thus, the viewer is entertained by having a central character upset by the resurfacing of a former lover for both emotional reasons, as in a classic earlier film, and *aesthetic* motives—funny stuff, indeed.

Eventually Ramada steers us back to *Casablanca*. Like Bergman's Ilsa, she tells Topper that when they had their affair, she thought her husband was dead. But when Ramada was informed otherwise, she had no choice but to leave her lover for the responsibilities of the marriage. An incredulous Topper is reduced to a stupefying, "You're joking?" Abrahams has effectively lulled the audience into the melodramatic mindset of a person torn by a dual love when the parody buzzer goes off and he has Ramada spoofingly floor us with the literal response to Topper's comment: "If I was joking I would say, 'A horse walks into a bar.' The bartender says, 'Why the long face?' "

The Topper/Ramada dialogue is interrupted by the enemy patrol boat. In the comic firefight that follows, Sheen's character plays the stereotypical war hero by sending his unit ashore to safety while he lays down a withering barrage of protective cover. So many bullets are expended that the shell casings at his feet form a midget island in the river. As parody luck would have it, a final explosion sends him flying toward shore and a cartoon-style rendezvous with his unit—landing headfirst at their feet like an arrow.

Recovering quickly from his head trauma (Topper briefly thinks he is a Stateside radio D. J.), the commando unit soon approaches the prison compound. Again, Ramada shares information with ties to *Casablanca*: her husband, Dexter Hayman (Rowan Atkinson, now famous as "Mr. Bean") is being held at the camp. Like Rick, the future safety of his lover's husband is in Topper's hands.

At first Sheen's character cannot believe it and finds himself asking again if she is "joking." This is a perfect set-up for Ramada to repeat a variation on her comic earlier literal answer. "If I was joking I would say, 'A rabbi, a priest, and a minister walk into a bar." With the exasperation of an Oliver Hardy, Topper accepts her claim. Like Laurel & Hardy, Topper and Ramada seem a perfect mental match, qualifying for the former team's comic definition—"Two minds without a single thought."

As a final *Casablanca* connection, Rowan Atkinson's character is a celebrated underground fighter, as was Ilsa's husband, Victor Laszlo (Paul Henreid; see the Woody Allen portion of the previous chapter). For a full parody treatment, however, Atkinson's Dexter also won the Nobel Prize for inventing something beyond worthless—the artificial appendix.

Ready to infiltrate the camp, Topper goes ahead to cut a hole in the gate. Again turning to his handy commando knife, with just the appropriate wire-slicing attachment, he prepares an opening for the unit. But before anyone can use it, the gate collapses, as if by its own volition. Normally, this gag would score as a modest laugh and/or smile. But Sheen the actor almost breaks from his stoical/stupid character with a near wisp of a grin. In that split second one better appreciates the parody discipline under which the genre's deadpan actors labor.

I was reminded of the outtakes that ran during the final credits of the satire *Being There* (1979), in which one sees numerous takes of Peter Sellers laughingly unable to maintain his simpleminded character Chauncey Gardiner. Those exit images made the viewer better appreciate Seller's performance. Although I am not suggesting Sheen's *Part Deux* role be equated with Seller's last great part, sometimes cracks in the mask elevate the comic significance of what has transpired, be it parody or another genre.

Inside the compound the enemy soldiers are dispatched with cartoonlike violence. Wanting to keep their infiltration secret as long as possible, the weapons of choice are relatively silent, such as a bazooka-sized gun that extends a boxing glove for the surprising knockout. Topper uses a bow and arrow, and when he runs out of arrows, he substitutes a *chicken* as a lethal projectile.

Tied to this quiet penetration is a takeoff on the ultimate invisible warrior—the Western's Native American. That is, various commando members communciate via animal sounds, which comically range from a horse to monkeys. During this action there is a brief cutaway to Lloyd Bridge's

President Benson and another commando unit. They, too, have come part way by boat. But we pick up their involvement in the operation (an eventual attack on Hussein's quarters) just as they are proceeding underwater in full scuba gear.

This legitimate aquatic commando slant (Charlie Sheen's 1990 *Navy SEALS* was just such a vehicle, about Middle Eastern terrorists) takes an amusing in-joke turn when the underwater sequence features connections to Bridge's popular television series *Sea Hunt* (1958–62). This action adventure program starred Bridges as a diver forever advancing the story in voice-over narration. The *Part Deux* footage of President Benson as a diver features both *Sea Hunt*'s patented suspense music and Bridge's standard voice-over.

Returning to *Part Deux*'s main action, the rescue of Crenna's Colonel Denton, Topper soon finds his former commander's cell. What follows is a diverting spoof of innumerable movie escape scenes where an out-of-the-way ring of keys must be speared. Using a broom handle, Sheen's character must snag the keys from under the nose of a sleeping guard. Everything goes comically wrong.

Topper manages to poke the slumbering soldier in both an eye and ear before sending the handle end up his nose. Things get only funnier as he next hits a radio dial that serves up a wonderfully unlikely instrumental rendition of "Dixie." (It it the best radio gag since Harpo mistook a radio for a safe and "dialed" himself some unwanted music in *Duck Soup*, 1933.) Eventually Topper bags the keys and tosses them to the colonel. But despite Sheen's buff body (a left-handed homage to Stallone), the throw is short, and Denton all but leaves his cell as he stretches to retrieve the keys—thus undercutting the need for them in the first place.

As the commandos free additional prisoners, they encounter increased enemy resistance. In the midst of this firestorm, unit tough guy, Harbinger (Miguel Ferrer) suffers a breakdown and Topper must talk his rescue mate through this shellshock. Using comically inappropriate nicknames, such as "you big bad G. I. Joe" and "Rainy Face," Topper manages to return Harbinger to his earlier "proud warrior" status in record time. Once again the film satirizes the war film's ability to compartmentalize killing and have the soldier suffer no psychological problems. Or, as Harbinger thanks Topper, "I can kill again. You've given me a reason to live." One might label this the Sergeant York factor, after the 1941 film of the same name, in which a former conscientious objector becomes America's most decorated World War I soldier.

This hooray for homicide spirit is an ideal set-up for spoofing the undefeatable hero shoot-out that follows. With a body count meter periodically appearing in the left-hand corner of the screen, Topper mows down an astronomical number of enemy soldiers—complete with the sound a pinball machine makes as it racks up points. Eventually the meter number causes Equal to *Robo Cop* to appear on the screen. This is soon followed by Equal to *Total Recall* and finally, Bloodiest Movie Ever.

The body count meter is an imaginative takeoff on any film bloodfest, especially the *Rambo* series inspiration for *Part Deux*, or the Arnold Schwarzenegger movies specifically noted above. It also brings to mind the spaghetti Westerns (see Chapter 4) that launched the first modern movie star of body count epics, Clint Eastwood. The latter films had teenage boys of the period keeping their own body count tallies as the Westerns were re-released in double and triple bills at the end of the 1960s.

On a darker satirical level, *Part Deux*'s meter also conjures up the body count numbers the national network news programs broadcast nightly as they reported on the Vietnam War in the late 1960s. The young male spaghetti Western fans with the macabre body counting habits were quite possibly borrowing from reality. Thus, even when the broadest of parodies, such as *Part Deux*, burlesques movie battles, a degree of real-world satire slips in.

As the meter mayhem closes down, Ramada takes a bullet intended for Topper. But instead of comically dying, to tweak the Western cliché of the hero's ethnic girlfriend giving her life for him (see Chapter 2), Ramada survives thanks to another cliché: the bullet is deflected by her locket, which contains pictures of her and Topper. Besides parodying stereotypical action adventure expectations, the reintroduction of the love theme is timely, since Sheen's character is just about to rescue the prisoner—Ramada's husband—Dexter Hayman.

Before Topper separates from the unit he lobs a verbal spoof at macho heroes' knee-jerk, self-sacrificing nature. He tells the now-free colonel, "If I'm not there [at the airfield where the group will be flown out] in fifteen minutes, you know what to do." Crenna's character responds with what is normally left unsaid—that they will leave the hero behind. But Topper comically derails that battle film cliché by requesting that the men wait an additional fifteen minutes.

Dexter is being held at Saddam's presidential compound. This allows for a comic confrontation between Topper and the dictator. Their weapons of choice are swords, though the American soon has to make do with a cordless phone antenna. Predictably, the dual is interrupted when Topper takes a call from Saddam's wife . . . Hillary Rodham Hussein (Ramada and Michelle also have Rodham for a middle name).

Showing a sporting nature, Sheen's character covers for the dictator, who does not want to take the call. When the fight resumes, Topper is soon in a dicey situation. But out of nowhere, President Benson appears to engage Saddam, allowing Topper to search for Dexter. The leaders' fight also takes on swashbuckling proportions, including a light saber duel à la the *Star Wars* trilogy.

Although having kingpins go one-on-one is played for broad parody laughs, it, too, touches on a familiar strand in previous war stories. For instance, Erich Remarque's classic antiwar novel *All Quiet on the Western Front* (1928) has soldiers wishing the leaders were the ones to fight, and the Oscar-showered *Patton* (1970) had the title character musing that World War II should be decided by a tank duel between himself and Germany's celebrated Field Marshal Rommel, "the Desert Fox."

Benson ultimately wins the fight by freezing Saddam with a fire repellent that renders the dictator as brittle as glass. Naturally, this invites the cinematically visual scene of his shattering. And by placing this in close proximity to a rip-roaring fireplace blaze, Saddam particles can melt into droplets that resemble the liquid mercury puddles linked to the "morphing" special effect in *Terminator 2* (1991). In this film Schwarzenegger's character has to do ongoing battle with a robot warrior from the future which, even when reduced to liquid metal, can recreate itself.

The *Part Deux* comedy slant in spoofing this phenomenon is that the Saddam puddle also contains elements of his pet pooch, which had been inadvertently frozen and shattered, too. Consequently, it brings to mind the campy sci-fi property *The Fly* (1958, remade 1986), in which a teleportation machine mixes the atomic makeup of its inventor and first passenger with an uninvited guest—a fly. The *Part Deux* result is that Saddam lives again as a cute dog-man, though still with an attitude.

The film's closing moments also feature a fight between Ramada and Michelle, as the former comes to realize Michelle is working for the enemy. Topper rescues Dexter, but the former prisoner is such a whiny sort that no one minds when he later accidentally falls to his death, allowing Ramada and Topper to be a couple again.

Before Dexter's surprise exit, there is one final *Casablanca* reference. Sheen's character does a variation on Bogart's Rick putting Ilsa on the plane, though it is more effectively integrated at the close of *Play It Again, Sam* (see Chapter 3). Topper's last contact with Michelle, before she is taken away in handcuffs, is also reminiscent of another Bogart film—*The Maltese Falcon* (1941). Michelle asks Topper to help get her off for "old times' sake." The line and situation is straight out of *The Godfather* (1972), in which Abe Vigoda's character begs for his life. *But* the Topper/Michelle sexual encounters have a film noir tone to them, similar to *Basic Instinct* and *No Way Out*. And when she asks Sheen's character for help, the noir fan is going to think of *The Maltese Falcon*'s duplicitous siren, Mary Astor, as she asks Bogart's Sam Spade for assistance, with the authorities ready to incarcerate her.

The film ends with the good guys flying to safety, but not before dropping a piano on the dictator and a cinema demise patterned on the first witch to die in *The Wizard of Oz* (1939), she of the curdled-up toes under

Dorothy's house. However, the spoofing continues through the final credits, including a listing for the "Secret of *The Crying Game*"!

Part Deux prompted film reviewer Ebert to observe, "Movies like this are more or less impervious to the depredations of movie critics. Either you laugh, or you don't. I laughed."[7] Most reviewers took Ebert's lead and laughed as well. *The* industry organ, *Variety*, gave it the highest praise: "If the first mission made roughly $50 million domestically, the sky could be the limit for this much better sequel—a clever spoof . . . [which] boasts a higher shooting percentage than its forebear."[8]

Sometimes the *Part Deux* review itself was funny, as if the movie's inspired silliness gave the critic license to join the world of cutups. One such example was Janet Maslin's *New York Times* critique, with the affectionate fun shining through even in the review's title—"From 'Rambo' to Rodham, Smirking All the Way."[9]

People called it "slick, hip and funny" and then praised the picture for occasionally challenging the viewer: "Abrahams and cowriter Pat Proft show more respect for the audience than most modern filmmakers do, assuming that moviegoers will get even subtle jokes . . . [such as] a gag involving Tojo, World War II prime minister of Japan."[10]

Coming full circle back to Ebert, this critic had the best take on the film, or any inventive parody. "One of the pleasures of watching a spoof like this is to spot the references; it's like a quiz on pop art."[11]

SCREAM

Although *Hot Shots! Part Deux* garnered solid reviews for assuming the standard parody take—the affectionately broad, over-the-top yet never controversial dissing of a focus genre and related topics—*Scream* received even better critiques by pushing the burlesque envelope.

In spoof film literature, nothing brings reviewers out like a provocative parody of reaffirmation. Though *Part Deux* reviews were uniformly good, many publications chose not to examine this traditional burlesque. One assumes they saw the picture as merely entertainingly diverting mind candy (see Chapter 1's look at parody's lack of respect). But seemingly every practicing critic in the Western world had a slant on reaffirmation's *Scream*, and the majority penned kudos. For instance, *Rolling Stone* called it "a delicious blend of fun and fright" and likened the opening murder of Drew Barrymore's character to "a tour de force that rivals Janet Leigh's [death] in *Psycho*."[12]

Variety described the film as both "sophisticated parody" and "an interesting stab at altering the shape of horror"—high praise, indeed.[13] Several magazines, including the tony British publication *Sight and Sound*, credited *Scream* with going "beyond parody into post-modernism."[14] Put less obtusely, the film explores contemporary horror by blurring the difference between art and reality.

Not even the incongruity of a Christmas release could dull the critical praise—"an amusingly twisted contrast to whatever sugary sentiments affect the yuletide," said the *San Francisco Chronicle*'s Peter Stack.[15] This review also praised the movie's intellectual aspirations; Kevin Williamson's script "turns the [parody] jabs at horror formula into wicked fun with flickers of intelligence."

As a working critic, I was most taken with *Scream*'s sorties into black humor. A book I had written on the genre (*American Dark Comedy: Beyond Satire*, Greenwood Press) was published just prior to the movie's release, and used Norwegian artist Edvard Munch's lithograph *The Shriek* (1896) as the volume's frontispiece. In *Scream* the murders are committed by a person wearing a mask portraying the central character in Munch's lithograph.

The Shriek, like a similar Munch lithograph called *The Cry*, or *The Scream* (1895, depending upon the translation), depicts an individual on a nighttime bridge whose caricaturelike face is caught in a terrible shriek. The hollow cheeks and staring eyes remind one of death's skull. (In the *Scream* story line the Munch-like mask and a black-robed Halloween costume are sold in stores as "Father Death.")

Expressionistic lithographs such as these sometimes illustrated early dark comedy literary works, especially the writings of Franz Kafka, a contemporary of Munch. Along those lines *The Shriek* can be interpreted as a visualization of the writer's metaphor for life as an ongoing "trial" ended only by death.

In dark comedy films the Munch connection sometimes moves beyond metaphor. For instance, in Martin Scorsese's *After Hours* (1985), Griffin Dunne's central character, Paul, meets a beautiful stranger whose roommate creates lifesize plaster-of-Paris versions of tormented, *Shriek*-like men. Although this is not the most reassuring artistic slant for your date's friend to take, it is important to the story. As Paul's evening from hell progresses, he becomes more and more like a Munch man. Eventually, his life depends upon literally becoming a Munch-like art object. Another sculptress conceals him from his now legion of enemies by plastering him into a figure like the plaster-of-Paris *Shriek* men. The implication here is that even in safety, life freezes you into something you are not.

Regardless, examples such as these document the ongoing link between Munch and dark comedy. What makes the *Shriek*-like mask in *Scream* innovative along black humor lines is that this face, formerly symbolic of victimization, is now doing the victimizing. Thus, the genre of shock effect (dark comedy) just became more shocking. And of course, the title *Scream* seems to underline this Munch tie, since it is the name sometimes given the 1895 lithograph.

Most *Scream* reviewers missed the Munch connection and its significance, though there were occasional asides. *The New York Times*' Janet Maslin entertainingly opined, "Among the droller touches . . . are the killer's mask, which is Edvard Munch by way of a trick-or-treat costume."[16]

The Munch-masked killer makes his first appearance in *Scream*'s Drew Barrymore prologue. The only bona fide star in the picture, her surprisingly quick demise occurs before viewers get comfortable. And that is just the point. The conscientious horror film, as well as one doubling as a parody, strikes graphically early. The audience is put on notice that no one is beyond the knife (not even stars) and that future violence could be just as disturbing (Barrymore's character is gutted), though it seldom is.

This prologue also addresses several traditional horror movie themes. The victim is a home-alone teenager in an isolated area. The voyeuristic killer can obviously see Barrymore's Casey as he terrorizes her by phone. The sexy high schooler is a disappointingly easy victim. (The first time I saw *Scream* at a theatre, during its initial run, one audience member yelled, "You can't go falling down, girl.") And adults are powerless to protect these young people: Casey's parents get home just as she is being murdered. The helplessness is accented when her mother attempts to call the police and hears her daughter's dying moments—Casey is still clutching her cordless phone.

In addition, the prologue embraces some new age horror film conventions. While there was nothing novel about the sinister caller/soon-to-be-murderer even when Barbara Stanwyck played victim in *Sorry, Wrong Number* (1948), *Scream*'s killer has a dark sense of humor (reinforced later by his mask choice). He turns the nightmare into a spoofing game by posing some questions which, if answered correctly, allegedly offer a safe way out. Casey is not good under pressure.

The second modern horror slant to surface in the prologue call, besides the murderer's black comedy mindset, is the fascination both he and Casey share for horror films. She is about to watch a "scary movie," which leads him to ask which is her favorite. After establishing Casey's pick as *Halloween* (1978), with his probably being *Nightmare on Elm Street* (1984, also by *Scream* director Wes Craven), questions are asked about *Halloween* and *Friday the 13th* (1980). This self-referential nature about horror films, as noted earlier, is central to both enjoying the parody and understanding *Scream*'s multiple levels.

If Casey and her soon-to-be-murderer sound somewhat chummy, they initially are. Both are openly flirtatious, with Barrymore's character forgetting her boyfriend (soon to be a victim, too), until she feels threatened. Casey's seemingly "easy" nature would throw her into the genre's standard vulnerable nonvirgin category, which is addressed at length later in the picture. Suffice it to say, past and present horror movie themes continuously vie for *Scream*'s center stage.

The next scene occurs the same night and introduces the film's leading lady, high schooler Sidney Prescott (Neve Campbell). Studying in her bed-

A PG-13 couple on the way to NC-17, Skeet Ulrich and Neve Campbell in *Scream* (1996).

room, she is surprised by boyfriend Billy Loomis (Skeet Ulrich), who comes through her window. Again, it is movie discussion time. Watching *The Exorcist* (1973) earlier on TV, reminded him of her—never a good sign in your horror film boyfriend.

It turns out, however, that this movie chitchat has broader implications. The version of *The Exorcist* that Billy was watching was edited for television. He feels their relationship had started at the near adult R rating, heading toward the provocative NC-17 status. But now her sexual mores had them back in an edited-for-TV category. Nothing is resolved, but Sidney gets in the film spirit of things by asking if Billy would settle for a PG-13 and flashes her breasts. Besides being funny cinema-extrapolated dialogue, the scene underlines the movie mentality of this picture's characters.

The next day at school Sidney runs into a media circus. As she learns about the Casey catalyst for this reporter feeding frenzy, the viewer receives cues that there is something dark in Sidney's past. The school segment also introduces *Scream*'s other primary characters: Sidney's best friend, Tatum Riley (Rose McGowan), Tatum's brother, Deputy Dewey Riley (David Arquette), Tatum's boyfriend, Stuart (Matthew Lillard), high school tag-along friend and video store clerk Randy (Jamie Kennedy), Principal Himbry (Henry Winkler), and TV tabloid reporter Gale Weathers (Courteney Cox).

After class the school bus drops Sidney off at her isolated country home. Her father is away on business, and one is reminded of the fatal setting Barrymore's character found herself in. For safety's sake Sidney is staying with Tatum. Her friend is late picking Sidney up, in part, because (fittingly) she stops to get some videos (movies). Sidney's downtime at home, before the predictable call from the killer, also allows news channel surfing, with Gail Weathers explaining the dark innuendos at school: Sidney's mother was brutally murdered a year ago. Thus, another horror theme surfaces; it is the anniversary of a grizzly killing.

Though Sidney's call from the murderer is foreseeable, her response when he enters the house is more novel; unlike passive Casey, she is aggressively elusive and survives. Television exit polls at the time of *Scream*'s initial release found Sidney's tougher stance, compared with the standard horror film victim, a key selling point for the movie. Her diverting phone dialogue with the killer also underlines this moxie, including a quote earlier in this chapter in which she disparages the genre's stereotypical dumb, big-breasted heroines.

Ironically, Sidney's friend Tatum is just such a well-endowed victim type, and she will ultimately pay the price. But that is several plot twists later. Sidney's first near-death experience ends with her boyfriend as a suspect— he showed up at the same time she was being stalked at the house. More importantly, the Munch-like mask and black accompanying robe are re-covered, which increases the dark comedy in several upcoming scenes.

The only additional story information that evening occurs at the police station, when Sidney, accompanied by Tatum and Dewey, attempts to leave but is confronted by reporter Weathers. After a brief exchange about the latter's forthcoming book, Sidney knocks her down for no apparent reason. It is a dramatic but still nebulous opening to a subplot concerning the murder of Sidney's mother.

The next scene finds Sidney back at school the following morning. But one wonders about the safety-in-numbers scenario when Dewey assures her she will be secure there. This spoofs the tendency of horror film guarantees to fall through. Not surprisingly, Sidney is again attacked. But when she shares this with Tatum it is discounted, because students dressed in the "Father Death"/Munch-like costume have appeared all over school this day. Indeed, things are so chaotic that Principal Himbry suspends classes.

This segment fleshes out the Weathers/Sidney connection, as well as serving up one more brutal murder. First, the viewer learns that the tabloid book both chronicles the murder of Sidney's mother *and* questions whether the person the girl helped convict of the crime, Cotton Weary (Liev Schrei-ber), is really guilty.

Second, with the movie long overdue for a killing, the principal is mur-dered in his office. This is a troublesome death, beyond the fact that a popular actor plays the character—Henry Winkler, "the Fonz" of *Happy Days* fame. His principal is a compassionate man genuinely concerned about the welfare of his students. Plus, he is also shown to be an amusingly human figure. Shortly before his death he puts on the mask and makes like a killer in the mirror. This small moment encapsulates the complex feeling viewers often have toward popular culture villains—appalled . . . with a touch of fascination.

The next major scene returns *Scream* to a pivotal theme—parodying young people's obsession with horror films. Appropriately, the setting is the video store where Randy clerks. There has been a run on mass murder tapes, and Randy is in his element as he shares his views on the recent killings with Tatum's boyfriend, Stuart.

Director Craven is a former college instructor, and Randy represents his in-house professorial type, a character trait that is embellished further at the bloodbath of a party that closes the movie, where Randy gives a quasi-lecture on horror movie basics. (Fittingly, in Craven's 1997 sequel, with the surviving characters moving on to college, one scene takes place in a university film class.)

Regardless, Randy's video store star turn is both entertaining and a productive exercise in self-referential scary movie criticism. And more to the point, he correctly labels Billy as the killer, though at this point Skeet Ulrich's character is no longer the suspect. Of course, Randy does not realize he is getting analytical with Billy's accomplice (Stuart). But when Stuart posits that Sidney's dad is the murderer (evidence will soon point to him), Randy continues to be professorially correct, right down to using the proper criticism terms—calling the father a "red herring" (the apparent answer that proves to be false).

The character dynamics get interesting at the video store after Billy overhears what Randy has been saying about him. When Billy physically threatens the nerdy Randy (who does a great young Jerry Lewis riff earlier in the film), Randy manages to comically defuse the tormentor (and impress the viewer) with both self-deprecating humor and his take on late 1990s motives in the horror genre: "It's the millenium; motives are incidental." (Among my college students, Randy is by far the most popular character in the first two installments of *Scream*.)

Before moving on to the lengthy party finale, which Stuart throws allegedly to celebrate the suspension of classes, several parody footnotes deserve attention. Fred, the school janitor, though seen only fleetingly, is made up to resemble Freddy Krueger, from the *Nightmare on Elm Street* series. *Exorcist* star Linda Blair also puts in a brief cameo. Billy is given the same last name, Loomis, as the psychiatrist played by Donald Pleasence in *Halloween*. And *Scream* is full of red herrings. For instance, shortly before Sidney is attacked at school, attention is drawn to the killer's boots. Later, it is revealed that Dewey's boss, Sheriff Burke (Joseph Whipp), has identical boots. Thus, Craven constantly spoofs the genre's tendency to manipulate the viewer.

So many major events take place in the finale, running the gamut from more murders, to ultimately revealing the responsible parties (accent always on parody), that the closing segment could be released as a mini-thesis on the genre. The first important incident is the killing of Sidney's best friend, Tatum. Her boyfriend, Stuart, sends her to the garage to get a beer, and it is never made clear whether he is responsible for her death, or if it is Billy (in mask and costume) who attacks her.

Initially, Tatum thinks her eventual killer is a clowning Randy. In a moment of horrific innocence she even asks if he wants to "play psycho killer," with her as the "helpless victim." Receiving a nod from her stalker, Tatum spoofs the stereotypical horror film victim by deadpanning, "No, please don't kill me, Mr. Ghost Face; I want to be in the sequel." But she soon realizes this is not a game when he sadistically cuts her arm.

Tatum does not, however, wilt under the terror of the situation. As Miramax (*Scream*'s production house) co-chairman Bob Weinstein observed, "Like *The Crying Game* [1992] or *Pulp Fiction* [1994], the *Scream* saga's a whole new approach to movies. It kills off all the old formulas."[17] Tatum goes on the offensive, bombarding "Mr. Ghost" with unopened beer bottles, smacking him with a refrigerator freezer door, and deftly outmaneuvering a frontal attack by flipping him over her back. It is only when she chooses an unwise retreat (escape through an undersized pet exit in the garage door) that she fits the genre's traditional big-breasted, small-brained heroine image. She becomes stuck in the opening, and the killer easily dispatches Tatum with a broken neck by sending the garage door (and victim) up.

Following her yet-to-be-discovered death, several party activities are going on simultaneously. Sidney and Billy go upstairs to a bedroom, Randy plays film instructor to a living room group watching a tape of *Halloween*, and Gale joins Dewey on a surveillance walk outside the house. Like the Sidney/Billy bedroom scene early in the story, the couple discuss life and relationships as filtered through the movies. As if to further foreshadow Billy's unstable nature, he is beginning to have difficulty differentiating between reality and film. And since all the young people in *Scream*'s fictional community of Woodsboro are movie freaks, too, the potential for future homegrown killers seems unlimited. (Unfortunately, this take on violence, as movie-made, plays into the hands of censorship-minded conservatives— a subject to be addressed later in the chapter.)

Director Craven teasingly cuts from Sidney and Billy just as the heroine seems willing to give up her status as a virgin. Next, Randy stops the *Halloween* tape for a mini-lecture on the rules for survival in a horror film: no sex, no sinful substance abuse, and never say, "I'll be right back." (Based on this, a sexual Sidney could be a dead Sidney.) The screening of *Hallow-een* resumes with what Randy calls the "obligatory tit shot," and Craven playfully cuts back to Sidney and Billy just as she is about the remove her bra.

A phone call breaks up this flirtation with soft porn. Principal Himbry has been found gutted and hanging from a goalpost at the school's football field. Randy is shocked to watch his *Halloween* audience leave; movies for him, even old movies, are superior to any other attraction. But the student exodus is a solid plot device. It thins the party, and by cutting to the teens driving away, there is a natural segue to Gale and Dewey walking outside.

The unlikely couple is nearly run down by the festive students—gutted principals are always a big draw. As the deputy and the reporter dive for cover, they discover the car of Sidney's missing father. Is he the killer lurking around this—yet another—isolated teen home? From this point the plot shifts to high gear.

The action cuts to a subdued Sidney and Billy, their sex scene regrettably over. As if in homage to Randy's horror movie rules (sex equals death), the masked killer suddenly joins them and appears to murder Billy. Sidney just barely escapes, going out a window and literally falling to safety . . . only to discover poor Tatum still hanging from the pet exit in the garage door.

Inside the house, one-track Randy continues to watch *Halloween*, oblivious to the violence around him. Here again, Craven has Randy's monologue working darkly comic double duty. That is, as the boy shouts advice to *Halloween* star Jamie Lee Curtis, such as, "He's right around the corner" and, "Look behind you," Randy's warnings apply equally to his own situation—the Munch-masked murderer is in the same room. But just as it appears Randy's luck has run out, the killer is distracted by the outside cries of the still-terrorized Sidney.

"Mr. Ghost" follows her to Gale's TV van, where he slits the camera-man's throat but again fails to kill Sidney, who manages to run away. Gale and Dewey return to this horrific but now mysteriously deserted setting. Spoofing the film's fascination with the horror genre, the deputy's investigation of screams from the house find them emanating from the TV and the still-playing *Halloween* tape. But whereas Dewey allows himself a bemused moment of relaxation at being fooled, the slaughterhouse van scene quickly sends Gale into hysterics, contributing to her car crash as she attempts to drive away.

Sidney, nearly run over by Gale, resurfaces at this point, in search of Dewey's quasi-authority-figure security. But as in so many horror films, whether peppered with parody elements or not, the law is a bust. As if cued by Sidney's calls, Dewey comes out of the house . . . with a knife in his back, closely followed by the costumed killer. Spoofing Curtis' many close calls in *Halloween*, Sidney gets away yet again.

As she contemplates the sudden disappearance of the Munch-like figure, Randy and Stuart resurface—each fingering the other as a suspect. Taking no chances (and packing Dewey's gun), Sidney locks both out of the house just as Billy makes his surprising return. Thinking she saw him murdered earlier, Sidney defers to Billy's request for the gun and autonomy in this parody war zone. Big mistake; read reviews of any horror film.

From now on broad burlesque rules, as Billy and Stuart reveal their murderous mentality. After letting Randy into the house, Billy casually shoots him. But more to the parody point, Sidney's boyfriend quotes *Psycho*'s Norman Bates: "We all go a little mad sometimes." Perhaps feeling a need to be the horror movie expert, given his almost immediate blasting of the professorlike Randy, Billy footnotes his quote by naming the actor who played Bates, Anthony Perkins. As if savoring the humor quotient of a horror movie killer spouting slasher film facts, Billy nonchalantly tastes the apparent blood on his T-shirt and pronounces it corn syrup, noting this was the substitute used for pig's blood in *Carrie* (1976).

Billy and Stuart proceed to taunt the incredulous Sidney by revealing their litany of crimes, starting with the murder of her mother exactly one year before. They also produce a bound and gagged Neil Prescott (Lawrence Hecht), Sidney's father. It is their plan to make him the fall guy. But their run of luck is about to change. The two are first distracted by a gun-toting Gale. Though they manage to disarm her, Sidney gets away.

Coming full parody circle from the prologue beginning, suddenly it is Sidney on the phone threatening the killers: she has called the police. And as Billy searches for her, the film pays its final spoofing salute to *Halloween*. The tape, which is still playing in the living room, has reached the clothes closet hiding place of Jamie Lee Curtis. Billy takes note and correctly guesses Sidney is in the closet, too. But he should have paid attention to the fact that Curtis at this point was taking the offensive.

Known as the "scream queen" for the run of horror movies that followed her *Halloween* introduction to features, Curtis's closet scene has her fashioning a weapon from a coat hanger and stabbing the murdering Michael as he investigates her hiding place. As if aping Curtis' turnabout but with a lancelike umbrella, Sidney explodes out of her closet and stabs Billy twice.

It is an effective scene for several reasons. First is the surprise factor. Despite the Curtis foreshadowing, the viewer never actually sees Sidney in her secret sanctum until she comes flying out. Second, it affectionately spoofs Curtis' timid self-defense by making Sidney much more aggressive. Third, it is a fitting footnote to *Halloween*, which greatly influenced Craven. Fourth, it is the ultimate in-your-face spoof of Billy and Stuart as murderers, because Sidney's closet counterattack finds her wearing *their* mask and costume.

Before one can fully process all this, Craven fastforwards Sidney and the viewer into another surprise onslaught, this time from Stuart. Coming at a run, it is reminiscent of Norman Bates' basement attack on Marion's sister in *Psycho*. But again Sidney reigns, with an assist, of sorts, from Curtis and *Halloween*. The first to her feet after being wrestled to the floor, Sidney pushes a TV over onto Stuart's head. Fittingly, the last thing he ever sees is an image of an aggressive Curtis from *Halloween*, which is still playing on the TV.

Parodying horror films finales that go on and on, Billy revives and is about to knife Sidney when Gale suddenly enters the picture and shoots him. Joined by the wounded Randy, he provides yet another teacher insight on horror films, warning that this is when the supposedly dead killer comes back to life for one last scare. And sure enough, Billy does just that. But Sidney ends it quickly with a fatal shot to his forehead, followed by the comment, "Not in my movie." Though a survivor, even Sidney now has a film mindset on life.

Scream might have best ended with Sidney's cryptic comment. But the close as filmed, Gale's on-location news report the following morning, is not without its pluses. Most specifically, since *Scream* is movie-driven (horror films on video), it seems appropriate to have a media ending. Today's shock crimes often become tomorrow's films. Indeed, the *Scream* sequel begins at the movie adaptation opening of Gale's murder-chronicling book.

Scream is a fun ride that, like so many parodies, both educates and manipulates. For instance, Randy "teaches" that sex equals death in the horror genre, especially if *Halloween* is a pivotal defining example. Consistent with this, he attributes his survival of the bloodbath finale to being a virgin. Yet, Sidney has sex—with one of the killers, no less—and still manages both to live and usurp their reign of terror.

For all the entertainingly insightful attributes equated with parody, one that is seldom addressed reflects its propensity to disperse potential censorship problems. For example, shortly after critic Roger Ebert mentioned *Scream*'s "incredible level of gore," he went on to observe, "Is the violence defused by the ironic way the film uses it and comments on it? For me it was."[18] Or, as *Entertainment Weekly* movie critic Lisa Schwarzbaum noted in her review of *Halloween: H20* (1998), "in a post-*Scream* . . . landscape, horror is never so blackly frightening that it's not a little, like, amusingly ironic, too . . . movie-mad younger audiences . . . are never so spooked that they can't simultaneously assess the mechanics behind the mood building."[19]

The positive critical spin on parody-conscious horror since *Scream* even has the genre's capable heroines being celebrated in a self-fulfilling manner. Jamie Lee Curtis said of her *H20* character, "There had to be a moment where Laurie could get away, but instead she recognizes that the only possible way for her to live is to face [longtime nemesis] Michael Myers and risk dying."[20] Or, as *H20* director Steve Miner more broadly defined it, "The theme of the whole thing is that your demons will always be with you unless you confront them."[21] *Scream* scripter and co-executive producer of *H20* Kevin Williamson was, fittingly, the most amusingly succinct in defining these pivotal heroine scenes, calling them "the Sigourney Weaver moment," after the actress' strong recurring figure in the *Alien* film series.[22]

As the original *Halloween* influenced *Scream*, that movie and its sequel are becoming the touchstone vehicles for the latest wave of horror films . . . a wave now strongly laced with parody.

NOTES

1. Damian Cannon, *Scream* review, IMDb (Internet Movie Database), *Scream* site, "Film Reviews UK 1998" citation, visited April 13, 1998.

2. Roger Ebert, *Scream* review, IMDb, *Scream* site, *Chicago Sun-Times* citation, visited April 13, 1998.

3. Dotson Rader, "How Steve Martin Wised Up," *Parade Magazine*, August 30, 1998, p. 5.

4. Jack Kroll, "Paint the Town White," *Newsweek*, March 9, 1998, p. 68.

5. Louis Menand, "What Is 'Art,'?" *The New Yorker*, February 9, 1998, p. 40.

6. *Hot Shots! Part Deux* review, IMDb, *Hot Shots, Part Deux* site, *Washington Post* citation (May 21, 1993), visited April 13, 1998.

7. Roger Ebert, *Hot Shots! Part Deux* review, *Chicago Sun-Times*, May 21, 1993.

8. *Hot Shots! Part Deux* review, *Variety*, May 24, 1993, p. 44.

9. Janet Maslin, "From 'Rambo' to Rodham, Smirking All the Way," *New York Times*, May 21, 1993, late edition.

10. *Hot Shots! Part Deux* review, *People*, May 31, 1993, p. 14.

11. Ebert, *Hot Shots! Part Deux* review.

12. "Holiday Hits and Misses," *Rolling Stone*, December 26–January 9, 1997, p. 206.

13. Leonard Klady, *Scream* review, *Variety*, December 16–22, 1996, p. 79.

14. Kim Newman, *Scream* review, *Sight and Sound*, May 1997, p. 53.

15. Peter Stack, *Scream* review, *San Francisco Chronicle*, December 20, 1996, p. C-5.

16. Janet Maslin, "Tricks of the Gory Trade," *New York Times*, December 20, 1996, p. C-22.

17. David Hochman, "Scream and Scream Again," *Entertainment Weekly*, November 28, 1997, p. 31.

18. Ebert, *Scream* review.

19. Lisa Schwarzbaum, "A Time to Kill," *Entertainment Weekly*, August 14, 1998, p. 45.

20. Chris Nashawaty, "Final Cut," *Entertainment Weekly*, August 14, 1998, p. 34.

21. Ibid.

22. Ibid.

6

Epilogue

Outnumbered by the enemy in *The Last Remake Of Beau Geste* (1977), French Foreign Legion soldier Beau Geste (Michael York) tells his "twin" brother and fellow legionnaire (Marty Feldman), "Remember, save your last bullet for yourself." Feldman's Digby Geste responds, "Yes, I would like a souvenir."

Though comedy by its very nature tends to receive less recognition than serious drama, parody gets the least respect of the comedy genres (which also include screwball, populist, black, and personality-driven). This short shrift is no doubt based on the fact that parody works from a given structure, such as the pun to a stand-up comedian. Put more succinctly, this genre affectionately spoofs a specific film, type of films, or auteur. The audience recognizes the parody target, say the phenomenally popular *Titanic* (1997), or the films of celebrated director Alfred Hitchcock, and often wrongfully assumes burlesque story construction is a no-brainer.

Chapter 1 addressed seven basic characteristics of parody, and two components stand out in any defense of the genre's importance. First is the topic of "creative criticism": to maximize the comic dismantling of a given film or films, the parodist must know and showcase all the fundamental properties of his target. Thus, the burlesque movie, if effectively done, becomes an entertaining study guide of a given film, genre, or auteur. Consequently, a student of the Western might better understand the genre if he or she screened the assortment of sagebrush spoofs examined in Chapters

2 and 3. Along related lines, laughing along with Bob Hope's *My Favorite Blonde* (1942) and Mel Brooks' *High Anxiety* (1977) can help one brush up on Hitchcock basics.

The second pivotal parody component embraces spoofs of reaffirmation. Some burlesques cut so close to the target that they are often perceived as the genre under affectionate attack. For instance, many viewers would instinctively label *Butch Cassidy and the Sundance Kid* (1969) a Western, or *Scream* (1996) a horror film. But to do so is to miss the fascinating tension between genre expectations and a more sophisticated parody that is comic without deflating the characters involved. And at times, such as Butch and Sundance's last dialogue, the reaffirmation approach offers up a high art poignancy not normally associated with parody. At a bare minimum, the reaffirmation burlesque takes the conscientious viewer on a more ambitiously complex "ride," fluctuating between broad parody points and a straight rendition of the type of target being kidded.

In sorting through a mountain of parody criticism for this book, a third component justifying the genre frequently surfaced. One might label this factor the "pop culture literacy experience." Parody films, by their very nature, are generously laced with references to both a given target and the popular culture from which they emerged, a veritable time capsule for the period. And the viewer receives a certain pleasure from recognizing these things, or, as film critic Lisa Schwarzbaum observed when writing about the late 1990s mix of parody and horror, "The more pop-culture references and inside jokes [which are understood], the more *hip* the viewing crowd feels."[1] Bob Hope said much the same thing years earlier when referring to Robert Benchley's comic comments in the *Road to Utopia* (1945), as well as other examples of movie spoofing, "They [the audience] love anything that gives them a little mental jerk and they want to be 'with it.' "[2]

This timeliness is integral to parody. For instance, the most consistent complaint against Mel Brooks' *Spaceballs* (1987) was that it appeared a full decade after the birth of the *Star Wars* (1977) phenomenon. Though still entertaining, it was not cutting-edge funny.

Initially I was bothered by praise for this "pop culture literacy experience," thinking of it as nothing more than a parody variation of Trivial Pursuit. But after I kept encountering critics embracing the argument (such as reviewer Roger Ebert's comments on the subject in the previous chapter), I decided it merited a second look.

After further contemplation, this parody pop culture slant seemed a valid—even traditional—value to endorse. Most art, from T. S. Eliot's *The Waste Land* (1922), to *M.A.S.H.* the TV show (1972–83), rewards the enthusiast with recognition points for understanding insider allusions within the work. *The Waste Land* reader is pleased to know even a modest percentage of its literary quotations and allusions, just as the *M.A.S.H.*

viewer is proud to find the humor in Hawkeye (Alan Alda) repartee that has an early 1950s connection, the time period in which *M.A.S.H.* is set.

The inclusion of the many literary references in *The Waste Land*, what writer and broadcaster Kenneth McLeish once called "the junkyard of the intellectual mind," does not make this poem a work of art, just as a historically based joke does not elevate *M.A.S.H.*[3] But the pop culture connection it makes with the bright admirer often assists in bringing across higher artistic aspirations.

These, then, have been some final thoughts on the significance of parody. But I must not forget the most basic lesson I learned from a humorous father: parody, like so many forms of comedy, is most valuable "because it makes us laugh at things we don't normally see as funny." Or, as Mel Brooks subtitled *Blazing Saddles* (1974), "Never Give A Saga An Even Break."

NOTES

1. Lisa Schwarzbaum, "A Time To Kill," *Entertainment Weekly*, August 14, 1998, p. 45.

2. Brooks Riley, "Words of Hope," *Film Comment*, May–June 1979, p. 24.

3. Kenneth McLeish, *Arts in the Twentieth Century* (1985; reprint, New York: Viking Penguin, 1986), p. 8.

Appendix: Selected Filmography

Parody Films Mentioned and/or Examined in the Text (chronological order also applies to films released in the same year).

1917	*Teddy at the Throttle* (approximately 18 minutes) Director: Clarence Badger. Stars: Bobby Vernon, Gloria Swanson, and Wallace Beery.
1922	*The Frozen North* (approximately 18 minutes) Director/Screenplay: Buster Keaton and Eddie Cline. Star: Keaton.
1923	*The Shriek of Araby* (approximately 45 minutes) Director: F. Richard Jones. Star: Ben Turpin.
1923	*Three Ages* (approximately 54 minutes) Director: Buster Keaton and Eddie Cline. Screenplay: Clyde Bruckman, Joseph Mitchell, and Jean Havez. Star: Keaton.
1924	*Two Wagons, Both Covered* (approximately 18 minutes) Director: Rob Wagner. Screenplay: Will Rogers. Star: Rogers.
1924	*Sherlock Jr.* (45 minutes) Director: Buster Keaton. Story: Clyde Bruckman, Joseph Mitchell, and Jean Havez. Star: Keaton.
1925	*The Gold Rush* (approximately 100 minutes) Director/Screenplay: Charlie Chaplin. Star: Chaplin.
1925	*Go West* (Approximately 63 minutes) Director: Buster Keaton. Screenplay: Raymond Cannon. Star: Keaton.

1927   *The General* (74 minutes)
            Director/Story: Buster Keaton and Clyde Bruckman. Star:
            Keaton.

1931   *Monkey Business* (77 minutes)
            Director: Norman McLeod. Screenplay: S. J. Perelman and
            Will B. Johnstone. Stars: Marx Brothers.

1937   *Way Out West* (65 minutes)
            Director: James W. Horne. Screenplay: Charles Rogers, Felix
            Adler, and James Parrott. Stars: Laurel & Hardy.

1939   *Gunga Din* (117 minutes)
            Director: George Stevens. Screenplay: Joel Sayre and Fred
            Guiol. Stars: Cary Grant, Victor McLaglen, and Douglas Fair-
            banks, Jr.

1939   *The Cat and the Canary* (72 minutes)
            Director: Elliott Nugent. Screenplay: Walter De Leon and
            Lynn Starling. Stars: Bob Hope and Paulette Goddard.

1939   *Destry Rides Again* (94 minutes)
            Director: George Marshall. Screenplay: Felix Jackson, Henry
            Meyers, and Gertrude Purchell. Stars: Marlene Dietrich,
            Jimmy Stewart, Charles Winninger, Mischa Auer, Brian Don-
            levy, Irene Hervey, Una Merkel, Warren Hymer, Samuel S.
            Hinds, and Jack Carson.

1940   *My Little Chickadee* (83 minutes)
            Director: Edward Cline. Screenplay: Mae West and W. C.
            Fields. Stars: W. C. Fields and Mae West.

1940   *Road to Singapore* (84 minutes)
            Director: Victor Schertzinger. Screenplay: Don Hartman and
            Frank Butler. Stars: Bob Hope and Bing Crosby.

1940   *Buck Benny Rides Again* (82 minutes)
            Director: Mark Sandrich. Screenplay: William Morrow and
            Edmund Beloin. Stars: Jack Benny, Eddie Anderson, Phil Har-
            ris, and Andy Devine.

1940   *The Ghost Breakers* (82 minutes)
            Director: George Marshall. Screenplay: Walter De Leon.
            Stars: Bob Hope and Paulette Goddard.

1940   *Go West* (80 minutes)
            Director: Edward Buzzell. Screenplay: Irving Brecher. Stars:
            Marx Brothers.

1941   *Road to Zanzibar* (92 minutes)
            Director: Victor Schertzinger. Screenplay: Frank Butler and
            Don Hartman. Stars: Bob Hope and Bing Crosby.

1942   *My Favorite Blonde* (78 minutes)
            Director: Sidney Lanfield. Screenplay: Don Hartman and

Frank Butler, from an original story by Melvin Frank and Norman Panama. Stars: Bob Hope and Madeleine Carroll.

1942   *Road to Morocco* (83 minutes)
Director: David Butler. Screenplay: Frank Butler and Don Hartman. Stars: Bob Hope and Bing Crosby.

1944   *The Princess and the Pirate* (94 minutes)
Director: David Butler. Screenplay: Don Hartman, Melville Shavelson, and Everett Freeman. Star: Bob Hope.

1945   *Road to Utopia* (90 minutes)
Director: Paul Jones. Screenplay: Norman Panama and Melvin Frank. Stars: Bob Hope, Bing Crosby, and Robert Benchley.

1946   *Monsieur Beaucaire* (93 minutes)
Director: George Marshall. Screenplay: Melvin Frank and Norman Panama. Star: Bob Hope.

1947   *My Favorite Brunette* (87 minutes)
Director: Elliott Nugent. Screenplay: Edmund Beloin and Jack Rose. Star: Bob Hope.

1947   *The Wistful Widow of Wagon Gap* (78 minutes)
Director: Charles Barton. Screenplay: Robert Lees, Frederic I. Rinaldo, and John Grant. Stars: Abbott & Costello.

1947   *Road to Rio* (100 minutes)
Director: Norman Z. McLeod. Screenplay: Edmund Beloin and Jack Rose. Stars: Bob Hope and Bing Crosby.

1948   *A Southern Yankee* (90 minutes)
Director: Edward Sedgwick. Screenplay: Harry Tugend, from a seventy page original story by Melvin Frank and Norman Panama. Stars: Red Skelton and Brian Donlevy.

1948   *The Paleface* (91 minutes)
Director: Norman Z. McLeod. Screenplay: Edmund Hartmann and Frank Tashlin. Stars: Bob Hope and Jane Russell.

1950   *Fancy Pants* (92 minutes)
Director: George Marshall. Screenplay: Edmund Hartmann and Robert O'Brien, from the Harry Leon Wilson novel. Stars: Bob Hope and Lucille Ball.

1952   *Son of Paleface* (95 minutes)
Director: Frank Tashlin. Screenplay: Frank Tashlin, Robert L. Welch, and Joseph Quillan. Stars: Bob Hope, Jane Russell, and Roy Rogers; unbilled cameo by Bing Crosby.

1952   *Road to Bali* (90 minutes)
Director: Hal Walker. Screenplay: Frank Butler, Hal Kanter, and William Morrow. Stars: Bob Hope and Bing Crosby; unbilled cameo by Jane Russell.

1953   *Scared Stiff* (106 minutes)
                Director: George Marshall. Screenplay: Herbert Baker and
                Walter De Leon; added dialogue: Ed Simmons and Norman
                Lear. Stars: Dean Martin, Jerry Lewis, Lizabeth Scott, and
                Carmen Miranda; unbilled cameo by Bob Hope and Bing
                Crosby.

1954   *Casanova's Big Night* (86 minutes)
                Director: Norman Z. McLeod. Screenplay: Hal Kanter and
                Edmund Hartmann. Star: Bob Hope.

1954   *Beat the Devil* (93 minutes)
                Director: John Huston. Screenplay: Huston and Truman Ca-
                pote. Star: Humphrey Bogart.

1956   *The Court Jester* (101 minutes)
                Director/Screenplay: Norman Panama and Melvin Frank.
                Stars: Danny Kaye, Glynis Johns, Basil Rathbone, and Angela
                Lansbury.

1956   *Pardners* (90 minutes)
                Director: Norman Taurog. Screenplay: Sidney Sheldon. Stars:
                Dean Martin and Jerry Lewis.

1959   *Alias Jesse James* (92 minutes)
                Director: Norman Z. McLeod. Screenplay: William Bowers
                and Daniel D. Beauchamp. Star: Bob Hope.

1962   *Road to Hong Kong* (91 minutes)
                Director: Norman Panama. Screenplay: Panama and Melvin
                Frank. Stars: Bob Hope and Bing Crosby.

1965   *Cat Ballou* (97 minutes)
                Director: Elliot Silverstein. Screenplay: Walter Newman and
                Frank R. Pierson. Stars: Jane Fonda and Lee Marvin.

1966   *Our Man Flint* (107 minutes)
                Director: Daniel Mann. Screenplay: Hal Fimberg. Stars: James
                Coburn and Lee J. Cobb.

1966   *The Silencers* (103 minutes)
                Director: Phil Karlson. Screenplay: Oscar Saul. Stars: Dean
                Martin, Stella Stevens, and Victor Buono.

1966   *What's Up, Tiger Lily?* (94 minutes)
                Original version: *Kagi No Kagi* (Japan, 1964). Re-release Di-
                rector: Woody Allen. Screenplay/Dubbing: Allen, Frank Bux-
                ton, Len Maxwell, Louise Lasser, Mickey Rose, Julie Bennett,
                and Bryna Wilson.

1967   *In Like Flint* (115 minutes)
                Director: Gordon Douglas. Screenplay: Hal Fimberg. Stars:
                James Coburn and Lee J. Cobb.

1967   *Bonnie and Clyde* (111 minutes)
                Director: Arthur Penn. Screenplay: David Newman and Rob-

ert Benton. Stars: Warren Beatty, Faye Dunaway, Michael J. Pollard, Gene Hackman, Estelle Parsons, and Gene Wilder.

1968   *The Producers* (88 minutes)
Director/Screenplay: Mel Brooks. Stars: Zero Mostel, Gene Wilder, Kenneth Mars, Dick Shawn, and Christopher Hewett.

1969   *Take the Money and Run* (85 minutes)
Director: Woody Allen. Screenplay: Allen and Mickey Rose. Star: Allen.

1969   *Butch Cassidy and the Sundance Kid* (112 minutes)
Director: George Roy Hill. Screenplay: William Goldman. Stars: Paul Newman, Robert Redford, Katharine Ross, and Strother Martin.

1972   *Play It Again, Sam* (87 minutes)
Director: Herbert Ross. Screenplay: Woody Allen, based on Allen's play. Stars: Allen, Diane Keaton, Tony Roberts, Jerry Lacy, and Susan Anspach.

1972   *The Cheap Detective* (92 minutes)
Director: Robert Moore. Screenplay: Neil Simon. Stars: Peter Falk, Ann-Margaret, Eileen Brennan, Sid Caesar, Stockard Channing, James Coco, Dom Deluise, Louise Fletcher, Marsha Mason, John Houseman, Madeline Kahn.

1972   *Everything You Always Wanted to Know About Sex (But Were Afraid to Ask)* (87 minutes)
Director/Screenplay: Woody Allen. Stars: Allen, Louise Lasser, Tony Randall, Burt Reynolds, and Gene Wilder.

1973   *The Long Goodbye* (111 minutes)
Director: Robert Altman. Screenplay: Leigh Brackett, from Raymond Chandler's novel. Stars: Elliott Gould and Sterling Hayden.

1973   *Sleeper* (88 minutes)
Director: Woody Allen. Screenplay: Allen and Marshall Brickman. Stars: Allen and Diane Keaton.

1974   *Blazing Saddles* (93 minutes)
Director: Mel Brooks. Screenplay: Brooks, Norman Steinberg, Andrew Bergman, Richard Pryor, and Alan Unger. Stars: Cleavon Little, Gene Wilder, Harvey Korman, Madeline Kahn, Brooks, and Slim Pickens.

1974   *Young Frankenstein* (108 minutes)
Director: Mel Brooks. Screenplay: Gene Wilder and Brooks. Stars: Wilder, Marty Feldman, Peter Boyle, Madeline Kahn, Cloris Leachman, Teri Garr, Kenneth Mars, and Gene Hackman.

1975   *Love and Death* (85 minutes)
Director/Screenplay: Woody Allen. Stars: Allen and Diane Keaton.

1975   *The Rocky Horror Picture Show* (100 minutes)
Director: Jim Sharman. Screenplay: Richard O'Brien and Sharman, based on O'Brien's play (O'Brien also wrote the music and lyrics, as well as playing the character Riff Raff). Stars: Tim Curry, Susan Sarandon, Barry Bostwick, O'Brien, Jonathan Adams, Nell Campbell, Peter Hinwood, Meat Loaf, Patricia Quinn, Charles Gray.

1975   *The Adventures of Sherlock Holmes' Smarter Brother* (91 minutes)
Director: Gene Wilder. Screenplay: Wilder. Stars: Wilder, Madeline Kahn, Marty Feldman, and Dom Deluise.

1975   *The Black Bird* (98 minutes)
Director/Screenplay: David Giler. Star: George Segal.

1976   *Murder By Death* (95 minutes)
Director: Robert Moore. Screenplay: Neil Simon. Stars: Peter Falk, Alex Guinness, Peter Sellers, David Niven, Maggie Smith, Elsa Lanchester, James Coco.

1977   *The Last Remake of Beau Geste* (85 minutes)
Director: Marty Feldman. Screenplay: Feldman and Chris J. Allen. Stars: Marty Feldman, Michael York, Ann-Margret, and Peter Ustinov.

1977   *The World's Greatest Lover* (89 minutes)
Director/Screenplay: Gene Wilder. Stars: Wilder, Carol Kane, and Dom DeLuise.

1977   *High Anxiety* (94 minutes)
Director: Mel Brooks. Screenplay: Brooks, Ron Clark, Rudy De Luca, and Barry Levinson. Stars: Brooks, Madeline Kahn, Cloris Leachman, Harvey Korman, and Ron Carey.

1980   *Airplane!* (87 minutes)
Director/Screenplay: Jim Abrahams, David Zucker, Jerry Zucker. Stars: Robert Hays, Julie Hagerty, Leslie Nielsen, and Lloyd Bridges.

1980   *The Nude Bomb* (94 minutes)
Director: Clive Donner. Screenplay: Arne Sultan, Bill Dana, and Leonard B. Stern, based on characters created by Mel Brooks and Buck Henry. Star: Don Adams.

1980   *The Man with Bogart's Face* (106 minutes)
Director: Robert Day. Screenplay: Andrew J. Fenady, from his novel. Star: Robert Sacchi.

1981   *An American Werewolf in London* (97 minutes)
Director/Screenplay: John Landis. Stars: David Naughton and Griffin Dunne.

1982   *Dead Men Don't Wear Plaid* (89 minutes)
Director: Carl Reiner. Screenplay: Phil Robinson. Star: Steve Martin.

1982   *My Favorite Year* (92 minutes)
                Director: Richard Benjamin. Screenplay: Norman Steinberg
                and Dennis Palumbo. Stars: Peter O'Toole, Mark Linn-Baker,
                Joseph Bologna, Lainie Kazan, and Bill Macy.

1983   *The Man with Two Brains* (93 minutes)
                Director: Carl Reiner. Screenplay: Reiner, Steve Martin, and
                George Gipe. Stars: Martin and Kathleen Turner.

1985   *The Purple Rose of Cairo* (82 minutes)
                Director/Screenplay: Woody Allen. Stars: Mia Farrow and Jeff
                Daniels.

1985   *Lust in the Dust* (85 minutes)
                Director: Paul Bartel. Screenplay: Philip John Taylor. Stars:
                Tab Hunter, Divine, and Lainie Kazan.

1986   *¡Three Amigos!* (105 minutes)
                Director: John Landis. Screenplay: Steve Martin, Lorne Mi-
                chaels, and Randy Newman. Stars: Chevy Chase, Steve Mar-
                tin, and Martin Short.

1987   *Spaceballs* (96 minutes)
                Director: Mel Brooks. Screenplay: Brooks, Thomas Meehan,
                and Ronny Graham. Stars: Brooks (two roles), John Candy,
                Rick Moranis, Bill Pullman, and Daphne Zuniga.

1988   *The Naked Gun: From the Files of Police Squad* (85 minutes)
                Director: David Zucker. Screenplay: Jerry Zucker, Jim
                Abrahams, David Zucker, and Pat Proft. Stars: Leslie Niel-
                sen, George Kennedy, Priscilla Presley, and Ricardo Mon-
                talban.

1989   *Crimes and Misdemeanors* (104 minutes)
                Director/Screenplay: Woody Allen. Stars: Allen, Alan Alda,
                and Mia Farrow.

1990   *The Freshman* (102 minutes)
                Director/Screenplay: Andrew Bergman. Stars: Marlon Brando,
                Matthew Broderick, and Bruno Kirby.

1991   *Naked Gun 2 ½: The Smell of Fear* (85 minutes)
                Director: David Zucker. Screenplay: Zucker and Pat Proft.
                Stars: Leslie Nielsen, Priscilla Presley, and George Kennedy.

1991   *Hot Shots!* (85 minutes)
                Director: Jim Abrahams. Screenplay: Pat Proft and Abrahams.
                Stars: Charlie Sheen, Kevin Dunn, Cary Elwes, Valeria Gol-
                ino, and Lloyd Bridges.

1993   *Hot Shots! Part Deux* (89 minutes)
                Director: Jim Abrahams. Screenplay: Abrahams and Pat Proft.
                Stars: Charlie Sheen, Lloyd Bridges, Valeria Golino, Richard
                Crenna, Brenda Bakke, Miguel Ferrer, Rowan Atkinson, and
                Jerry Haleva.

1993
Manhattan Murder Mystery (105 minutes)
Director: Woody Allen. Screenplay: Allen and Marshall Brickman. Stars: Allen, Diane Keaton, and Alan Alda.

1996
Scream (110 minutes)
Director: Wes Craven. Screenplay: Kevin Williamson. Stars: Neve Campbell, David Arquette, Courteney Cox, Matthew Lillard, Skeet Ulrich, Rose McGowan, Drew Barrymore, Jamie Kennedy, and Henry Winkler.

1997
Austin Powers: International Man of Mystery (90 minutes)
Director: Jay Roach. Screenplay: Mike Myers. Stars: Myers, Elizabeth Hurley, and Michael York.

1997
Scream 2 (120 minutes)
Director: Wes Craven. Screenplay: Kevin Williamson. Stars: David Arquette, Neve Campbell, Courteney Cox, Sarah Michelle Gellar, Jamie Kennedy, Laurie Metcalf, and Jerry O'Connell.

Selected Bibliography

Adamson, Joe. *Groucho, Harpo, Chico and Sometimes Zeppo*. New York: Simon & Schuster, 1973.

Adler, Bill, and Jeffrey Feinman. *Mel Brooks: The Irreverent Funnyman*. New York: Playboy Press, 1976.

Agee, James. *Agee on Film*. vol. 1. New York: Grosset and Dunlap, 1969.

Allen, Woody. *Side Effects*. New York: Random House, 1980.

Alpert, Hollis. "The Wild Man Is Coming." *Saturday Review* (August 9, 1952), p. 36.

Atlas, Jacoba. "New Hollywood: Mel Brooks Interview." *Film Comment* (March–April, 1975), p. 57.

"Babbling Brooks." *Newsweek* (December 23, 1974), p. 79.

Bach, Steven. *Marlene Dietrich: Life and Legend*. New York: William Morrow, 1992.

Barnes, Howard. *My Favorite Brunette* review. *New York Herald-Tribune* (March 20, 1947).

Barnum, P. T. *Struggles and Triumphs; Or, Forty Years' Recollections of P. T. Barnum*. 1855. Reprint, ed. Carl Bode, New York: Penguin Classics, 1987.

Barr, Charles. *Laurel & Hardy*. 1968. Reprint, Los Angeles: University of California Press, 1974.

Beebe, Lucius. "Sitting In At the Try-Outs of 'Stars in your Eyes' [*Gunga Din* review]." *New York Herald-Tribune* (February 5, 1939), p. 2.

Benchley, Robert. "Carnival Week in Sunny Las Los." In *The Treasurer's Report and Other Aspects of Community Singing*. New York: Grosset and Dunlap, 1930, pp. 37–46.

Boehnel, William. "Laurel & Hardy in Lively Comedy." *New York World-*

Telegram (May 4, 1937). In the *Way Out West* file, Billy Rose Theatre Collection, New York Public Library at Lincoln Center.

———. *Destry Rides Again* review. *New York World-Telegram* (November 30, 1939). In the *Destry Rides Again* file, Billy Rose Theatre Collection, New York Public Library at Lincoln Center.

———. "Mae West and W. C. Fields Co-Star in *My Little Chickadee.*" *New York World-Telegram* (March 16, 1940). In the *My Little Chickadee* file, Billy Rose Theatre Collection, New York Public Library at Lincoln Center.

Bogdanovich, Peter. *John Ford.* Los Angeles: University of California Press, 1970.

Brooks, Tim, and Earle Marsh. *The Complete Directory to Prime Time Network TV Shows 1946–Present.* New York: Ballantine Books, 1979.

Brosnan, John. *Future Tense: The Cinema of Science Fiction.* New York: St. Martin's Press, 1978.

Burdett, Winston. *Way Out West* review. *Brooklyn Daily Eagle* (May 4, 1937). In the *Way Out West* file, Billy Rose Theatre Collection, New York Public Library at Lincoln Center.

"Butch Cassidy: Tardy Movie Salute." *Newark Evening News* (December 23, 1968). In the *Butch Cassidy and Sundance Kid* file, Billy Rose Theatre Collection, New York Public Library at Lincoln Center.

"Butch Cassidy and the Sundance Kid." *Filmfacts* vol. 12, no. 15 (1969), p. 338.

"Buzzell, Brecher Set Up Big Laugh Fest." *Hollywood Reporter* (December 11, 1940), p. 3.

Buzzell, Edward. "Mocked and Marred By The Marxes." *New York Times* (December 15, 1940), p. 6

Caesar, Sid (with Bill Davidson). *Where Have I Been: An Autobiography.* New York: Crown Publishers, 1982.

Cameron, Kate. "Dietrich Rides Again to Screen Triumphs." *New York Daily News* (November 30, 1939). In the *Destry Rides Again* file, Billy Rose Theatre Collection, New York Public Library at Lincoln Center.

———. "Mae West and Fields Give *Destry* a Ride." *New York Daily News* (March 16, 1940). In the *My Little Chickadee* file, Billy Rose Theatre Collection, New York Public Library at Lincoln Center.

Canby, Vincent. *Butch Cassidy and the Sundance Kid* review. *New York Times* (September 25, 1969), p. 54.

———. *Young Frankenstein* review. *New York Times* (December 16, 1974), p. 48.

Cannon, Damian. *Scream* review, IMDb (Internet Movie Database), *Scream* site, "Film Reviews UK 1998" citation, visited April 13, 1998.

Carroll, Kathleen. "A Funny Thing Happened to Frankenstein." *New York Daily News* (December 8, 1974), Leisure section, p. 9.

Cawelti, John G. *The Six-Gun Mystique.* Bowling Green, Ohio: University Press, 1971.

———. "The Question of Popular Genres." *Journal of Popular Film and Television* (Summer, 1985), pp. 55–56.

Cocks, Jay. "Monster Mash." *Time*, p. 104.

Cohn, Herbert. "*My Little Chickadee* Pairs Fields, Mae West." *Brooklyn Daily Eagle* (March 16, 1940). In the *My Little Chickadee* file, Billy Rose Theatre Collection, New York Public Library at Lincoln Center.

Coleman, Robert. "Destry Rides Again: Comedy With A Wallop." *New York Daily*

Mirror (November 30, 1939). In the *Destry Rides Again* file, Billy Rose Theatre Collection, New York Public Library at Lincoln Center.

Copeland, Elizabeth. "Human Marlene Revealed in Rowdy *Destry*." (January 12, 1940). In the *Destry Rides Again* file, Billy Rose Theatre Collection, New York Public Library at Lincoln Center.

Couchman, Jeffrey. "Bob Hope: More Than A Gagster?" *New York Times* (May 6, 1979), section 2, pp. 1, 15.

Creelman, Eileen. "A Smashing Good Melodrama at the Music Hall, *Gunga Din*." *New York Sun* (January 27, 1939). In the *Gunga Din* file, Billy Rose Theatre Collection, New York Public Library at Lincoln Center.

———. *Destry Rides Again* review. *New York Sun* (December 1, 1939). In the *Destry Rides Again* file, Billy Rose Theatre Collection, New York Public Library at Lincoln Center.

Crosby, Bing (with Pete Martin). *Call Me Lucky*. New York: Simon & Schuster, 1953.

Crowther, Bosley. *Destry Rides Again* review. *New York Times* (November 30, 1939), p. 25.

———. *My Favorite Brunette* review. *New York Times* (March 20, 1947), p. 38.

———. *Son of Paleface* review. *New York Times* (October 2, 1952), p. 32.

Curtis, James. *Between Flops: A Biography of Preston Sturges*. New York: Harcourt Brace Jovanovich, 1982.

Dane, Joseph A. "Parody and Satire: A Theoretical Model." *Genre* (Summer 1980), p. 153.

Darrach, Brad. "*Playboy* Interview: Mel Brooks," *Playboy* (February 1975), pp. 16–17, 19, 21–22, 26, 28, 30–31.

Davis, Joe Lee. "Criticism and Parody." *Thought* (Summer 1951), p. 180.

Destry Rides Again review. *Variety* (December 6, 1939).

Dunning, John. *Tune In Yesterday: The Ultimate Encyclopedia of Old-Time Radio, 1925–1976*. Englewood Cliffs, NJ: Prentice-Hall, 1976.

Durgnat, Raymond. *The Crazy Mirror: Hollywood Comedy and the American Image*. 1969. Reprint, New York: Dell, 1972.

Ebert, Roger. *Young Frankenstein* review. *Chicago Sun-Times* (June 9, 1974), section 3, p. 2.

———. *Hot Shots! Part Deux* review. *Chicago Sun-Times* (May 21, 1993).

———. *Scream* review, IMDb (Internet Movie Database), *Scream* site, *Chicago Sun-Times* citation, visited April 13, 1998.

Eells, George, and Stanley Musgrove. *Mae West: A Biography*. New York: William Morrow, 1982.

Everson, William K. *The Art of W. C. Fields*. New York: Bonanza Books, 1967.

"Everybody's Favorite Hope." *Newsweek* (March 31, 1947), p. 92.

Eyles, Allen. *The Marx Brothers: Their World of Comedy*. 1969. Reprint, New York: Paperback Library, 1971.

———. *James Stewart*. 1984; reprint, New York: Stein and Day, 1986.

Faith, William Robert. *Bob Hope: A Life in Comedy*. New York: G. P. Putnam's Sons, 1982.

Ferguson, Otis. "Methods of Madness." *New Republic* (January 27, 1941), p. 117.

Fields, Ronald J. *W. C. Fields: A Life on Film*. New York: St. Martin's Press, 1984.

Fleishman, Philip. "Interview with Mel Brooks." *Macleans* (April 17, 1978), pp. 6, 8, 10.

Fowler, Gene. *Minutes of the Last Meeting*. New York: Viking Press, 1954.

Frank, Melvin, and Norman Panana. Unpublished story treatment for *A Southern Yankee* (1948). In the *Southern Yankee* Collection, Archives of the Performing Arts, Doeheny Library, University of Southern California (USC), Los Angeles, California.

Garland, Robert. "Laurel & Hardy Hit New High in Hilarity With *Way Out West*. *New York American* (May 4, 1937). In the *Way Out West* file, Billy Rose Theatre Collection, New York Public Library at Lincoln Center.

Gehring, Wes D. *Leo McCarey and the Comic Anti-Hero in American Film*. New York: Arno Press, 1980.

———. "Correspondence with William Goldman." (August 28, 1980).

———. "Correspondence with William Goldman." (October 5, 1980).

———. *Charlie Chaplin: A Bio-Bibliography*. Westport, CT: Greenwood Press, 1983.

———. *W. C. Fields: A Bio-Bibliography*. Westport, CT: Greenwood Press, 1984.

———. *Screwball Comedy: A Genre of Madcap Romance*. Westport, CT: Greenwood Press, 1986.

———. *The Marx Brothers: A Bio-Bibliography*. Westport, CT: Greenwood Press, 1987.

———, ed. and chief contributor. *Handbook of American Film Genres*. Westport, CT: Greenwood Press, 1988.

———. *Laurel & Hardy: A Bio-Bibliography*. Westport, CT: Greenwood Press, 1990.

———. *Mr. "B" or Comforting Thoughts About the Bison: A Critical Biography of Robert Benchley*. Westport, CT: Greenwood Press, 1992.

———. *Groucho and W. C. Fields*. Jackson: University Press of Mississippi, 1994.

———. *Populism and the Capra Legacy*. Westport, CT: Greenwood Press, 1995.

———. *Dark Comedy: Beyond Satire*. Westport, CT: Greenwood Press, 1996.

———. *Personality Comedian as Genre: Selected Players*. Westport, CT: Greenwood Press, 1997.

Gelmis, Joseph. "But Seriously, Folks, *Mel Brooks* Is One of the Brightest People You're Gonna Run Into In Your Life." *Newsday* (January 21, 1971), p. 3A.

Gertner, Richard. *Butch Cassidy and the Sundance Kid* review. *Motion Picture Daily* (September 10, 1969), pp. 1, 6.

Glut, Donald F. *The Frankenstein Legend: A Tribute to Mary Shelley and Boris Karloff*. Metuchen, NJ: Scarecrow Press, 1973.

Gold, Herbert. "Funny Is Money." *New York Times Magazine* (March 30, 1975), pp. 16–17, 19, 21–22, 26, 28, 30–31.

Goldman, William. "William Goldman on the Craft of the Screenwriter." *Esquire Film Quarterly* (October 1981), pp. 121–22, 124, 126–27, 129.

———. *The Princess Bride*. 1973. Reprint, New York: Ballantine Books, 1992.

Go West review. *Showman's Trade Review* (December 14, 1940). In the *Go West* Special Collection file, Margaret Herrick Library, Academy of Motion Picture Arts and Sciences, Beverly Hills, California.

Go West review. *Variety* (December 18, 1940), p. 16.

Go West review. *New York World Telegram* (February 21, 1941). In the *Go West* file, Billy Rose Theatre Collection, New York Public Library at Lincoln Center.

Gow, Gordon. *Blazing Saddles* review. *Film and Filming* (August 1974), p. 43.

Hale, Wanda. "Marx Bros. In Stride In Their New Comedy." *New York Daily News* (February 21, 1941). In the *Go West* file, Billy Rose Theatre Collection, New York Public Library at Lincoln Center.

Hamilton, Sara. " 'Destry' Film On Screen At Two Theatres." *Los Angeles Examiner* (January 13, 1940), section 1, p. 8.

———. "Folks, Meet Sam Hinds, That Judge in 'Destry.' " *Los Angeles Examiner* (January 14, 1940), section 5, p. 5.

Hartung, Philip T. *Destry Rides Again* review. *Commonweal* (December 15, 1939), p. 187.

Haskins, Jim. *Richard Pryor: A Man and His Madness*. New York: Beaufort Books, 1984.

Higham, Charles. *Marlene: The Life of Marlene Dietrich*. New York: W. W. Norton, 1977.

Himes, Chester. *My Life of Absurdity: The Later Years*. New York: Thunder Mouth Press, 1976.

Hochman, David. "Scream and Scream Again." *Entertainment Weekly* (November 28, 1997), pp. 28–34.

"Holiday Hits and Misses." *Rolling Stone* (December 26–January 9, 1997), p. 206.

Holtzman, William. *SEESAW: A Dual Biography of Anne Bancroft and Mel Brooks*. Garden City, NY: Doubleday, 1979.

Hope, Bob. *They Got Me Covered*. Hollywood, CA: privately published, 1941.

Hope, Bob (with Melville Shavelson). *Don't Shoot, It's Only Me*. New York: Simon & Schuster, 1953.

Hope, Bob, and Bob Thomas. *The Road to Hollywood*. Garden City, NY: Doubleday, 1977.

Horn, Maurice, ed. *The World Encyclopedia of Comics*. 1976. Reprint, New York: Avon Books, 1977.

Hot Shots! Part Deux review, IMDb (Internet Movie Database), *Hot Shots! Part Deux* site, *Washington Post* citation (May 21, 1993), visited April 13, 1998.

Hot Shots! Part Deux review. *People* (May 31, 1993), p. 14.

Hubbard, Kin. *Abe Martin's Almanack For 1908*. Indianapolis: privately published, 1907.

———. *Abe Martin's Brown County Almanack*. Indianapolis: privately published, 1909.

Hutcheon, Linda. *A Theory of Parody*. New York: Methuen, 1985.

Jenkins, Henry. *What Made Pistachio Nuts? Early Sound Comedy and The Vaudeville Aesthetic*. New York: Columbia University Press, 1992.

Johaueson, Blaud. "*Way Out West*: Laurel & Hardy Go Western." *New York Daily Mirror* (May 4, 1937). In the *Way Out West* file, Billy Rose Theatre Collection, New York Public Library at Lincoln Center.

———. "Thrills, Tears, Comedy Make *Gunga Din* a Great Show." *New York Daily Mirror* (January 26, 1939). In the *Gunga Din* file, Billy Rose Theatre Collection, New York Public Library at Lincoln Center.

Johnson, Erskine. " 'Destry Rides Again' Great Entertainment." *Los Angeles Examiner* (November 29, 1939), section 1, p. 17.

Johnston, Claire, and Paul Willemen (eds.). *Frank Tashlin*. London: Vineyard Press, 1973.

Kael, Pauline. "Spoofing: Cat Ballou." In her *Kiss Kiss Bang Bang*. Boston: Little, Brown, 1968.

———. *Blazing Saddles* review. *The New Yorker* (February 18, 1974), pp. 100, 103.

———. "A Magnetic Blur." *The New Yorker* (December 30, 1974), pp. 58–59.

———. *Reeling*. New York: Warner Books, 1976.

King, Stephen. *Danse Macabre*. 1979; reprint, New York: Berkley Publishing, 1982.

Kiremidjian, David. *A Study of Modern Parody*. New York: Garland Publishing, 1985.

Kitses, Jim. *Horizons West*. Bloomington: Indiana University Press, 1970.

Klady, Leonard. *Scream* review. *Variety* (December 16–22, 1996), p. 79.

Kracauer, Siegfried. *Theory of Film: The Redemption of Physical Reality*. New York: Oxford University Press, 1960.

Kroll, Jack. "Paint the Town White." *Newsweek* (March 9, 1998), p. 68.

Krutnick, Frank. "Jerry Lewis: The Deformation of the Comic." *Film Quarterly* (Fall 1994), pp. 12–26.

Kuhlmann, Susan. *Knave, Fool, and Genius: The Confidence Man as He Appears in Nineteenth Century American Fiction*. Chapel Hill: University of North Carolina Press, 1973.

Lahr, John. "PROFILE; The C.E.O. of Comedy [Bob Hope]." *The New Yorker* (December 21, 1998), pp. 62–70, 72–76, 78–79.

"Laughing With and At." *Commonweal* (April 4, 1947), p. 614.

Lax, Eric. *On Being Funny: Woody Allen and Comedy*. New York: Manor Books, 1975.

Leach, Jim. "The Screwball Comedy." In *Film Theory and Criticism*, ed. Barry K. Grant. Metuchen, NJ: Scarecrow Press, 1977, pp. 75–89.

Lindberg, Gary. *The Confidence Man in American Literature*. New York: Oxford University Press, 1982.

McArthur, Colin. *Underworld USA*. New York: Viking Press, 1972.

McCann, Graham. *Woody Allen: New Yorker*. 1990. Reprint, New York: Polity Press, 1992.

McLeish, Kenneth. *Arts in the Twentieth Century*. 1985. Reprint, New York: Viking Penguin, 1986.

"Mae and Bill Out West." *Newsweek* (February 26, 1940), p. 30.

Maltin, Leonard. *The Great Movie Comedians*. New York: Crown Publishers, 1978.

"Marlene in Hoss Opera: 'Destry Rides Again' Puts on a Lively Two-Gun Show." *Newsweek* (December 11, 1939), p. 33.

Marx, Arthur. *The Secret Life of Bob Hope*. New York: Barricade Books, 1993.

Marx, Groucho. *The Groucho Letters: Letters From and to Groucho Marx*. New York: Simon and Schuster, 1967.

Maslin, Janet. "From 'Rambo' to Rodham, Smirking All The Way." *New York Times* (May 21, 1993, late edition), p. C-6.

———. "Tricks of the Gory Trade." *New York Times* (December 20, 1996), p. C-22.

Mast, Gerald. *The Comic Mind: Comedy and the Movies*, 2d ed. Chicago: University of Chicago Press, 1979.

Masters, Dorothy. "Laurel-Hardy Comedy Jeopardizes Theatre." *New York Daily News* (May 4, 1937). In the *Way Out West* file, Billy Rose Theatre Collection, New York Public Library at Lincoln Center.

Matthiessen, F. O. *American Renaissance: Art and Expression in the Age of Emerson and Whitman.* 1941. Reprint, New York: Oxford University Press, 1954.

Mauro, Tony. "Parody Hits Right Note With Court." *USA Today* (March 8, 1994), p. 1-A.

Memorial, Keith. *My Little Chickadee* review. *Boston Herald* (March 11, 1940). In the *My Little Chickadee* file, Billy Rose Theatre Collection, New York Public Library at Lincoln Center.

"Mirth of a Nation." *Entertainment Weekly* (October 16, 1992), p. 17.

Moffitt, Jack. "Back to Utopia." *Esquire* (April 1946), p. 63.

Moritz, Charles, ed. "Gene Wilder." In *Current Bibliography*. New York: H. W. Wilson, 1979, pp. 454–57.

Mortimer, Lee. "Mae West, Fields Cut Up in *Little Chickadee.*" *New York Daily Mirror* (March 16, 1940). In the *My Little Chickadee* file, Billy Rose Theatre Collection, New York Public Library at Lincoln Center.

"Movie of the Week: *My Little Chickadee*: Mae West and W. C. Fields Burlesque the Westerns." *Life* (February 19, 1940), pp. 63–65.

"Movie of the Week: The Paleface." *Life* (January 3, 1949), p. 61.

Murphy, Kathleen. "Sam Peckinpah: No Bleeding Heart." *Film Comment* (April 1985), pp. 74–75.

Murray, Edward. "Chapter 6, Pauline Kael and the Pluralist, Aesthetic Criticism." In his *Nine American Film Critics*. New York: Frederick Ungar, 1975.

My Favorite Brunette review. *Time* (March 31, 1947), pp. 99–100.

My Little Chickadee review. *Variety* (February 14, 1940), p. 18.

My Little Chickadee review. *Time* (February 26, 1940), p. 66.

My Little Chickadee review. *New York Post* (March 16, 1940). In the *My Little Chickadee* file, Billy Rose Theatre Collection, New York Public Library at Lincoln Center.

Newman, Kim. *Scream* review. *Sight and Sound* (May, 1997), p. 53.

Nichols, Nina. "Destiny Rides Again." *Cinema Texas Program Notes* (February 4, 1980). In the *Destiny Rides Again* Special Collection file, Margaret Herrick Library, Academy of Motion Picture Arts and Sciences, Beverly Hills, California.

Nielsen, Leslie, and David Fisher. *The Naked Truth*. New York: Pocket Books, 1993.

Nolan, William F. *John Huston: King Rebel*. Los Angeles: Sherbourne Press, 1965.

Nugent, Frank S. *Way Out West* review. *New York Times* (May 4, 1937), p. 29.

———. *My Little Chickadee* review. *New York Times* (March 16, 1940), p. 8.

Olson, Scott R. "College Course File: Studies in Genre—Horror." *Journal of Film and Video* (Spring-Summer, 1996), pp. 67–79.

Parsons, Louella. "Paulette Goddard and Bob Hope Scheduled for Another Thriller, 'The Ghost Breakers.' " *Los Angeles Examiner* (November 22, 1939), section 1, p. 17.

Paul, William. "Film: *Way Out West.*" *Village Voice* (January 29, 1970), p. 58.
———. *Laughing Screaming: Modern Hollywood Horror and Comedy.* New York: Columbia University Press, 1994.
Pelswick, Rose. "Latest Marx Lunacy." *New York Journal American* (February 21, 1941). In the *Go West* file, Billy Rose Theatre Collection, New York Public Library at Lincoln Center.
"Premiere Set for Western" and "Preview of W. C. Fields Latest Feb. 6." *Los Angeles Examiner* (January 31, 1940), section 1, p. 11.
Ray, Robert B. *A Certain Tendency of the Hollywood Cinema, 1930–1980.* Princeton, NJ: Princeton University Press, 1985.
"Reite Ihn, Cowboy!" *New York Times* (December 3, 1939), section 9, p. 8.
Riley, Brooks. "Words of Hope." *Film Comment* (May-June, 1979), p. 24.
Riva, Maria. *Marlene Dietrich: By Her Daughter.* New York: Alfred A. Knopf, 1993.
"Road to Singapore," review. *Hollywood Reporter* (February 21, 1940), p. 3.
Road to Utopia, The, review. *New York Herald-Tribune* (February 28, 1946).
Road to Utopia, The, review. *The New Yorker* (March 2, 1946), p. 81.
Rose, Margaret A. *Parody II Meta-Fiction.* London: Croom Helm, 1979.
Rosenblum, Ralph, and Robert Karen. *When The Shooting Stops . . . The Cutting Begins: A Film Editor's Story.* New York: Penguin, 1979.
Rowe, Kathleen. *The Unruly Woman: Gender and the Genres of Laughter.* Austin: University of Texas Press, 1995.
Sanello, Frank. *Jimmy Stewart: A Wonderful Life.* New York: Pinnacle Books, 1997.
Sarris, Andrew. *The American Cinema: Directors and Directions, 1929–1968.* New York: E. P. Dutton, 1968.
Schickel, Richard. "Hi-Ho, Mel." *Time* (March 4, 1974), pp. 62–63.
———. *Clint Eastwood: A Biography.* New York: Alfred A. Knopf, 1996.
Schjeldahl, Peter. "How The West Was Won By Mel." *New York Times* (March 17, 1974), section 2, p. 15.
Schwarzbaum, Lisa. "A Time To Kill." *Entertainment Weekly* (August 14, 1998), pp. 44–46.
Shelley, Mary. *Frankenstein: Or, The Modern Prometheus.* 1818. Reprint, New York: New American Library, 1965.
Siegel, Larry. "Mel Brooks Interview." *Playboy* (October 1966), pp. 71–72, 76, 78, 80.
Siska, William C. "The Art Film." In *Handbook of American Film Genres,* ed. Wes D. Gehring. Westport, CT: Greenwood Press, 1988, pp. 353–70.
Smurthwaite, Nick, and Paul Gelder. *Mel Brooks and the Spoof Movie.* New York: Proteus Books, 1982.
Spoto, Donald. *Blue Angel: The Life of Marlene Dietrich.* New York: Doubleday, 1992.
Stack, Peter. *Scream* review. *San Francisco Chronicle* (December 20, 1996), p. C-5.
Stang, Joanne. "And Then He Got Smart." *New York Times* (January 30, 1966), section 2, p. 17.
Sterritt, David. "It's a Whole New Career for Gene Wilder." *The Christian Science Monitor* (January 29, 1975), p. 9.

Stevick, Philip. "Frankenstein and Comedy." In *The Endurance of Frankenstein: Essays on Mary Shelley's Novel*, ed. George Levine and U. C. Knoepflmacher 1979. Reprint, Los Angeles: University of California Press, 1982.

Tashlin, Frank. "*Son of Paleface* Went Thataway." *New York Times* (October 5, 1952), section 2, p. 5.

Taylor, Robert Lewis. *W. C. Fields: His Follies and Fortunes*. Garden City, NY: Doubleday, 1949.

Thomas, Bob. "Mel Brooks 'Salutes' *Young Frankenstein*." *New York Post* (May 28, 1974), p. 22.

Thompson, Charles. *Bob Hope: Portrait of a Superstar*. New York: St. Martin's Press, 1981.

Thompson, Jack. *My Favorite Brunette* review (March 30, 1947), p. 16.

Thurber, James. "The Secret Life of Walter Mitty." In *The Thurber Carnival*. New York: Harper and Brothers, 1945, pp. 47–51.

———. *The Beast in Me and Other Animals*. 1948; reprint, New York: Harcourt Brace Jovanovich, 1973.

Trapp, Martin. *Mary Shelley's Monster*. Boston: Houghton Mifflin, 1976.

Warshow, Robert. *The Immediate Experience*. Edited by Sherry Abel. New York: Atheneum, 1962.

Way Out West review. *Variety* (May 5, 1937), p. 16.

Werner, Edith. "For Laughter, Go West With the Marx Brothers." *New York Mirror* (February 21, 1941). In the *Go West* file, Billy Rose Theatre Collection, New York Public Library at Lincoln Center.

Westerbeck, Colin L., Jr. "Flying High and at Bargain Rates." *Commonweal* (September 12, 1980), p. 502.

"Westerns Aid Film Industry." *New York Morning-Telegraph* (June 15, 1941). In the *Destry Rides Again* file, Billy Rose Theatre Collection, New York Public Library at Lincoln Center.

West, Mae. *Goodness Had Nothing to Do With It*. 1959. Reprint, New York: MacFadden-Bartell, 1970.

Wilde, Oscar. "The Decay of Lying." In *Criticism: The Major Texts*, ed. W. J. Bate. Chicago, IL: Harcourt Brace Jovanovich, 1970, pp. 638–42.

Wilson, Marilyn. "*The Paleface*." In *Magill's Survey of Cinema*, 2d ser., vol. 4, ed. Frank Magill. Englewood Cliffs, NJ: Salem Press, 1981.

Winston, Archer. "Laurel and Hardy Panic Rialto With Their Act." *New York Post* (May 4, 1937). In the *Way Out West* file, Billy Rose Theatre Collection, New York Public Library at Lincoln Center.

———. *Destry Rides Again* review. *New York Post* (November 30, 1939). In the *Destry Rides Again* file, Billy Rose Theatre Collection, New York Public Library at Lincoln Center.

Yacowar, Maurice. *Loser Take All*. New York: Frederick Ungar, 1979.

———. *Methods in Madness: The Comic Art of Mel Brooks*. New York: *Mel Brooks*. New York: St. Martin's Press, 1981.

You Can't Cheat an Honest Man review. *Variety* (February 22, 1939), p. 12.

You Can't Cheat an Honest Man review. *Newsweek* (February 27, 1939), p. 25.

Zimmerman, Paul D. "Wild, Wild West. *Newsweek* (February 18, 1974), pp. 101, 104.

———. "The Mad Mad Mel Brooks." *Newsweek* (February 17, 1975), p. 55.

Index

About the Author

WES D. GEHRING is Professor of Film at Ball State University and Associate Media Editor at *USA Today Magazine*. He is the author of a dozen books, including *Screwball Comedy: A Genre of Madcap Romance* (Greenwood, 1986), *Personality Comedians as Genre* (Greenwood, 1997), *American Dark Comedy* (Greenwood, 1996), *Populism and the Capra Legacy* (Greenwood, 1995), and *Handbook of American Film Genres* (Greenwood, 1988). He has also written biographies of W. C. Fields, Charlie Chaplin, The Marx Brothers, and Laurel and Hardy.

Recent Titles in
Contributions to the Study of Popular Culture

ISBN 0-313-26186-5

EAN

9 780313 261862

HARDCOVER BAR CODE